T0192029

Communications
in Computer and Information Science 1520

More information about this series at https://link.springer.com/bookseries/7899

Magali Bigey · Annabel Richeton ·
Max Silberztein · Izabella Thomas (Eds.)

Formalizing Natural Languages: Applications to Natural Language Processing and Digital Humanities

15th International Conference, NooJ 2021
Besançon, France, June 9–11, 2021
Revised Selected Papers

 Springer

Editors
Magali Bigey
Université de Franche-Comté
Besançon, France

Annabel Richeton
Université de Franche-Comté
Besançon, France

Max Silberztein (iD)
Université de Franche-Comté
Besançon, France

Izabella Thomas
Université de Franche-Comté
Besançon, France

ISSN 1865-0929   ISSN 1865-0937   (electronic)
Communications in Computer and Information Science
ISBN 978-3-030-92860-5   ISBN 978-3-030-92861-2   (eBook)
https://doi.org/10.1007/978-3-030-92861-2

This Springer imprint is published by the registered company Springer Nature Switzerland AG
The registered company address is: Gewerbestrasse 11, 6330 Cham, Switzerland

Preface

NooJ is a linguistic development environment that provides tools for linguists to construct linguistic resources that formalize a large gamut of linguistic phenomena: typography, orthography, lexicons for simple words, multiword units and discontinuous expressions, inflectional, derivational and agglutinative morphology, local, phrase-structure and dependency grammars, and transformational and semantic grammars. For each linguistic phenomenon to be described, NooJ proposes a set of computational formalisms, the power of which ranges from very efficient finite-state machines (that process regular grammars) to very powerful Turing machines (that process unrestricted grammars). NooJ also contains a rich toolbox that allows linguists to construct, maintain, test, debug, accumulate, and share large linguistic resources. This makes NooJ's approach different from most other computational linguistic tools that typically offer a unique formalism to their users and are not compatible with each other.

NooJ provides parsers that can apply any set of linguistic resources to any corpus of texts, to extract examples or counter-examples, annotate matching sequences, perform statistical analyses, and so on. Because NooJ's linguistic resources are neutral, they can also be used by NooJ to generate texts automatically. By combining NooJ's parsers and generators, one can construct sophisticated NLP (Natural Language Processing) applications, such as Automatic Machine Translation and Automatic Paraphrasing software.

Since its first release in 2002, several private companies have used NooJ's linguistic engine to construct business applications in several domains, from business intelligence to opinion analysis. To date, there are NooJ modules available for over 50 languages; more than 140,000 copies of NooJ have been downloaded. In 2013, an open-source version for NooJ was released, based on the Java technology, which is available to all as a GPL project and supported and distributed by the European Metashare platform.

NooJ has been recently enhanced with new features to respond to the needs of researchers who analyze texts in various domains of human and social sciences (history, literature and political studies, psychology, sociology, etc.), and more generally of all the professionals who need to explore their corpus of texts.

This volume contains 20 articles selected from the papers and posters presented at the International NooJ 2021 conference organized in Besançon, France. Because of the COVID-19 pandemic, the conference was organized virtually as a video conference. However, this did not hinder the quality of the presentations or the success of the event, as over 70 participants were able to attend and participate in the ten thematic sessions.

The following articles are organized in three parts: "Linguistic Formalization and Analysis" contains six articles; "Digital Humanities and Teaching" contains seven articles, and "Natural Language Processing Applications" contains seven articles.

The articles in the first part involve the construction of electronic dictionaries and grammars to perform various linguistic analyses, in several languages:

— In his article "Tweaking NooJ's Resources to Export Morpheme-level or Intra-word Annotations", Prihantoro presents a set of lexical, morphological, and syntactic resources for Indonesian that can be used to automatically perform morphological analysis of Indonesian texts and represent the complex results of the various levels of analysis in a standard, interoperable way.

— In "Intensive Comparisons of the PECO and PVCO Classes in Old French", Xavier Blanco and Yauheniya Yakubovich describe a set of linguistic resources aimed at formalizing adjectival predicates (PECO) and verbal predicates (PVCO) in Old French.

— In "Lexicon-Grammar Tables for Modern Arabic Frozen Expressions, Asmaa Kourtin, Asmaa Amzali, Mohammed Mourchid, Abdelaziz Mouloudi, and Samir Mbarki present a set of lexicon-grammar tables that describe Arabic frozen expressions and show how to implement it as NooJ dictionaries.

— In "Syntactic Analysis of Sentences Containing Arabic Psychological Verbs", Asmaa Amzali, Asmaa Kourtin, Mohammed Mourchid, Abdelaziz Mouloudi, and Samir Mbarki formalize the structure of Arabic sentences that contain psychological verbs as a lexicon-grammar table, transform the lexicon-grammar table into a dictionary, and show how to use that dictionary to implement a syntactic parser using NooJ.

— In "Formalizing Italian Negation for Sentiment Analysis", Mario Monteleone and Ignazio Mauro Mirto present a set of NooJ dictionaries, comprising morphological and syntactic grammars that describe the various ways negation can be expressed in Italian. These precisely formalized resources can then be used to perform automatic sentiment analysis that is more reliable than the results produced using sentiment analysis software based on statistical methods.

— In "Formalizing Predicates for Discovery under the Lexicon Grammar Framework", Javiera Jacobsen, Walter Koza, Mirian Muñoz, and Francisca Saiz present a transformational grammar that describes Spanish sentences that express a discovery (e.g. the verbs *encontrar*, *hallar*); the grammar can be used by NooJ both to automatically recognize sentences and identify their semantic roles (who discovers what) with a very good f-measure (92%), as well as generate a large number of sentences that correspond to a given semantic scheme.

The articles in the "Digital Humanities and Teaching" section show how NooJ can be used to help analyze corpora in various applications in the social sciences (gender studies, literature, and pedagogy):

— In "Who is to Blame for What? An Insight within the French Yellow Vests' Movement through Dole's Books of Grievances", Marion Bendinelli explores Dole's book of grievances written during the Yellow Vest Movement, developing various specific linguistic resources and methods to study expressions of blame.

— In "Sensitivity to Fake News: Reception Analysis with NooJ", Magali Bigey and Justine Simon show how they have used NooJ to study the reception of infox by first-year students.

— In "Negation Usage in the Croatian Parliament, Kristina Kocijan and Krešimir Šojat discuss the usage of negation in parliamentary discussions, taking into consideration gender, time, and political party.

— In "Locating Traces of Subjectivity in Diplomatic Discourse: The Example of the French Ministry of Foreign Affairs", Annabel Richeton shows how NooJ can help to find traces of subjectivity in diplomatic discourse, using specifically developed lexical resources.

— In "Construction of an Educational Game 'VocabNooJ'", Héla Fehri, Lazhar Arroum, and Sameh Ben Aoun present the educational game software "VocabNooJ", which proposes several word games based on linguistic resources implemented with NooJ.

— In "Approach to the Automatic Treatment of Gerunds in Spanish and Quechua: A Pedagogical Application", Andrea Rodrigo, Maximiliano Duran, and María Yanina Nalli present a pedagogical application aimed at teaching both Spanish to Quechua speakers and Quechua to Spanish speakers. The application is based on a set of NooJ morphological grammars that describe how gerunds are expressed in Quechua, as well as a set of morphological and syntactic grammars that describe how gerunds are expressed in Spanish.

— In "Using NooJ to formalize French cooking expressions", Tong Yang presents the construction of a set of linguistic resources that describe the French vocabulary used in the domain of cooking, to be used to teach French cooking to foreign cooks.

The last section, dedicated to the presentation of "Natural Language Processing Applications", contains the following articles:

— In "Paraphrasing Tool Using the NooJ Platform", Amine Alassir, Sondes Dardour and Héla Fehri present a software application capable of recognizing and generating French paraphrases automatically, taking into account relations of synonymy, antonymity, and passivation.

— In "The Recognition and the Automatic Translation of Dative Verbs", Hajer Cheikhrouhou presents a Nooj application capable of recognizing French dative constructions (using the LVF dictionary) and producing the equivalent structure in Arabic, using bilingual syntactic grammars.

— In "From Laws and Decrees to a Legal Dictionary", Ismahane Kourtin, Samir Mbarki, and Abdelaaziz Mouloudi present a terminological resource built with NooJ that will be used by a question-answering system in the legal domain.

— In "Automatic Detection and Generation of Argument Structures within the Medical Domain", Walter Koza and Constanza Suy present a semantic analyzer that parses medical texts in gynecology and obstetrics, recognizes a hundred biomedical verbs (formalized in lexicon-grammars), and produces the corresponding semantic representation (predicates and their arguments).

— In "Meaning Extraction from Strappare Causatives in Italian", Ignazio Mauro Mirto and Mario Monteleone present a prototype of a semantic analyzer that uses a formalization of the various syntactico-semantic contexts of the Italian verb *strappare*, which automatically produces an annotation of the semantic roles of its arguments.

— In "Terms and Appositions: What Unstructured Texts Tell Us", Giulia Speranza, Maria Pia di Buono, and Johanna Monti present a software capable of detecting technical terms for specific domains (starting with archeology), using a combination of a dictionary used as a starting anchor and various local grammars to extend the terminological database.

— In "Automatic generation of intonation marks and prosodic segmentation for Belarusian NooJ Module", Yauheniya Zianouka, Yuras Hetsevich, David Latyshevich, and Zmicier Dzenisiuk show how to build a system that can segment texts automatically, generating prosodic transcription and delimiting long sentences, aimed at being inserted in a text-to-speech automatic system.

This volume should be of interest to all users of the NooJ software because it presents the latest development of its linguistic resources, as well as a large variety of applications, both in the digital humanities and in NLP software.

Linguists as well as computational linguists who work on Arabic, Belarusian, Croatian, English, Indonesian, Italian, Medieval French, Quechua, or Spanish will find advanced, up-to-the-minute linguistic studies for these languages.

We think that the reader will appreciate the importance of this volume, both for the intrinsic value of each linguistic formalization and the underlying methodology, as well as for the potential for developing NLP applications along with linguistic-based corpus processors in the social sciences.

Magali Bigey
Annabel Richeton
Max Silberztein
Izabella Thomas

Contents

List of Contributors

Amine Alassir University of Gabes, Gabes, Tunisia

Asmaa Amzali Computer Science Research Laboratory, Faculty of Science, Ibn Tofail University, Kenitra, Morocco

Sameh Ben Aoun University of Gabes, Gabes, Tunisia

Lazhar Arroum University of Gabes, Gabes, Tunisia

Marion Bendinelli Université Bourgogne Franche-Comté/ELLIADD (UR 4661), Paris, France

Magali Bigey ELLIADD (UR 4661), University of Franche-Comté, Besançon, France

Xavier Blanco Universitat Autònoma de Barcelona, Cerdanyola del Vallès, Spain

Hajer Cheikhrouhou University of Sfax, LLTA, Sfax, Tunisia

Sondes Dardour MIRACL Laboratory, University of Sfax, Sfax, Tunisia

Maria Pia di Buono UniOr NLP Research Group, University of Naples "L'Orientale", Naples, Italy

Maximiliano Duran Université de Franche-Comté, Besançon, France

Zmicier Dzenisiuk United Institute of Informatics Problems of the National Academy of Sciences of Belarus, Minsk, Belarus

Héla Fehri MIRACL Laboratory, University of Sfax, Sfax, Tunisia

Yuras Hetsevich United Institute of Informatics Problems of the National Academy of Sciences of Belarus, Minsk, Belarus

Javiera Jacobsen Pontificia Universidad Católica de Valparaíso, Valparaíso, Chile

Kristina Kocijan Department of Information and Communication Sciences, Faculty of Humanities and Social Sciences, University of Zagreb, Zagreb, Croatia

Asmaa Kourtin Computer Science Research Laboratory, Faculty of Science, Ibn Tofail University, Kenitra, Morocco

Ismahane Kourtin ELLIADD Laboratory, Bourgogne-Franche-Comté University, Besançon, France; MISC Laboratory, Faculty of Science, Ibn Tofail University, Kenitra, Morocco

Walter Koza Pontificia Universidad Católica de Valparaíso, Valparaíso, Chile

David Latyshevich United Institute of Informatics Problems of the National Academy of Sciences of Belarus, Minsk, Belarus

Samir Mbarki MISC Laboratory, Faculty of Science, Ibn Tofail University, Kenitra, Morocco; EDPAGS Laboratory, Faculty of Science, Ibn Tofail University, Kenitra, Morocco

Ignazio Mauro Mirto Dipartimento Culture e Società, Università di Palermo, Palermo, Italy

Mario Monteleone Dipartimento di Scienze Politiche e della Comunicazione, Università di Salerno, Fisciano, Italy

Johanna Monti UniOr NLP Research Group, University of Naples "L'Orientale", Naples, Italy

Abdelaaziz Mouloudi MISC Laboratory, Faculty of Science, Ibn Tofail University, Kenitra, Morocco

Abdelaziz Mouloudi EDPAGS Laboratory, Faculty of Science, Ibn Tofail University, Kenitra, Morocco

Mohammed Mourchid Computer Science Research Laboratory, Faculty of Science, Ibn Tofail University, Kenitra, Morocco

Mirian Muñoz Pontificia Universidad Católica de Valparaíso, Valparaíso, Chile

María Yanina Nalli Facultad Regional Rosario, Universidad Tecnológica Nacional, Rosario, Argentina

Prihantoro Universitas Diponegoro, Semarang, Indonesia

Annabel Richeton ELLIADD, Bourgogne Franche-Comté University, Besançon, France

Andrea Rodrigo Facultad de Humanidades y Artes, Universidad Nacional de Rosario, Rosario, Argentina

Francisca Saiz Pontificia Universidad Católica de Valparaíso, Valparaíso, Chile

Justine Simon ELLIADD (UR 4661), University of Franche-Comté, Besançon, France

Krešimir Šojat Department of Linguistics, Faculty of Humanities and Social Sciences, University of Zagreb, Zagreb, Croatia

Giulia Speranza UniOr NLP Research Group, University of Naples "L'Orientale", Naples, Italy

Constanza Suy Pontificia Universidad Católica de Valparaíso, Valparaíso, Chile

Yauheniya Yakubovich Universitat de València, Valencia, Spain

Tong Yang North China Electric Power University, Beijing, China

Yauheniya Zianouka United Institute of Informatics Problems of the National Academy of Sciences of Belarus, Minsk, Belarus

Linguistic Formalization and Analysis

Tweaking NooJ's Resources to Export Morpheme-Level or Intra-word Annotations

Prihantoro[(✉)] [iD]

Universitas Diponegoro, Semarang, Indonesia
prihantoro@live.undip.ac.id

Abstract. NooJ's [1, 2] export function allows its users to convert NooJ output from a binary file to a text file format. However, at present, the NooJ export function does not fully export intra-word units. My solution to this problem is demonstrated using SANTI-morf [3], a new morphological annotation system for Indonesian, written as a package in NooJ's Indonesian language module. While the solution is dedicated to Indonesian morphology, I argue that the method I propose can be replicated by other NooJ users facing the same challenge. A new syntactic grammar whose rules capture morphotactic combinations that form Indonesian polymorphemic words is devised. Dictionaries and morphological grammars are modified to allow all morphemes and their associated analytical attributes to be automatically transferred using the new syntactic grammar as single units, like monomorphemic words. Some symbols that are special to NooJ must be replaced by non-standard symbols as these special symbols are not acceptable in syntactic annotations. This experimentation successfully exports more than 99% of word tokens from the test-bed corpus into full morpheme-level annotations. While successful, the concatenation of these morphemes as single units and the use of non-standard symbols confuse morpheme boundaries and annotations, causing the readability of the output to be low. A small program is then written to improve the readability of the output, which can easily be adapted to users' anticipated needs.

Keywords: NooJ · Morpheme · Annotation · Export · Resources · Indonesian

1 Export Function in NooJ

NooJ [1, 2] is a rule-based linguistic text analyzer within which a finite-state engine is one of its core components. When NooJ is used to annotate a text or corpus, its output is stored in a binary file, rather than a text file. This output is readable in NooJ, but not other programs. It is thus impossible for a user to index a binary file using corpus query programs other than NooJ, such as CQPweb [4], Sketch Engine [5], AntConc [6], Wordsmith [7], or LancsBox [8].

Anticipating this, NooJ provides an export function, which allows NooJ's annotation output to be converted into a text rather than a binary file, which is thus readable, even to commonly used simple text-editor programs such as Notepad or Gedit. This export function makes NooJ output more accessible.

© Springer Nature Switzerland AG 2021
M. Bigey et al. (Eds.): NooJ 2021, CCIS 1520, pp. 3–14, 2021.
https://doi.org/10.1007/978-3-030-92861-2_1

The resulting annotation of the text file is presented in an XML document format. While many programs can index a corpus presented in XML document format, some cannot. However, this is not the main concern as the output is already in a text file, not binary. It is thus possible to write a small program to convert the XML format into another format, such as Text Encoding Initiative [9] or Corpus Encoding Standard [10], or any format acceptable in the corpus query program that will be used to index the corpus.

2 Exporting Morpheme Level Annotation: Challenges and Opportunities

NooJ can perform annotation, not only at the word level (e.g., POS tagging or morphosyntactic annotation) or beyond it (e.g., phrase structure annotation) but also at the morpheme level. For instance, NooJ can tokenise a polymorphemic word into its corresponding morpheme(s) and associate each morpheme with a morphological tag. In NooJ, this phenomenon is termed *intra-word annotation*, as illustrated in the annotation of *cannot* (see Fig. 1[1], below), a string composed of connected letters. This string is decomposed into two Atomic Linguistic Units (ALUs), <can, V> and <not, ADV>.

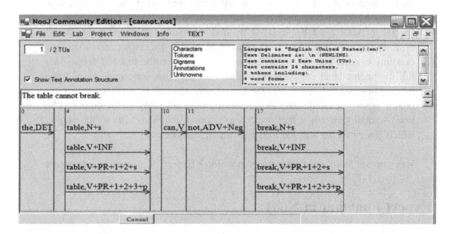

Fig. 1. Intra word annotation of *cannot* into two units

In this case, the ALU is defined at the word level. However, in morphological annotation, the ALU is defined at the intra-word level, i.e., morphemes. While the export function works well for word-level annotation or beyond, for morpheme-level annotation, the export function in NooJ only exports the annotation of the final morpheme of each word. For instance, in the case of the three-morpheme Indonesian word *memberikan*, 'to give (sth)', only the last morpheme, the suffix *-kan*, is exported (see LEMMA = "kan" below). The active prefix *mem-* and the root *beri* 'to give' are not exported.

<LU LEMMA = "**kan**" CAT = "SFX" TYPE = "R_VER" TYPE = "CAUS" RL = "112500" TYPE = "YumiA1">**membersihkan**</LU>

Likewise, for *secepat*, 'as quick as', a two-morpheme Indonesian word, only its root *cepat*, 'quick', is exported. The equative prefix *se-* 'as (any adjective) as' (see LEMMA="cepat" below) is not exported. Note that the standard NooJ term *lemma* is still used to refer to morphemes in the annotation output. However, in conjunction with the aim of this paper, the term *morpheme* is used from this point onwards.

<LU LEMMA = "**cepat**" CAT = "ROOT" TYPE = "ADJ" TYPE = "PS" TYPE = "AC" TYPE = "ACS" TYPE = "TX" TYPE = "DykaA1">**secepat**</LU>

This means that all polymorphemic words are only partially exported. This is one of my main concerns as I implement SANTI-morf [3], a morphological annotation system for Indonesian text, using NooJ. To address this problem, there are at least two potential solutions.

The first solution is to access NooJ's source code and modify the export function or add a new export function that can properly generate all morphemes. The benefit of implementing this approach is that there will be no need to use any external program. Once revised, the export function can be accessed normally.

Despite the aforementioned benefit, implementing this solution is also challenging. The modification must not result in any conflict with other functions, particularly word-level export, which so far has been stable. It might be useful to just add a new export function alongside the existing export function. Then, an extra radio button in the NooJ interface export panel can be added to confirm whether a user wants to export morpheme-level annotation. When selected, NooJ will run the additional export function. Thus, the already-existing export function remains intact. While this solution seems straightforward, note that it can only be done by someone who has access and technical programming skills to modify NooJ source code. End-users who have no access or technical skills to modify NooJ's source code cannot implement this solution.

The second solution is to modify or 'tweak' NooJ resources so that the current export function can produce all morphemes. The reason why I use the term 'tweak' is because the modification is somewhat atypical. Despite that, I will demonstrate in Sect. 3 that this 'tweak' produces the expected outcome, which normal procedures cannot achieve.

Despite the complexity imposed by this uncommon modification, this solution can be carried out independently by users without needing to access NooJ's source code. In addition, no technical programming skills are required. It means that all NooJ users can immediately implement this solution. It is also less likely that this solution will result in a conflict with the existing export function, as the function in NooJ's source code is not modified at all. In this paper, we will explore this option, as further discussed in Sect. 3.

3   Tweaking Resources

3.1   About the Experiment

This experiment is part of the SANTI-morf (*Sistem Analisis Teks Indonesia – morfologi*) or in English ('A morphological analysis system for Indonesian Text') project, which aims to build a system of morphological analysis for Indonesian texts at the morpheme level, with a multi-module pipeline architecture [3]. The language targeted by the system, Indonesian, is a standard variety of Malay, one of the Austronesian languages in Southeast Asia that is widely used in Indonesia [11]. Words in Indonesian can be formed using a variety of morphological processes such as affixation, reduplication, compounding, and cliticisation [12]. SANTI-morf aims to annotate the morphemes involved in these morphological processes. NooJ is used to implement SANTI-morf. SANTI-morf resources are available as a NooJ package in an Indonesian language module. The NooJ version used in this project is NooJ version 7.

3.2   The Logic Behind the Tweaking

There are two conditions worth noting in the current output. The first one is the failure to properly export all morphemes from each polymorphemic word. However, NooJ successfully exports all morphemes of monomorphemic word annotations. Thus, theoretically, if the tweak causes NooJ to successfully process all words as 'monomorphemic' words, it is expected that all morphemes will be exported properly. This statement is explained in more detail as follows.

The tweaking of NooJ resources must allow multiple ALUs to be analyzed as one unit. This is, in fact, a common practice in NooJ. Users can implement syntactic annotations, such as phrase-structure annotations, which in essence combine multiple ALUs as single units. However, such annotation typically accesses word-level ALUs. For instance, noun-phrase annotation is applied to a combination of an article and a noun; a time-expression annotation might be a combination of prepositions, adverbs, nouns, numeral or punctuation marks, as in *at approximately five o'clock*. Given that the current ALU I am targeting is at the morpheme, not the word, level, the implementation of this argument is: 'annotating multiple morphemes that form a polymorphemic word as one unit'.

Note that this is not a standard NooJ procedure. The result, if successful, is more likely to be incorrectly formatted. However, the prime objective of this experiment is to export all morphemes. Once all morphemes are successfully exported (even if incorrectly formatted), the next step is to decompose single-analytic-unit annotations back into corresponding morphemes, by reformatting the result of the export, into a proper format desired by the user.

3.3   Implementation

The first step is to create a syntactic grammar rule that will access and combine all morphemes and their corresponding baseline annotations which have initially been supplied by dictionary and morphological grammar rules. The new syntactic rule will have an arbitrary attribute, W (for word). This is not an analytic attribute, it is merely required for implementation purposes.

```
Rule = <E>/<W   <E>/>
```

The next step is to incorporate the morphotactic rules of Indonesian into this rule. To this end, I use variables. These variables are used to specify morphotactically correct morpheme combinations that form Indonesian polymorphemic words. Variable names in this rule are letters in alphabetical order that correspond to the position of each morpheme. Thus, in the case of *secepat*, which is a combination of an equative adjective prefix *se-* followed by an adjective root *cepat* 'quick', the two morphemes are then assigned variables A and B, respectively, in the rule. A hash is inserted between variables to ensure that the morphemes are agglutinated without any spaces.

```
Rule = <E>/<W
$(A <PFX> )$ #  $(B <ROOT> $)
<E>/>
```

When exported using the NooJ standard procedure, all morphemes are expected to be agglutinated without clear delineators. Thus, we need to provide overt morpheme boundary delineation markers. For this purpose, the arbitrary code MM (for morpheme marker) is added. This code is then followed by a numeric digit signifying the position of the morpheme, such as MM1 (first), MM2 (second), etc. See MM1 below. MM1 is prepended with +, because it is written in the rules as secondary attributes following W.

```
Rule = <E>/<W
$(A <PFX> )$ # $(B <ROOT> $)
<E>/+MM1>
```

The elements present in baseline annotations must be transferred into syntactic annotations. These elements are morphemes and their corresponding morphological tags (which are combinations of morphological analysis attributes and values). In NooJ, attributes begin with plus symbols (except in the first position), while values for corresponding attributes begin with equals symbols =. To illustrate this, see the attributes and values in the annotation of the equative prefix *se-* in <se,PFX+R_ADJ +EQTV+RL=010200+YumiA1>, given by SANTI-morf's morphological grammar.

The morpheme *se-* in the annotation can easily be transferred using the syntactic rule transfer code $A_. In the code below, the equals sign preceding the code (=$A_) functions as a demarcation symbol between the morpheme order MM1 and the actual morpheme form, transferred using $A_.

```
Rule = <E>/<W
$(A <PFX> )$ # $(B <ROOT> $)
<E>/+MM1=$A_>
```

While the above rule successfully transfers the morpheme *se-*, we still need to assign the analytical attributes associated with the morpheme, that is: PFX+R_ADJ +EQTV. The rest of the attributes and values (+RL=010200+YumiA1) do not need to be exported because they are created for SANTI-morf implementation. For example, RL = 010200 is the rule number's value, created for debugging purposes. YumiA1 is an attribute that informs the name of the morphological grammar file into which the morphological grammar rule is written; it is also created for debugging purposes.

Rewriting these attributes directly in the syntactic rule as +MM1=$A_,PFX +R_ADJ+EQTV fails, giving an UNDEFINED error code. It seems that the error is caused by the comma, and *plus* symbols, which in NooJ might not be allowed in syntactic annotations. To overcome this, I incorporated an arbitrary attribute ' + ID' into the morphological grammar rule, from which the analysis of the equative adjective se- is initially written (here ADJ_se- rule in the morphological grammar). The original rule which produced the initial annotation is shown below.

```
varX= $(X <L>* $) ;
out1= <E>/<$1L,$1C$1S$1F>;
#rule 010200
ADJ_se- = se/<se,PFX+R_ADJ+EQTV+RL=010200+YumiA1>
:varX   <E>/<$X=:ROOT+DykaA1+ADJ> :out1   ;
```

The required attributes are rewritten as + ID's corresponding values (see below). However, because the plus and comma symbols seem to prevent the annotation from being automatically transferred, percentage symbols are used. This symbol is proven to be acceptable in syntactic grammar. The improvement to the morphological grammar rule is illustrated in bold below (compared with the initial rule above).

```
#rule 010200
ADJ_se-=
se/<se,PFX+R_ADJ+EQTV+RL=010200+YumiA1+ID=se%PFX%R_ADJ%EQ
TV>       :varX   <E>/<$X=:ROOT+DykaA1+ADJ> :out1   ;
```

In the values, you can see that I also rewrite the morpheme (se). This is because the SANTI-morf morphological annotation scheme distinguishes the unit's orthographic and citation forms. For this unit, both forms are identical, *se-*. However, for a certain unit, such as the active prefix morpheme *meng-*, its orthographic and citation forms differ, namely *meng* and *meN*, respectively. While the modification to the morphological grammar will differ slightly, the main principle of supplying an additional attribute ID does not change.

Let us now return to the syntactic grammar. To transfer the attributes of the first morpheme (given by the modified morphological grammar), the following element, =AID, is added to the syntactic grammar. The equals sign is used again as it can be accepted in a syntactic annotation. The element =AID means: transfer all annotation values under +ID that belong to the ALU within variable A.

```
Rule = <E>/<W
$(A <PFX> )$ # $(B <ROOT> $)
<E>/+MM1=$A_=$A$ID>
```

The rule is now half-complete as we still need to incorporate the second morpheme (the adjective root *cepat*) and its corresponding tag into the syntactic grammar. To do this, the same procedure is repeated and adapted. Again, I use an equals sign (a sign acceptable in a syntactic annotation) to connect the first and second ALUs. At the end, an extra element, =MM, is added. This is simply to mark the end of the analysis, as without this an UNDEFINED error code occurs.

```
Rule = <E>/<W
$(A <PFX> )$ $(B <ROOT> $)
<E>/+MM1=$A_=$A$ID=$B_=$B$ID=MM>
```

As the second morpheme is a root verb, we need to update the entry lines in the dictionary file within which the root is originally written. The same procedure is implemented. Only the required attributes (in bold below) are incorporated into the + ID's values in the entry.

```
cepat,ROOT+ADJ+PS+AC+ACS+TX+DykaA.
```

The part written in bold above shows the relevant attributes to be transferred to the syntactic annotation. In the modified entry line below, the attributes are added as corresponding values of + ID. Again, the morpheme is rewritten for the purposes of adhering to SANTI-morf's morphological annotation scheme.

```
cepat,ROOT+ADJ+PS+AC+ACS+TX+DykaA1+ID=cepat%ROOT%ADJ
```

This modification finalises the syntactic rule for *secepat,* and also other words comprising a prefix + a root combination. Once the rule is applied, NooJ provides the expected syntactic annotation. As shown in the upper segment of the figure below, the syntactic annotation shows that all the morphemes congregate as one unit (Fig. 2).

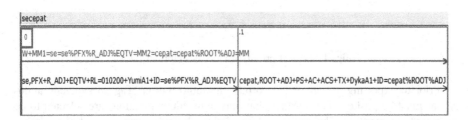

Fig. 2. Syntactic annotation of *se-cepat*

Because the experiment was successful, new syntactic rules to cover the remaining morphotactic combinations are then added. It considers the combination of Indonesian affixes, compounds, reduplications, and clitics. At present, the syntactic grammar file contains 169 rules representing 168 morpheme combinations (Figs. 3).

```
Main = :rule1|:rule2|:rule3|:rule4|:rule5|:rule6|:rule7|:rule8|:rule9|:rule10|:rule11|
|:rule21|:rule22|:rule23|:rule24|:rule25|:rule26|:rule27|:rule28|:rule29|:rule30|:rul(
|:rule41|:rule42|:rule43|:rule44|:rule45|:rule46|:rule47|:rule48|:rule49|:rule50|:rul(
|:rule61|:rule62|:rule63|:rule64|:rule65|:rule66|:rule67|:rule68|:rule69|:rule70|:rul(
|:rule81|:rule82|:rule83|:rule84|:rule85|:rule86|:rule87|:rule88|:rule89|:rule90|:rul(
|:rule101|:rule102|:rule103|:rule104|:rule105|:rule106|:rule107|:rule108|:rule109|
|:rule121|:rule122| :rule123 | :rule124 | :rule125| :rule126 | :rule127 | :rule128 | :
|:rule141 | :rule142 |:rule143 |:rule144 |:rule145 |:rule146 |:rule147 | :rule148 |:rι
|:rule163 |:rule164 |:rule165 |:rule166 | :rule167 |:rule168 ;
rule1 = <E>/<W $(A <ALU+PCLT> $) # $(B <CFX+A> $) # $(C <ROOT> $) (<E>|-) #
rule2 = <E>/<W $(A <ALU+PCLT> $) # $(B <CFX+A> $) # $(C <ROOT> $) (<E>|-) #
rule3 = <E>/<W $(A <ALU+PCLT> $) # $(B <PFX> $) # $(C <ROOT> $) (<E>|-) # $(
rule4 = <E>/<W $(A <ALU+PCLT> $) # $(B <PFX> $) # $(C <ROOT> $) (<E>|-) # $(
rule5 = <E>/<W $(A <CFX+A> $) # $(B <ROOT> $) # $(C <CFX+Z> $) (<E>|-) # $(
rule6 = <E>/<W $(A <CFX+A> $) # $(B <ROOT> $) # $(C <CFX+Z> $) (<E>|-) # $(
```

Fig. 3. Syntactic grammar rules in file EN-v4-reformat1.nog

The syntactic grammar file (within which the rules are stored) must be placed lowest in the priority. I name the grammar EN-v4-reformat1. The code EN-v4 is SANTI-morf's version code (Fig. 4).

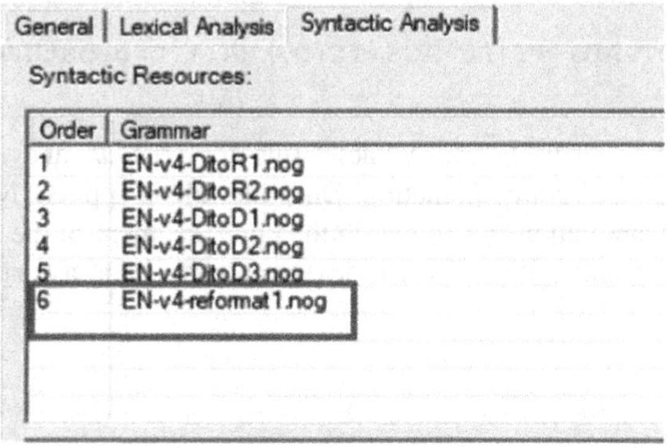

Fig. 4. Lowest priority for EN-v4-reformat1.nog

Prior to exporting the annotated corpus, the radio button 'Tag all syntactic annotation' must be pushed. This ensures that only syntactic annotations are selected to be generated in the output. The output is shown below. It demonstrates that all morphemes (for *mem-bersih-kan,* and *se-cepat* below) are exported.

```
<W
MM1="mem=meN%PFX%R_VER%ACV=MM2=bersih=bersih%ROOT%ADJ=MM3
=kan=kan%SFX%R_VER=MM">membersihkan</W>
<W
MM1="se=se%PFX%R_ADJ%EQTV=MM2=cepat=cepat%ROOT%ADJ=MM">se
cepat</W>
```

While all morphemes are fully exported, the annotation looks very untidy. This is caused by the presence of the equals and percentage signs previously used to export all analytical attributes. To improve the readability of the text file, we need to implement a number of search-and-replace operations to obtain the desired output format. For instance, % needs to be replaced with + so that all attributes can be properly connected using the standard NooJ connector symbol. The parts = MM2 and =MM3 need to be replaced with (newline)MM2 and (newline)MM3 to allow morpheme boundaries to be overtly shown.

To implement these, and other required changes, I wrote a small program in PHP. Note that this task can also be carried out using any program which supports regular expression functions. As this procedure is, in essence, a multiple find-and-replace operation, it can even be performed using text editor programs such as Notepad or Gedit, or even NooJ's REGEXP (even though each find-and-replace operation must be executed individually). See the final output below (subsequent to applying for the program), which is more readable. Each annotation for each morpheme begins with MM followed by a numeric digit. The output below consists of MM1, MM2, and MM3 (these are the three attributes of tag W) given on three separate lines. Thus, there are three morphemes. The word formed by these morphemes *membersihkan* 'to clean (sth)' is specified by a W tag (inside the angle brackets).

```
<W
MM1="mem,meN,PFX+R_VER+ACV"
MM2="bersih,bersih,ROOT+ADJ"
MM3="kan,kan,SFX+R_VER"
>membersihkan</W>

<W
MM1="se,se,PFX+R_ADJ+EQTV"
MM2="cepat,cepat,ROOT+ADJ"
>secepat</W>
```

This final output is not given in standard XML format as used in NooJ, but I argue that the format is quite straightforward. The full word is enclosed in <W> XML tags. The XML attributes in the tag are used to inform the order of the morphemes (MM1, MM2, etc.), and associated XML values are used to contain the morphemes and their corresponding tags (orthographic form, citation form, morphological tag). With this format, other users can easily adapt the output for use in their preferred corpus-query program.

4 Evaluation and Known Issues

SANTI-morf is applied to a 10K+ word-token testbed corpus. I manually inspect the output and discover that more than 99% of the word tokens in the testbed are correctly exported. The less than 1% of words that NooJ cannot properly export can be categorised into two different types.

The first type consists of words that are ambiguously tokenised. For instance, in the original annotation, the word *mencari*, 'to look for', is correctly analysed as a combination of a prefix and a root, but an alternative analysis as a combination of a prefix, a root, and a suffix is also present (Fig. 5).

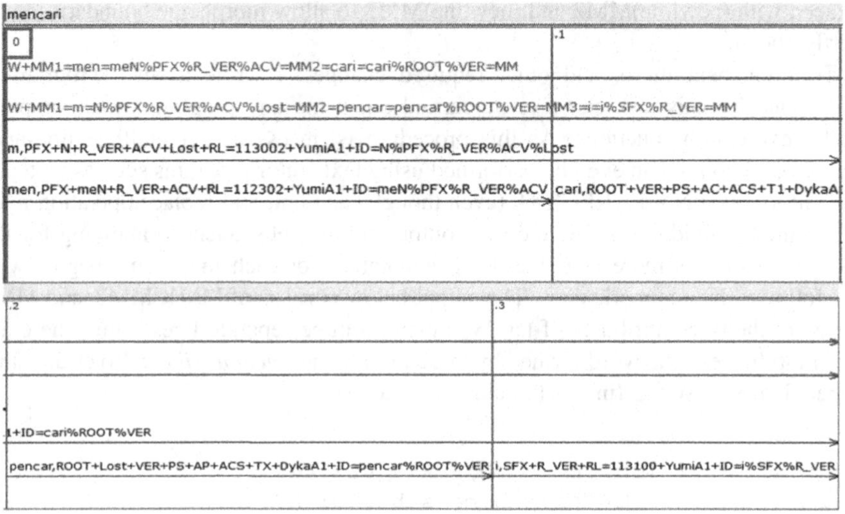

mencari	
0	.1
W+MM1=men=meN%PFX%R_VER%ACV=MM2=cari=cari%ROOT%VER=MM	
W+MM1=m=N%PFX%R_VER%ACV%Lost=MM2=pencar=pencar%ROOT%VER=MM3=i=i%SFX%R_VER=MM	
m,PFX+N+R_VER+ACV+Lost+RL=113002+YumiA1+ID=N%PFX%R_VER%ACV%Lost	
men,PFX+meN+R_VER+ACV+RL=112302+YumiA1+ID=meN%PFX%R_VER%ACV	cari,ROOT+VER+PS+AC+ACS+T1+DykaA
.2	.3
1+ID=cari%ROOT%VER	
pencar,ROOT+Lost+VER+PS+AP+ACS+TX+DykaA1+ID=pencar%ROOT%VER	i,SFX+R_VER+RL=113100+YumiA1+ID=i%SFX%R_VER

Fig. 5. Ambiguous syntactic annotations

The syntactic grammar does indeed manage to capture these two analyses but, when exported, the XML tags are oddly structured. As shown below, the structure is <W Attribute1 = values1><W Attribute2 = values2>word</W></W>. Therefore, my program fails to properly reformat it.

```
<W
MM1="men=meN%PFX%R_VER%ACV=MM2=cari=cari%ROOT%VER=MM"><W
MM1="m=N%PFX%R_VER%ACV%Lost=MM2=pencar=pencar%ROOT%VER=MM
3=i=i%SFX%R_VER=MM">mencari</W></W><W >
```

If the tokenisation is ambiguous and produces multiple sequences with different numbers of morphemes, only the longest sequence is exported, even though that longest sequence might be incorrect. This is caused by NooJ's syntactic grammar configuration, which prioritises the longest sequence. Once the longest sequence in the annotation output is detected, other sequences are ignored.

The second type of error refers to words whose analyses are obtained from a dictionary entry containing an equals sign, such as *aba = aba*, 'cue'. In the NooJ dictionary, the equals sign is one of NooJ's special symbols, equivalent to an optional hyphen in the text. Thus, an entry can capture both *aba aba* and *aba-aba*. However, this turns out to cause errors in the export, as the orthographic and citation forms are not properly delineated.

```
<W MM1="aba=aba=aba=aba%ROOT%NOU=MM">aba-aba</W>
```

5 Conclusion

In this paper, I have described the logic behind the tweaking of NooJ resources, the outcome, and implementation. The outcome is a new syntactic grammar, and a set of modified dictionaries and morphological grammars, that can properly export NooJ's morphological annotation output. The implementation is successful, as shown by the results of the evaluation. My paper here, thus, presents a novel finding on NooJ's interoperability, as it allows NooJ's results to be used by systems other than NooJ. The procedure followed in this paper can be adapted by NooJ users who want to make their morphologically annotated corpora more accessible beyond the NooJ community.

It seems that NooJ's morphological grammar is understudied. This is shown by the use of the LEMMA attribute in the XML attributes present in standard NooJ's text-file output, which is applied to all annotations, even those at the morpheme level. Many experiments use NooJ morphological grammars, but they are typically used to complement morphosyntactic analyses (rather than a full-scale implementation of morphological annotation, up to export).

The known limitations of this experiment are ambiguous export of words that are ambiguously analysed and the use of equals signs in dictionary entries. There are several alternatives to remedy this problem. First, more rigorous disambiguation rules can be created to prevent ambiguities, even before applying the modified syntactic grammar. This will reduce the number of errors as unambiguous analyses can be correctly exported. Second, in the case of retained ambiguities, a new format to describe ambiguous morphemes should be designed. This format will guide the creation of a small program to reformat annotation output into a tidy format. Third, the use of equals signs in the dictionary should be reconsidered or replaced with another symbol. Alternatively, the small program to reformat annotation needs to be revised to accommodate this, so that the program can also output the desired format.

Acknowledgments. This paper was written during my PhD candidacy at Lancaster University, Lancaster, United Kingdom. I would like to extend my deepest gratitude to the Indonesia Endowment Fund for Education (https://www.lpdp.kemenkeu.go.id/ (last accessed 07/08/2021)) (*Lembaga Pengelola Dana Pendidikan*, or LPDP) for fully sponsoring my PhD studies at Lancaster University. I am also highly indebted to Andrew Hardie, my PhD supervisor, for his useful feedback. All errors are mine.

References

1. Silberztein, M.: NooJ Manual (2003). www.NooJ4nlp.org

2. Silberztein, M.: Formalizing Natural Languages NooJ Approach. Wiley, London (2016)
3. Prihantoro: SANTI-morf: a new morphological annotation system for Indonesian. A Ph.D. thesis: forthcoming. Lancaster University Press, Lancaster (2021)
4. Hardie, A.: CQPweb – combining power, flexibility and usability in a corpus analysis tool. Int. J. Corpus Linguist. **17**(3), 380–409 (2012)
5. Kilgarriff, A., et al.: The Sketch Engine: ten years on. Lexicography **1**(1), 7–36 (2014). https://doi.org/10.1007/s40607-014-0009-9
6. Anthony, L.: Concordancing with AntConc: An introduction to tools and techniques in corpus linguistics. JACET Newsl. (55), 155–185 (2006). Version 3.2.0
7. Scott, M.: WordSmith Manual. Lexical Analysis Software Ltd., Gloucestershire (1996)
8. Brezina, V., Timperley, M., McEnery, T.: #LancsBox, v.4.x [software] (2018). http://corpora.lancs.ac.uk/lancsbox
9. Ide, N., Veronis, J. (eds.): Text Encoding Initiative: Background and Contexts. Computers and the Humanities, vol. 29, p. 1 (1995)
10. Ide, N.: Corpus encoding standard: SGML guidelines for encoding linguistic corpora. In: Proceedings of the First International Language Resources and Evaluation Conference, LREC1998, pp.463–470. ELRA, Granada (1998)
11. Tadmor, U.: Malay-Indonesian. In: Major World Languages, pp. 791–818. Routledge, New York (2004)
12. Mueller, F.: Indonesian morphology. In: Morphologies of Asia and Africa, pp. 1207–1230. Eisenbrauns, Winnona (2007)

Intensive Comparisons of the PECO and PVCO Classes in Old French

Xavier Blanco[1($\boxtimes$)] and Yauheniya Yakubovich[2]

[1] Universitat Autònoma de Barcelona, 08193 Cerdanyola del Vallès, Spain
Xavier.Blanco@uab.cat
[2] Universitat de València, 46019 Valencia, Spain
Yauheniya.Yakubovich@uv.es

Abstract. In this article, we study intensive comparisons of the PECO (adjectival predicate) and PVCO (verbal predicate) classes in Old French (primarily focusing on texts from the 12th and 13th centuries). We have proceeded by emptying and analysing a base corpus, completed with other sources, in order to offer the broadest possible overview of the topic. Intensive collocations are presented in accordance with the second term of the comparison: Humans, Animals, Vegetables, Inanimates and Abstracts. We offer numerous annotated examples of the type of collocations studied and of some similar collocations. This is a propaedeutic study that will give rise to various modules of electronic dictionaries that can be integrated into the NooJ linguistic engineering system. It is part of a broader research project to create a global description of intensive collocations in Medieval French that is being conducted within the framework of the COLINDANTE (*Intensive Collocations in Old French and Their Translations into Contemporary French and Spanish*, PID2019-104741GB-100) project funded by the *Ministerio de Ciencia e Innovación*, Spain).

Keywords: Phraseology · Lexicography · Old French · Frozen adverbs

1 Introduction

Within the framework of the research project on *Intensive Collocations in Old French and Their Translations into Contemporary French and Spanish* COLINDANTE, PID2019-104741GB-100) (*Ministerio de Ciencia e Innovación*, Spain), we are producing the most complete description possible of intensive collocations in Old French [4]. Among such collocations, we find those which are based on a comparison, for example: *rouge comme sang* ('red as blood') and *fuir comme un lièvre* ('to flee like a hare'). Following the description in [8], the former belong to the PECO (adjectival predicate) class and the latter to the PVCO (verbal predicate) class.

In this article, we present an overview of such intensive collocations found in the French medieval literature of the 12th and 13th centuries. To do so, we have systematically scoured the Frantext database [2] and, albeit to a lesser extent, we have also integrated a certain number of examples from the BFM database [9], and from dictionaries, phraseological catalogues and personal readings of texts not contained in the aforesaid databases. For reasons of brevity, and in order to homogenise the presentation

© Springer Nature Switzerland AG 2021
M. Bigey et al. (Eds.): NooJ 2021, CCIS 1520, pp. 15–27, 2021.
https://doi.org/10.1007/978-3-030-92861-2_2

as much as possible and be able to offer approximate but comparable quantified data, we shall primarily be presenting examples extracted from Frantext, which we shall cite in abbreviated form as per the textual database itself: *title, text reference number, year, page number or verse/line number* (abbreviated *p.* or *v.*). We should specify that we use an approximate total of 250 examples extracted from the said database. When we cite examples from other sources, they shall be accompanied by their abbreviated references following the pattern: *title, editor, publisher, year, page number or verse/line number*.

The propaedeutic research that we are presenting in this article will subsequently enable us to produce different modules of electronic dictionaries of Old French that can be integrated into the NooJ linguistic engineering environment [11], which will, in turn, allow us to proceed with automatic analysis of texts in order to enrich those dictionaries and annotate the analysed texts. Lexicography of Old French must account for a much greater diversity of forms than there is in contemporary languages (whose spelling and morphosyntax are much more fixed). However, studies like [1] (for Middle French) show that NooJ is a perfectly suitable environment for this type of work.

We have already presented the notion of intensive collocation in [5] and [6]. We therefore see no need to repeat it here, especially when the examples give a clear enough idea of the type of semantic value being studied. We should specify, however, that each comparison consists of four components. We can illustrate this with the example *Saietes volent come pluie* ('the arrows flew like rain') (*Roman de Brut*, A114, 1155, p. 216). The first term of this collocation corresponds to the object to which a certain action or quality is predicated (*saietes*). The second term corresponds to the item to which the first component is compared (*pluie*). The third term corresponds to the *tertium comparationis*, i.e. the quality common to the first two terms (in our example *volent*). The fourth component corresponds to the connector used to make the comparison (*come*).[1]

Our article is organised into five sections in accordance with the syntactic-semantic trait of the second term of the comparison: Human, Animal, Vegetable, Inanimate and Abstract.

2   Humans

16% of our corpus corresponds to intensive comparisons whose second term is a human name. We should immediately make it clear that we are referring to occurrences in absolute terms (not to types of occurrences). Thus, for example, *courir comme desvee* ('to run like a madman') appears twice: *Comme desvee va courant* in *Miracles de notre Dame* (A142, 1218, t. 4, p. 50) and *Ele corut comme desvee* in *Le Roman de la Rose* (E133, 1230, p. 214).

We should note that we prefer to work from precise occurrences than from regroupings of occurrences, since the former have an effective existence, while the

---

[1] In some cases where the example was particularly representative, we have included collocations with other comparative connectors, e.g. *plus que* 'more than': *Roge est la maille plus que n'est feus ardenz* (*Le Couronnement de Louis*, E173, 1130, v. 2478–2479).

latter depend on the researcher's criterion. So, for example, it could be agreed that only sequences that contain the same lexical components (leaving aside what are purely variations in spelling, and which are so numerous in medieval texts) correspond to a collocation. Or, it could be considered advantageous to regroup the collocations that contain the same *tertium comparationis* and different but synonymous or quasi-synonymous second terms. Thus, we could consider (or not) that the two examples presented above form a set with the sequence *Parmi le bois cuerent come esragiét* (*Moniage Guillaume. Seconde Rédaction*, A105, 1180, p. 150), given that *esragiet* and *desvee* have very similar meanings: 'mad, demented'.

Different regrouping criteria are possible (and may be useful depending on one's purpose), but working directly with occurrences means remaining open to the possibility of proposing groupings of different types depending on research needs. In fact, the comments that we make below are in themselves a kind of grouping of examples with a view to their panoramic presentation.

Returning to the specific matter of intensive comparative collocations with a second term corresponding to a name that designates a human being, we basically have four types of comparisons that use such a term. The first and most frequent corresponds to synonymic variants of 'mad' and is combined with verbs whose meaning is 'to run' or 'to shout': *si s'escria come esbahie* (*Le Roman de Renart*, R027, 1180, p. 63); *Et crioit come fors del san* (*Yvain ou Le chevalier au lion*, A002, 1177, p. 84a); *Et s'escrie com forsenez* (*Le Roman de la Rose*, E133, 1230, p. 184). *Cf.* also the two examples above with *esragiet* and *desvee*.

The second group features family relationships that are combined with predicates[2] reflecting positive feelings, such as 'to love': *vous amera autant comme li peres aimme le fil* (*La suite du Roman de Merlin*, R019, 1235, p. 200); *vous tenés chiers comme freres* (*La suite du Roman de Merlin*, R019, 1235, p. 202); *et tant l'anmoie de bon cuer comme freres doit amer autre* (*La mort le roi Artu*, A121, 1230, p. 84).

The third group introduces human types that, due to their profession, age or social status, are taken as paragons of certain actions: *Vos mentés comme gars* (*Roman d'Alexandre*, A111, 1180, p. 274); *Or pleurent ambedui comme petit tousel* (*Roman d'Alexandre*, A111, 1180, p. 241); *Devant l'ymage ensi se ploye / Devotement com une none* (*Miracles de Notre-Dame*, A142, 1218, p. 350). The word *gars* designates a young man of low social standing, who does subordinate jobs. It is also used as an insult. It is not unusual, then, for it to be combined with 'to lie'. A *tousel* is also a very young lad, but the word does not have the negative connotations associated with *gars*, and arises in the cited example combined with 'to cry', in an expression meaning something like 'to cry like a child'. A 'nun' is considered a paragon of devotion.

The fourth and final group of human-based intensive comparisons (treating 'human' here as a syntactic-semantic trait that includes any anthropomorphic being) takes the devil as a paragon, who appears with various names: 'the adversary' (*aversier*), 'he of evil destiny' (*maufé*), the 'demon', and so on. It goes without saying that these are

---

[2] We make an approximate reference to the different classes of predicates, in order to avoid the formalism of semantic labels, which would not make matters any clearer here. However, our basis is a complete hierarchy of semantic labels presented in [3].

expressions that introduce negative predicates or present them as such: 'ugly, horrible' (*hisdos come aversier, Le Couronnement de Louis*, E173, 1130, p. 17); 'strong-limbed' (*menbru comme dïable, Moniage Guillaume. Seconde Rédaction*, A105, 1180, p. 272); 'to howl' and 'to roar' (*Il hulle et brait conme maufez, Roman de Renart*, A122, 1175, p. 10).

3 Animals

With 44% of the cases, names that designate animals are the most frequent type of second term of comparison. The generic *beste* appears in combinations like *crier come beste; battre qqn come beste* ('to scream like a beast', 'to strike someone like a beast'). Note that these comparisons have a strong pejorative component. In fact, some comparisons are not part of this study because they do not present an intensive sense, but only a pejorative one: *(vivre, se comporter) come beste (mue, sauvage); traiter qqn come une beste (sauvage); (tuer, occire) qqn come beste*, 'to live, behave like a beast' (reinforced with 'mute', since one of the inherent characteristics of a 'beast' is the inability to speak; the spoken word is thus presented as a distinctively human property), 'to treat someone like a wild beast', 'to kill someone like a beast'.

The most common intensive comparison with *beste* is 'hairy as a beast'. In *Roman d'Alexandre* (A111, 1180, branche 3, p. 198 and p. 213), certain inhabitants of India (such as yogis) are described as follows: *Quelque tans que il face, tous jors vont ainsi nu / Et sont par tout le cors comme bestes pelu; Chascuns iert par le cors dusq'au nombril fendus / Et environ le dos comme bestes velus.*

In the medieval mentality, there were five main categories of animal [10]: quadrupeds, birds, fish, serpents (in the broader sense) and a residual category (*vermine, vermes*), which includes all kinds of generally small creatures not included in the previous categories: insects, worms, amphibians and even molluscs. We shall briefly consider the main animal-based comparisons in each of these categories.

3.1 Quadrupeds

This is by far the best represented category in terms of intensive comparisons. We could not possibly present them all here, not even slightly, but we shall highlight the main ones. At the top of the pile comes the lion, which rose to the throne of the animal kingdom in the 12th century, displacing the bear.[3] The lion is the prototype of courage, strength and valour (*fiers*[4], *hardi*): *Et Guillaume d'Orenge, qui est fiers com lyons; / As portes et as murs souvent les assaurrons* (*Buevon de Conmarchis*, Frantext A119, 1271, p. 63); *Bons chevaliers et larges, hardis comme lion* (*Roman d'Alexandre*, branche 4, A112, 1180, p. 336). Both adjectives are used in the following example: *Gorvains fu preuz e Meraugis / Fier et hardis comme lïons* (*Méraugis de Portlesguez*, ed. Szkilnik, Champion Classiques, ~ 1230, v. 690–693). The leopard also presents

---

[3] Which is presented to us as a hairy animal: *Velu sont commë ours, poil ont dur et poignant* (*Roman d'Alexandre*, A111, branche 3, 1180, p. 206).

[4] We should specify that *fiers* appears here in the sense of 'courageous, fearless', and not 'proud'.

these attributes, albeit to a lesser extent than the lion:[5] *Et, d'autre part, / plus estoit hardiz d'un liepart* (*Roman de la Rose ou Guillaume de Dole*, A129, 1228, p. 3).

In turn, the wolf and the wild boar are impetuous; they enter the fray in a rash, impulsive manner, although the wolf does so to attack and the wild boar does so in self-defence: *Couroit comme pors forsenés, / Qu'il ne prent garde ou il se fiere.* (*Yvain ou Le Chevalier au Lion*, ed. Hult, Libraire Générale Française, 1177, v. 3518–3519); *Atainz les a, si les assaut; Come lous qui a proie saut* (*Cligès*, ed. Luttrell & Gregory, Brewer, 1176, v. 3731–3732). The fox is a thief and coward, but also cunning, and gained widespread fame after *Roman de Renart*.

Of note among the domestic quadrupeds are the donkey and the ox. Both animals have a strong symbolic load (note that they were both close to child at the Nativity, the ox warming the new-born baby with its breath and the donkey being a means of transport). In comparisons, the donkey is an animal that is beaten (*sel batirent com asne a pont, Roman de Renart*, R027, 1180, branche I, p. 36) and the ox is the prototype of meekness.

Then there are ovine animals. The lamb and the goat are opposites. The former is a sweet, meek and Christological animal, and the latter is presented as a foul-smelling, lewd beast, and later on as a mad one too. Another curious opposition is that between the deer and the hare. Both are considered fast and fearful, but the former (which did not enjoy the best of reputations in Classical Antiquity) was highly esteemed in the Middle Ages as game for great lords and as an animal that symbolises resurrection, due to its antlers growing back every summer. The latter, on the other hand, is a cowardly, scavenging creature (*Plus est coars de lievre que chacent li mastin, Roman d'Alexandre*, A111, 1180, branche 3, p. 285). One should not have the 'heart of a hare', for that means being a coward: *Ne doi mie avoir cuer de lievre* (*Lancelot ou Le Chevalier à la Charrette*, A001, 1177, p. 31c).

Finally, there are two animals that were held in very poor regard: the dog and the pig. The dog is vile, miserable, flea-ridden and, on occasions, rabid (*Et plus le tienent vil c'un chien, Miracles de Notre-Dame*, A142, 1218, t. 4, p. 113). Only the hunting dog (for example, the speedy *lévrier* 'hound') is held in high esteem. The pig is an animal that ignores the sky and always stares at the ground. It represents dirtiness and materialism.

We can conclude this subsection with the horse, a fundamental animal in medieval French literature, but one that does not seem to have given rise to intensive comparisons. We only find it (and belatedly) in a few unspecific comparisons of the 'big as a horse' kind.

3.2   Birds

There is a fundamental distinction between birds of prey and other birds. Falconry (like hunting) is a privilege of the ruling classes. The falcon (and falconiformes in general,

---

[5] The gradation between the two animals reflected in the following context is interesting. The lion surpasses the leopard in power and courage: *Li uns des trois passera son pere autant come li lyons passe le liepart de pooir et de hardement* (*La Queste del Saint Graal*, S985, 1220, p. 77).

such as the *gerfaut* and *émerillon*) are vital, vigorous: *De la presse ist, bruiant come faucon, Aspremont*, A157, 1190, p. 540). Other birds flee from the falcon: *Autresi com la grue fuit devant le faucon, L'en porte Bucifal par l'estor de randon* (*Roman d'Alexandre*, 1180, branche 2, p. 125); *Si le fuient paien com gierfaut fait la grue* (*Buevon de Conmarchis*, A119, 1271, p. 89); *Que a merci venir l'estuet, / Come l'aloe qui ne puet / Devant l'esmerillon durer* (*Lancelot ou Le Chevalier à la Charrette*, A001, 1177, p. 37d). The hawk is not a falconiform (it is an accipitriform) but is also part of this category: *Que autresi l'eschievent com l'ostor fait la quaille* (*Roman d'Alexandre*, A110, 1180, branche 4, p. 138).

As well as birds of prey, two other birds were symbolically fundamental in the Middle Ages: the dove and the raven. The former is always a positive biblical element, a symbol of fidelity, humility and peace, as well as the main iconographic motif of the Holy Spirit. It is associated with the colour white, like the swan, but the latter is more typical of Antiquity. The raven, in contrast, is the opposite to the dove. It is a paragon of blackness and symbolises distance from God; it is a pagan bird, sacred to the Germanic and Celtic peoples. Like the raven, the magpie, the crow and the owl (*choue*) are also associated with darkness: *Et l'autre noir come choe* (*Erec et Enide*, A006, 1170, p. 20f).

3.3   Fishes

Medieval man knew less about fishes than about birds. Sea fish were little appreciated (as opposed to river fish, which were a common part of the diet). There are very few intensive comparisons associated with fish. Only the generic name seems to have engendered the common comparison, 'healthy as a fish': *Li mires du garir i mist grant espison, / Q'ains vint jors les rendra si sains comme poisson* (*Roman d'Alexandre*, A110, 1180, branche 2, p. 108); *Que en un moment fu si seine / Comme poisson qui noe en Seine* (*Miracles de Notre-Dame de Chartres*, A137, 1262, p. 203).

One might suppose that the whale (famous because of the Jonah story in the Bible, as well as that of the false island in *Navigation de saint Brendan*) would be an ideal candidate to be a paragon of largeness. However, the only example of 'big as a whale' that we know is a late one, dating from the end of the 15th century: *Qui est plus gro que une baleyne* (*Le Mystère de saint Sébastien*, ed. Mills, Droz, p. 46).

3.4   Snakes and Vermin

In this section we regroup two major categories of medieval zoology: 'serpents' and 'vermin'. The 'king' of serpents is the dragon, a diabolical animal. Therefore, it is no surprise to find 'horrible, ugly as a dragon': *Conversent un oisel qui sont nomé griffon, / D'orible forme sont, hideus comme dragon* (*Roman d'Alexandre*, A111, 1180, branche 3, p. 254). Note that this comparison refers to the griffin, a mythological half eagle, half lion creature. The Middle Ages had no strict separation between imaginary and real animals. After all, many of the animals that seem common to us (particularly the great African fauna) were causes of wonder. Why should dragons, griffins and unicorns not exist too? Nevertheless, only the dragon seems to be used in intensive comparisons.

The serpent is associated with the devil for obvious reasons. But its evil stems not so much from its aggressiveness as from its cunning. Hence we find 'clever as a serpent' in Boethius's translation (*Del Confortement de Philosophie*, A152, 1240, p. 164): *Por ce dist Jhesu Crist a sez deciples: "Soiez sage come serpent"*. The names of the different species (*coulevre, dipsas, guivre, vipère...*) do not seem to have engendered intensive comparisons.

It is interesting to note that *nu comme un ver* ('naked as a worm'), which is common in contemporary French, is not documented until the 15th century. In contrast, we do find an occurrence of 'naked as ivory, an ivory statue': *Mes nuz se voit com un yvoire* (*Yvain ou Le chevalier au lion*, A002, 1177, p. 90f).

Finally, there is the following curious occurrence: 'more whorish than a fly'. Undoubtedly, the choice of 'fly' stems from the need to make a rhyme: *Mout par estes de mavés estre, / de paior ne poez vos estre, / que plus estes pute que mouche / qui en esté les genz entouche* (*Roman de Renart*, R027, 1180, branche I, p. 107).

4   Vegetables

12% of the sequences in our base corpus are intensive comparisons whose second term is the name of a plant. Of particular note, we have flowers. The fleur-de-lis is the image of whiteness *par excellence* (*Dalés la dame l'ont assis / Qui est blance com flours de lis*, *Le Conte du Graal*, ed. Potvin, Dequesne-Masquillier, 1182–1190, p. 220). The rose generally represents redness (*La face vermellete comme rose de pré, Fierabras*, ed. Kroeber & Servois, Vieweg, s. XII, p. 61). These comparisons often refer to the female face and are clearly ameliorative. The following example, from *Li roumans de Berte aus grans piés* (ed. Scheler, Closson & Muquardt, 1273–1274, v. 789), regroups both comparisons in a single line: *Vermeille ert comme rose, blanche com flours de lis*.

We should specify that the adjective *rose* in reference to the colour comes late (no earlier than the 15th century). Medieval roses were red or white. The colour pink is considered a shade of red. A lady's complexion is therefore 'rosy', i.e. red, as in the following example from *Le Bel inconnu* (ed. Perret & Weill, Champion Classiques, s. XIII, v. 1541–1542): *Le vis avoit si colouré / Come la rose el tans d'esté*. Note here a reinforcement of the second term of the comparison: 'in the summertime'. Such reinforcements are frequent and varied (we already saw in §2 how 'mute' and 'wild' were reinforcements applied to *beste*). The interested reader will find numerous annotated examples of this type of comparison in [5].

Flowers are generally the paragon of what is beautiful and pleasing to the senses, be that sight or smell. The rose is *nete* ('pure, unblemished'): *Se tu vielz faire mon commant, / Je t'amonest, di et commant / Que nete soyes comme rose* (*Miracles de Notre-Dame*, A142, 1218, p. 297). The *esglentiers* ('sweet-brier') is fragrant: *Ele est fleiranz comme esglentiers, / Ele est ausi com li rosiers* (*Le Roman de l'Estoire dou Graal*, A113, 1199, p. 2).

After flowers, we have fruit, and especially the apple, an emblematic fruit (note here that the form *pomme* comes from the Latin collective neutral plural *poma*, which can be used for various tree fruits: *pomme d'orange, pomme grenade...*). Intensive combinations include 'healthy as an apple', 'round as an apple': *Sainz iert ancui com une pomme* (*Miracles de Notre Dame*, A141, 1218, t.3, p. 426); *Gras et reont com une pome* (*Lancelot ou le Chevalier à la Charrette*, A001, 1177, p. 35f).

Another frequent expression is 'black as a blackberry'. In its descriptive use it is applied to fabrics, defensive weapons, animal fur and human skin. *Martes zibellina* (also called *marta sable*; *sable* is what the colour black is called in heraldry) is described in various cases by means of this comparison, for example: *ceste chape de vair fourree / et ciz sables noirs come meure* (*Roman de la Rose ou Guillaume de Dole*, A129, 1228, p. 57). The black knight of *Vengeance Raguidel* (A130, 1200, p. 32) rides a horse 'blacker than a blackberry' and wears armour 'blacker than a ripe blackberry' (*madura* serves here to reinforce the intensive): *Ses cevax fu plus noirs que meure / et trestote s'autre armëur / plus noire que meure mëure. / Ses cevax ert noirs con corbiax / et li chevaliers fu mout biax.* Note that his hair is also 'black as a raven' (cf. § 3.2).

In *Aliscans* (ed. Regnier & Subrenat, Champion Classiques, s. XII, v. 6276–6279), the fourteen sons of Borel, one of the pagan chiefs, are described as 'blacker than a ripe blackberry' and also 'marvellously handsome: *Par la bataille ez vos poignant Borrel. / O lui estoient si.XIIII. chael, / Tuit chevaliers adoubé de novel, / Noirs comme more, merveilles furent bel.* It is interesting to note that, both in this example and in the previous one, it is specified that knights are very handsome.

Branches are long and brittle. Something (as an enemy) can be said to break or snap like a branch (*rain, raim*); i.e. easily: *Li cuens Guillelmes tret l'espee d'acier; / Fiert un paien en travers par derrier, / Ausi le cope comme un rain d'olivier* (*La Prise d'Orange*, A102, 1200, p. 85).

Leaves are the prototype of green, although it is important to note that the comparison 'green as a leaf' tends to have a psychological meaning and is used to describe the manifestation of a negative emotion, especially when describing a human face. In *Roman de Thèbes* (ed. Mora-Lebrun, Librairie Générale Française, 1150, v. 6835–6836), Ismène suffers a severe emotional setback caused by the death of Aton. The physical manifestation of this emotion is described thus: *vert esteit comme foille d'ierre / point de colour n'ot en sa face.* The ivy leaf is the most common sort in intensive comparisons, but we also find the vine leaf, walnut leaf, cabbage leaf and simply the leaf of a tree with no further details: *Einz est si froidie corne marbres / Et verz com est la fuille es arbres* (*Li romanz d'Athis et Prophilias*, ed. Hilka, Halle, Niemeyer, s. XII, v. 3015–3018).

Albeit less frequently than leaves, grass is also the paragon of greenness. In *Aspremont* (A157, 1190, p. 166), we find: *Et lor espié par sont si aceré / Qu'il sont plus vert que nule herbe de pré.* We should specify that 'chives' and 'leeks' are also prototypes of green, but these appear in far fewer comparisons. And there are still other plant names that appear more rarely as a second term in intensive comparisons. Because it combines two comparisons with more unusual forms, we could cite the examples of the following context (taken from *La chanson du Chevalier au Cygne et de Godefroid de Bouillon*, ed. Hippeau, Aubry, s. XII, v. 6780–6782) where we find *savine* (a type of juniper) and *fordine* (a wild plum): *Quant la dame l'entent, verde fu com savine; / Li cuers li est falis, pasmee chiet sovine; / La fache devint noire come fordine.*

5   Inanimates

Approximately 27% of the occurrences in our corpus use a concrete inanimate noun as the second term of comparison. This is unquestionably the syntactic-semantic trait for which the semantic diversity of second terms is greatest. We should particularly note the distinction between inanimate concrete countable and inanimate concrete uncountable (or mass) nouns. We shall therefore divide these subclasses into two subsections. The number of contexts that we have identified is similar for both.

5.1   Countable

Of the wide variety of syntactic-semantic classes of inanimate concrete countable nouns, we shall present two types of examples corresponding to lighting systems and cutting tools, two basic elements for life.[6]

As expected, words like 'torch' (*brandon*) and 'candle' (*estaval*, the large, thick type used in church, or the more generic *chandele*) are combined with 'to burn', 'to shine' or 'to illuminate': *A mont envers le ciel en guise de tisons / Virent venir les rais ardans comme brandons* (*Roman d'Alexandre*, A111, 1180, branche 3, p. 214); *Desus un escharboucle luisant comme estaval* (*Roman d'Alexandre*, A111, 1180, branche 3, p. 208); *Plus getent de clarté ne fait chandele esprise* (*Buevon de Conmarchis*, A119, 1271, p. 57).

Cutting tools, such as a 'knife' (*coutiaus*) or 'razor' (*rasor*), are naturally combined with 'to cut' (*trancher*), 'cutting' (*tranchant*): *De Durendal fiert grans caus a estrouz, / Qui trainche fer conme coutiaus fait trouz* (*Aspremont*, A157, 1190, p. 236); *Chascuns a trait le branc d'acier, / Cler et tranchant conme rasor* (*Deuxième Continuation de Perceval*, A117, 1210, p. 129). In both cases, the first term of the comparison is used to sing the praises of a sword's blade.

Another important subclass of inanimate concrete countable nouns corresponds to those with a locative interpretation. We have not included any specific section for *stricto sensu* locatives (e.g. 'landscape', 'plain'), since these do not seem to be used in fixed comparisons (although some would be good candidates, e.g. 'mountain' as a paragon for highness). The only exception seems to be 'clear as the moon':[7] *El ne fu oscure ne brune, / Ainz fu clere comme la lune* (*Le Roman de la Rose*, E133, 1230, p. 90). On the other hand, the concrete inanimate nouns that designate buildings do appear as second terms of intensive comparisons. Such is the case of *chastel* 'castle' ('safe as a castle on a hill') (*Or soions tuit seür comme chastel seur mote*, *Roman d'Alexandre*, A110, 1180, branche 2, p. 78), 'tower' ('supported as upon a tower') (*Sor la gambe senestre li jut comme une tor*, *Roman d'Alexandre*, A110, 1180, branche 2,

---

[6] As an example of another concrete inanimate noun, we have 'to tear (chainmail) as if it were a (bed) sheet' (*Lor haubers lor derompent autresi comme dras*, *Roman d'Alexandre* A111, 1180, branche 3, p. 298) or 'tense as a drum' (*Quant tendanz est comme tabours*, *Miracles de Notre-Dame*, A142, 1218, t.4, p. 479).

[7] The moon is also a symbol of change, hence 'lunatic': *Le fol se mue comme la lune* (*Le Livre de Ethiques d'Aristote*, 5903, 1370, p. 472). Note, however, that this is an example from the 14th century.

p. 93) or 'prison' ('shut away like in a prison') (*et fu trays a son cloistre aussi comme a une prison, La vie et les Epistres [de Pierres Abaelart et Heloys sa fame]*, A100, 1290, p. 26).

5.2 Uncountable

The main comparisons whose second term is an inanimate concrete uncountable noun include those that take the name of a colour as their *tertium comparationis*, in particular the following three: 'white as snow', 'red as blood' and 'black as coal'. It is not hard to find numerous examples of these comparisons in Medieval French literature, beyond the main corpus discussed here. We studied these comparisons in some detail in [5] and [6], so here we shall merely present an example of each with no further comment: *ses chevaus estoit plus blans que nege* (*La suite du Roman de Merlin*, R019, 1235, p. 185); *Et quant il l'ot tornee, si virent que ele [ceste espee] estoit rouge come sanc de l'autre part* (*La Queste del Saint Graal*, S985, 1220, p. 203);[8] *la dame en ot la char plus noire que charbon* (*Les enfances de Doon de Mayence*, B018, 1250, p. V].

The simile between the hair of a blonde lady and the colour of gold is also very common, but the form of the comparison seems somewhat less fixed than in the three aforementioned cases, for there are variations not only in the lexeme used as the *tertium comparationis* (*blont, sor, cler*), but also in the comparative connector, which recurs, in various cases, to the verb *sembler, ressembler* ('to seem'): *Le chief avoit si blont de blondeur esmeree / Que ce sambloit fins ors* (*Buevon de Conmarchis*, A119, 1271, p. 105); *Ses crins, qui tant sunt blont et sor / Que de coulor resamblent or* (*Les merveilles de Rigomer*, ed. Foerster, Halle Niemeyer, v. 5465–5466).

Other less frequent comparisons that use the names of colours are 'black as ink' and 'yellow as wax': *Quan Rollant veit la contredite gent, / Ki plus sunt neirs que nen est arrement* (*La Chanson de Roland*, E174, 1125, p. 150); *Mere, ce dist la serve, je suefre tel martire / Que j'en suis aussi jaune devenue com cire* (*Berte aus grans piés*, ed. Henry, Droz, v. 2116–2117).

We also encounter comparisons like: 'cold as ice' (*Assés en petit d'eure fu si frois comme glace, Roman d'Alexandre*, A110, 1180, branche 2, p. 113), 'heavy as iron' (*Vaslez, c'est mes haubers, s'est ausi pesanz come fers, Conte du Graal*, A128, 1181, p. 362r) and 'drunk as a soup' (*Et tantes fois baisa sa coppe / Qu'il estoit yvres comme soppe, Miracles de Notre Dame*, A141, 1218, t. 3, p. 68). Some examples are unique, such as 'to fry like butter in a pan', which has a figurative meaning, since it describes a negative emotion (indignation, as a result of which the blood crackles in the veins as if it were bacon fat used for cooking): *Li sans li bout et frit comme lars en paiele* (*Roman d'Alexandre*, A112, 1180, branche 4, p. 338).

Other PVCO comparisons are 'to burn like wax' (*Ou noiera en mer ou ardra comme cire, Roman d'Alexandre*, A109, 1180, p. 66) and 'to melt like ice' (*Et li escuz peçoie et font come glace, Yvain ou Le chevalier au lion*, A002, 1177, p. 100e).

---

[8] The form *vermeil come sanc* is even more frequent than *rouge come sanc*. Shortly before the cited example, we can read in the same text: *et voient autres letres vermeilles come sanc, qui disoient [...]* (*La Queste del Saint Graal*, S985, 1220, p. 203).

6 Abstracts

Only 1% of our corpus is made up of intensive comparisons whose second term is an abstract noun. And there is very little semantic variety between them. Of particular note are atmospheric phenomena, such as 'storm', 'thunder' and 'lightning'. Storms are 'violent' (*roide*) and 'rumbling' (*bruianz*): *coroit une eve si parfonde, / roide et bruianz come tanpeste* (*Erec et Enide*, A006, 1170, 21b).

Lightning is *bruyant* 'noisy, thunderous' (nowadays, we would expect something like 'quick'). In *La suite du Roman de Merlin* (R019, 1235, p. 564 and 565), we find: *Et le Morholt luy revient, bruyant comme le fouldre* and *Et le Morholt [...] qui venoit bruyant comme le fouldre.* It seems more natural to us for thunder to be loud: *Comme tonnoirres bruiant vint* (*Miracles de Notre-Dame*, A142, 1218, t. 4, p. 20). We could cite yet more comparisons associated to atmospheric phenomena, such as the one already mentioned in §1 *Saietes volent come pluie* (*Roman de Brut*, A114, 1155, p. 216) and its variant *Saietes volent come grelle* (*grelle* means 'hail'),[9] and also: *Tenve et legiere comme vens* (*Miracles de Notre-Dame*, A141, 1218, t. 3 p. 66) 'tenuous and light like the wind'.

We also have 'fire' (*feu, fu*) as the second term of a certain number of comparisons. We saw earlier that the association of blood with the colour red seems natural, while its association with fire (present, all the same, in various languages and cultures) is more symbolic, since the embers are reddish, but fire itself (i.e. the flame) features different shades of yellow, blue and orange, and cannot really be considered red. However, the French *chanson de geste* does like to employ the comparison 'red as fire' to describe the eyes of evil or, at least, threatening characters. In *Les Enfances Renier* (ed. Cremonesi, Instituto Editoriale Cisalpino, s. XIII, v. 8126), the pagan chieftain Corbon's eyes are red like fire: *Les yeux ot gros et rouges conme fus.* Le Roman d'Alexandre (1180, v. 235–236) contains another interesting case: *L'un des ieus ot vermel comme fu de carbon / Et l'autre ot ausi vair com d'un müé faucon.* Both the choice of colours and the heterochromia of his eyes give the protagonist a disturbing appearance. It is also poignant that in *Le Roman de la Rose* (ed. Strubel, Librairie Générale Française, 1225–1268, v. 2921) it is the personification of *Danger* who has red eyes: *Si ot les ielz roges come feus.*

Defensive weapons can also be red like fire, as in this example from *Le Couronnement de Louis* (E173, 1130, v. 2478–2479): *El dos li vestent son halberc jaserenc / Roge est la maille plus que n'est feus ardenz.*

In *Voyage de Saint Brendan* (ed. Short & Merrilees, Union générale d'éditions, s. XII, v. 1143–1144) the second term of the comparison is not 'fire', but 'flame': *Revint mult tost od sa lamme / Tute ruge cume flamme.* The blade (*lamme*) of a red-hot sword is described by the expression 'red as a flame'. Alliteration was a clear motive for choosing this *tertium comparationis*.

---

[9] In the following occurrence it is specified that they fly 'thickly': *Saietes volent tant espesse[e]ment / Conme la pleuue qui de menut descent* (*Aspremont*, A157, 1190, p. 226).

7 Conclusion

Intensive collocations in the French language have been (and will foreseeably continue to be) the subject of a large number of lexicological, lexicographical and semantic studies. But that is not the case with collocations in medieval language. We should emphasise, however, that a historical perspective is essential for a complete description of the phraseology. In [4] we show how collocation in medieval language is very different to that of the modern day and explain why it is so essential to study these initial stages of French phraseology.

Such a study must necessarily begin with a long period of systematic data collection [7]. The different classifications and arrangements of this data, as well as its formalisation with a view to integration in a linguistic engineering and corpus analysis environment like NooJ, will constitute the basis for an explanatory description of the phraseological phenomenon, which is dynamic and must therefore include the diachronic dimension.

On the one hand, the study of medieval collocations raises questions that push the notion of phrasema to the limits. Given the impossibility of recurring to the linguistic intuition of native speakers and acknowledging that the corpus will always be limited, no matter how much it is expanded to include the maximum number of available sources, the question arises as to how to distinguish effectively between a unit of language and the creation of discourse. It seems advisable to start by examining all discursive phenomena. However, after deciding to include a certain collocation as part of the language system, the usual lemmatisation problems arise, and which are particularly awkward in the case of Old French.

On the other hand, we should not forget that a good knowledge of phraseology is essential in order to understand and interpret any text. Detailed philological studies of the founding texts of the French language have made this very clear and have brilliantly and ingeniously answered many questions. However, by their very nature, philological descriptions have always tended to analyse the difficulties posed by a given text, rather make a general study of a certain type of phraseological unit. Therefore, systematic study of a certain semantic value (such as intensity) can offer a different and complementary perspective.

We shall end with one final quote that illustrates the extent to which intensive comparisons can play a crucial role in a literary work. This is the extremely famous description of Alexander the Great's tent, for which three of these collocations are used in just four lines:

> Li quatre pan sont fet chascuns d'une façon;
> L'uns est plus blans que nois et plus clers d'un glaçon,
> Li autres de travers est plus noirs que charbon,
> Et li tiers fu vermeus, tains de sanc de dragon,
> Et li quars fu plus vers que fueille de plançon.
> (Roman d'Alexandre, A109, 1180, p. 44).

Acknowledgments. The present research has been funded by the *Ministerio de Ciencia e Innovación* (Spain) in the framework of the Project I+D+i COLINDANTE (PID2019-104741GB-100).

References

1. Aouini, M.: Approche multi-niveaux pour l'analyse des données tex-tuelles non-standardisées: corpus de textes en moyen français. These de doctorat, Université Bourgogne Franche-Comté (2018)
2. ATILF. Base textuelle Frantext (en ligne). ATILF-CNRS & Université de Lorraine (1998–2019). http://www.frantext.fr. Accessed 24 Sept 2021
3. Blanco, X.: A hierarchy of semantic labels for Spanish dictionaries. In: Okrut, T., Hetsevich, Y., Silberztein, M., Stanislavenka, H. (eds.) NooJ 2015. CCIS, vol. 607, pp. 66–73. Springer, Cham (2016). https://doi.org/10.1007/978-3-319-42471-2_6
4. Blanco, X.: Remarques sur la variation diachronique des collocations. Cahiers Lexicol. **116**, 71–94 (2020)
5. Blanco, X.: Le sang, le feu et la rose. La couleur rouge comme *tertium comparationis* en français médiéval. In: Gross, G., Neveu, F., Fasciolo, M. (eds.) Décrire une langue: objectifs et méthodes. Classiques Garnier, Paris (forthcoming)
6. Blanco, X.: Le charbon, l'encre et la mûre. La couleur noire comme *tertium comparationis* en français médiéval. Zeitschrift für französische Sprache und Literatur (forthcoming)
7. Gross, M.: Méthodes en syntaxe. Hermann, Paris (1975)
8. Gross, M.: Grammaire transformationnelle du français. 3 - Syntaxe de l'adverbe. ASSTRIL, Paris (1986)
9. Guillot-Barbance, C., Heiden, S., Lavrentiev, A.: Base de français médiéval: une base de référence de sources médiévales ouverte et libre au service de la communauté scientifique. Diachroniques **7**, 168–184 (2020)
10. Pastoureau, M.: Bestiaires du Moyen Âge. Éditions du Seuil, Paris (2011)
11. Silberztein, M.: La formalisation des langues: l'approche de NooJ. ISTE Editions, Londres (2015)

Lexicon-Grammar Tables for Modern Arabic Frozen Expressions

Asmaa Kourtin[1]([✉]), Asmaa Amzali[1], Mohammed Mourchid[1], Abdelaziz Mouloudi[2], and Samir Mbarki[2]

[1] Computer Science Research Laboratory, Faculty of Science, Ibn Tofail University, Kenitra, Morocco
[2] EDPAGS Laboratory, Faculty of Science, Ibn Tofail University, Kenitra, Morocco

Abstract. Frozen or idiomatic expressions play a very important role in natural language processing, they are very important in focusing the meaning and expressing it clearly and precisely, away from the ambiguity's problem. They also enrich the language with enormous possibilities to express different meanings. Thus, the interest of linguistics in the study of the meaning is no longer limited to the vocabulary, but rather to the frozen expressions. The Arabic language is very rich in frozen expressions. We can find them dispersed in Arabic books, such as the Quran, the linguistic heritage's and literary's books, the books of proverbs, etc., which has led some researchers to collect, classify and explain them. Indeed, several classifications have been proposed according to the needs of each linguist. Our aim is to create, for the modern Arabic language, lexicon-grammar tables of fixed and continuous frozen expressions such as "مسك الختام" (misku al-khitam; Save the best for last). For that, we start by collecting and studying these expressions (about 800 frozen expressions). Then, we classified them into two classes and create their lexicon-grammar tables that will be implemented in NooJ by generating their NooJ dictionaries.

Keywords: Lexicon-grammar tables · Natural Language Processing (NLP) · Frozen expressions · Idiomatic expressions · Idioms · Modern Arabic · NooJ platform · NooJ dictionary · Syntactic and semantic analysis

1 Introduction

Natural language processing is a field of computer science concerned with interactions between computers and human natural languages. For several decades, the applications related to automatic natural languages processing have attracted particular attention, such as automatic translation, orthographic and grammar correction, corpus analysis, automatic question answering (QA), etc. For this, there are two techniques, the statistical and the linguistic approach.

Today, statistical techniques are the most used, but they do not give satisfaction, which requires the development of a natural language processing platform based on the linguistic approach such as NooJ, which contains different levels of analysis such as the lexical, morphological, syntactic, and semantic analyses.

© Springer Nature Switzerland AG 2021
M. Bigey et al. (Eds.): NooJ 2021, CCIS 1520, pp. 28–38, 2021.
https://doi.org/10.1007/978-3-030-92861-2_3

The language lexicon is not only made up of single words like nouns, verbs, etc. but also frozen expressions. Therefore, we should not be limited to the vocabulary study and the lexical meaning analysis of a language to process it. The language treatment must include the study of the syntactic meaning, including the study of frozen or idiomatic expressions. This recognition will help to solve many problems related to automatic natural language processing, such as the problem of automatic translation.

The frozen or idiomatic expressions have attracted the attention of several researchers in the last few years, leading to various researches for different languages. The Arabic language is very rich in frozen expressions which it inherited from the pre-Islamic era and early Islam, and whose use has persisted to this day. They are used in the daily communication language of Arabic speakers, and the works of writers and poets.

We can find these expressions dispersed in Arabic books, such as the Quran, in the linguistic heritage and literary's books, in the books of proverbs, etc., which has led some researchers to collect, classify and explain them. Indeed, several classifications have been proposed according to the needs, such as continuous expressions, discontinuous expressions, expressions that do not admit variations, expressions allowing variations, etc.

Our main objective is to create, for the modern Arabic language, lexicon-grammar tables of frozen expressions. For that, we will start by collecting and studying the fixed and continuous modern Arabic frozen expressions, such as "مسك الختام" (misku al-khitam; Save the best for last). Then, we will create lexicon-grammar tables for them that will be implemented in the NooJ platform by transforming them into NooJ dictionaries [1] and building their corresponding syntactic grammars [2] allowing to detect these expressions in texts and corpora.

This paper is structured as follows: In the second section, we will begin by reviewing existing works on frozen expressions for different languages. In the third section, we will explain the lexicon-grammar approach. In the fourth section, we will give an overview of the modern Arabic frozen expressions, then we will present our lexicon-grammar tables proposed for fixed and continuous modern Arabic frozen expressions. In the fifth section, we will explain how the lexicon-grammar tables are integrated into the NooJ platform, and then we will implement our proposed tables by generating their dictionaries. Finally, in the sixth section, we will conclude this paper with an evaluation and discussion of the benefits of this work, and then we will give some perspectives.

2 Related Works

The frozen or idiomatic expressions have attracted the attention of several researchers in the last few years, leading to various researches for different languages. In [3], Maurice Gross studied the French frozen expressions; he classified them into sentences with only one fixed nominal group in any syntactic position, and sentences with any number of fixed groups in any position.

In [4], Jorge Baptista focused on the syntactic properties that can be used to distinguish compound nouns from ordinary noun phrases and explained how the same methodology can be applied to the identification of compound adverbs. In [5], Jorge Baptista et al. built an electronic dictionary of the European Portuguese frozen expressions by focusing on the problems arising from the description of their formal variation in view of natural language processing.

For the Arabic language, several researchers have worked on the frozen expressions and their translation especially their French translation. In [6], Hijab Mohammad Alqahtni worked on the Saudi newspaper "Al Riyadh", when he analyzed a sample of idiomatic expressions sourced from this newspaper by focusing on their structure and context. In [7], Ali boulaalam studied the verbal sentence's category of Arabic frozen expressions and their French translation.

In [8], Sameh Yaiche dealt with the issue of emergence and interlanguage comparison by carrying out a psycholinguistic and experimental study being conducted on native and non-native French-speaking adults (Tunisian Arabic speakers), in order to determine whether linguistic factors facilitate the processing of fixed language during a memorization task.

In [9], Minko Mi Nseme Sylver Aboubakar made a theoretical study of the Arabic frozen expressions by classifying their morphosyntactic structures and analyzing the various elements composing these expressions as well as their degree of syntactic-semantic frozenness in order to build a lexical database.

In [10], Mohamed Saad Ali worked on the translation of the frozen expressions taken from the Qur'an in the French language by identifying the problems raised by this translation. In [11], Mennat-Allah Abdelmaksoud studied idioms in the Qur'an, by analyzing their French translation and the process of frozenness that characterizes them.

3   The Lexicon-Grammar Approach

The lexicon-grammar approach plays a very important role in automatic natural language processing (ANLP). It was initiated by Maurice Gross within the Laboratory of Documentary and Linguistic Automation (LADL) in 1975 [3, 12–14]. He built a syntactic lexicon of the French language by covering several lexical categories like verbs, nouns, adjectives, frozen expressions, etc.

The language's lexicon is classified into several classes grouping together a number of entries that accept the same definitional construction. In addition, the lexicon-grammar table code a class and it is represented by a matrix, where the lines depict the lexical entries, the columns depict the syntactic, semantic, distributional, morphological, and transformational properties, and the cells contain, either a lexical element, "+" or "−" to specify whether the corresponding lexical entry has the property of the corresponding column or not. If a lexical element has more than one meaning, then it must have multiple lexical entries, one per sense.

For instance, the C1D class represents French frozen expressions that have the basic construction "N0 V Det1 C1", where "N0" means the subject, "V" means the verb, "Det1" means the first determinant, and "C1" means a constant object (see Fig. 1).

<V ID>	N0 =: Nhum	N0 =: N-hum	Ppv =: se figé	Ppv =: en figé	Ppv =: y figé	Ppv =: Neg	<ENT>Ppv	<ENT>V	N0 V	<ENT>Det1	N0 V Det1 C1 Prép2 N2	<ENT>C1	C1 =: Npc	[passif]	Exemple
1	+	-	-	-	-	-	<E>	abandonner	-	la	-	compétition	-	+	§abandonner§la compétition
2	+	-	-	-	-	-	<E>	abandonner	-	le	-	domicile conjugal	-	+	§abandonner§le domicile conjugal
3	+	-	-	-	-	-	<E>	abandonner	-	les	-	lieux	-	+	§abandonner§les lieux
4	+	-	-	-	-	-	<E>	abandonner	+	la	-	partie	-	+	§abandonner§la partie
5	+	-	-	-	-	-	<E>	abandonner	-	la	+	pose	-	+	§abandonner§la pose
6	+	-	-	-	-	-	<E>	abandonner	-	le	-	terrain	-	+	§abandonner§le terrain
7	+	-	-	-	-	-	<E>	abjurer	-	la	-	foi catholique	-	+	§abjurer§la foi catholique
8	-	+	-	-	-	-	<E>	abolir	-	le	-	temps	-	+	§abolir§le temps
9	+	+	-	-	-	-	<E>	accélérer	-	le	-	mouvement	-	+	§accélérer§le mouvement

Fig. 1. Excerpt from the lexicon-grammar table C1D for French frozen expressions

4 Lexicon-Grammar Tables for Modern Arabic Frozen Expressions

4.1 Overview of the Modern Arabic Frozen Expressions

The common use of the frozen expressions is what made them semantic and structural stability. They are very important in focusing the meaning and expressing it clearly and precisely, away from the ambiguity's problem. These expressions also enrich the language with enormous possibilities to express different meanings.

The interest of modern linguistics in the study of the meaning is no longer limited to the vocabulary's study and the analysis of its lexical meaning, but rather to the study of the syntactic meaning including the study of frozen expressions, which led to the development of frozen expressions dictionaries.

The linguists used several terms to designate these expressions depending on the adopted approach [11]. The frozen expressions (التعبيرات الثابتة) are called also idiomatic expressions or idioms (التعبيرات الإصطلاحية), welding expressions (التعبيرات المسكوكة), ready-made sentences (العبارات الجاهزة), collocations (المتلازمات اللفظية), phrasemes, etc.

Different definitions have been provided to the frozen expressions from the syntactic and semantic points of view by Dubois, Maurice Gross, Gaston Gross, etc. [3, 15, 16]. From these definitions, we have adopted that the term "frozen" is reserved for expressions whose global meaning is not deduced by joining the meanings of its components; it is a group of words that, in their entirety, form a meaning that is coming from the accord of a group of linguists, e.g.:

(Iswaddati al-dounia fi 'aynay Zayd) اسودت الدنيا في عيني زيد

N2   C1   Prép   C0 Det   V

This sentence contains the frozen expression "اسودت الدنيا في عيني" when "اسودت" (iswaddati) is the verb, "الدنيا" (al-dounia) is the subject, "في" (fi) is the preposition, "عيني" ('aynay) is the first object and "زيد" (Zayd) is the second object.

The meanings of the components of this sentence are:

اسودت = Have darkened

الدنيا = The life

في = In

عيني = The eyes of

زيد = Zayd (A male human name)

However, the global meaning of this sentence is "Zayd faces hardship and loses hope in life". As shown, this meaning is a special meaning coming from the accord of a group of linguists that could not been deduced by joining all the meanings of the component.

The Arabic language is very rich in frozen expressions which it inherited from the pre-Islamic era and early Islam, and whose use has persisted to this day. These expressions are used in the daily communication language of Arabic speakers, in the newspapers, in the works of writers and poets, etc.

Many frozen expressions have their origins in Arabic books such as the Holy Qur'an and Al-Hadith al-sharif. For instance, the expression "أضغاث أحلام" (Adghathu ahlamin) that means "Confused dreams and illusions" and "اخفض جناحك" (Ikhfid janahaka) that means "Be kind".

Some frozen expressions are derived from the linguistic heritage and literary's books like poetry or classical Arabic sources. For instance, "لقي حتفه" (laqiya hatfahu) that means "He is dead" and "رجع بخفي حنين" (Raja'a bi khoffay Hanin) that means "He failed".

Others have their origin in the books of proverbs, such as «مصائب قوم عند قوم فوائد» (massa'ibu qawmin 'inda qawmin fawa'idu) that means "One man's meat is another man's poison" and "بيته من زجاج و يقذف الناس بالحجارة" (Baytoho min zojajin wa yaqdifu al-naasa bi alhijarati), this proverb is given to the one who has faults and talks about those of others. etc.

The Arabic language is very rich in frozen expressions which have led some researchers to collect, classify and explain them. Indeed, several classifications have been proposed according to the needs. Some researchers classified them according to the degree of frozenness such as fixed, semi-flexible, and flexible frozen expressions. Others classified the frozen expressions according to their structures such as "C0 C1" (Noun Noun), "V C0" (Verb Subject), "V C0 C1", etc., or according to their category like noun phrases (جمل اسمية), verbal phrases (جمل فعلية), genitive (الإضافة), etc. (see Table 1).

Our main objective is to create linguistic resources for modern Arabic frozen expressions. Thus, we will create lexicon-grammar tables for those expressions allowing us to describe all the grammatical, syntactic, and semantic features of the language lexicon. For that, we started by studying fixed and continuous frozen expressions then creating lexicon-grammar tables for them.

Table 1. Classification of frozen expressions

Degree of frozenness	Structure	Category	....
• Fixed • Semi-flexible • Flexible	• C0 C1 • V C0 • V C0 C1 • V C0 Prép C1 •....	• Noun phrases (جمل اسمية) • verbal phrases (جمل فعلية) • Genitive (الإضافة) • Adjective (نعت) • Preposition phrases (الجار و المجرور) • Single word (كلمة واحدة) •....	

Afterward, we did extensive research in some Arabic dictionaries of frozen expressions such as "معجم التعبير الإصطلاحي في العربية المعاصرة" that means "the dictionary of idioms in the Modern Arabic" [17]. Thus, we collected about 2400 frozen expressions. Then, we extracted and studied the fixed and continuous frozen expressions by describing their linguistic properties, and we obtained about 800 frozen expressions until now, e.g.:

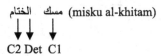

This expression means "to save the best for last", and it is a noun phrase made of Noun + Det + Noun.

4.2 Lexicon-Grammar Tables for Modern Arabic Frozen Expressions

As mentioned in the previous section, several classifications have been proposed for the frozen expressions according to the needs of each linguist.

In this paper, we worked on the fixed and continuous modern Arabic frozen expressions. For that, we studied these expressions by describing their syntactic-semantic properties. Then, we have classified them into two classes according to their categories (nominal or verbal expressions), the first one is "EFA1" and the second one is "EFA2". These two classes will be in turn subdivided into subclasses containing the entries sharing the same definitional construction.

• **The class "EFA1":**

This class groups the nominal fixed and continuous modern Arabic frozen expressions, e.g.:

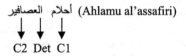

أحلام العصافير (Ahlamu al'assafiri)

↓ ↓ ↓

C2 Det C1

This frozen expression expressing "mental weakness and recklessness" is constituted of "Noun + Det + Noun".

Fig. 2. Excerpt from the lexicon-grammar table "EFA1"

The Fig. 2 shows an excerpt from our first lexicon-grammar table "EFA1". The
grammatical category of the entries of this table is a noun represented by "N". The
columns of this table contain the syntactic-semantic features, where "Prép" denote the
preposition, "Conj" denote the conjunction, "Det" means the determinant represented
by "الـ" (al) in Arabic, "C" is a noun used for frozen expressions and the features "C0
W", "C0 C1", "C0 Det1 C1", "C0 Prép1 C1", etc., represents the structures of the
frozen expressions contained in this table.

For instance, the frozen expression "أبا عن جدّ" (aban 'an jaddin) is used to express
"belonging and originality in something and praise them". This expression is a noun
phrase having the structure "C0 Prép1 C1" where "C0" is "أبا" (aban), "Prép1" is "عن"
('an) and "C1" is "جدّ" (jaddin).

- **The class "EFA2":**

This class groups the verbal fixed and continuous modern Arabic frozen expressions, e.g.:

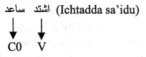

اشتدّ ساعد (Ichtadda sa'idu)

C0   V

This frozen expression that means "become stronger" is constituted of "Verb + Noun".

Fig. 3. Excerpt from the lexicon-grammar table "EFA2"

The Fig. 3 shows an excerpt from our second lexicon-grammar table "EFA2". The grammatical category of the entries of this table is a verb represented by "V".

For instance, the frozen expression "اتسع الخرق على الراتق" (ittasa'a alkharqu 'ala al-ratiqi) is used to express that "it's getting difficult, it can't be cured". This expression is a verbal phrase having the structure "V Det0 C0 Prép1 Det1 C1" where "V" is "اتسع" (ittasa'a), "Det0" is "ال" (al), "C0" is "خرق" (kharqu), "Prép1" is "على" ('ala), "Det1" is "ال" (al) and "C1" is "راتق" (ratiqi).

5 Implementation

The integration of the lexicon-grammar tables in the NooJ platform is a two-step process. First, each table must be converted into a NooJ dictionary, then we have to build for each one a syntactic grammar using the linguistic knowledge encoded in the table to identify the sentences as proposed by Max Silberztein [2, 18]. In addition, we note that the dictionary and syntactic grammar should have the same name and be created in the same folder of the NooJ platform that is "Lexical Analysis".

```
# NooJ V5
# Dictionary
#
# Language is: ar
#
# Alphabetical order is not required.
#
# Use inflectional & derivational paradigms' description files (.nof), e.g.:
# Special Command: #use paradigms.nof
#
# Special Features: +NW (non-word) +FXC (frozen expression component) +UNAMB (unam
#                   +FLX= (inflectional paradigm) +DRV= (derivational paradigm)
#
# Special Characters: '\' '"' ' ' ',' '+' '-' '#'
#|

أبا,N+EFA1+FXC+Prép1=عن+C1=جد+C0=N+C0Prép1C1
ابتسامة,N+EFA1+FXC+C1=ابتسم+C0=N+C1=Adj+C0C1
أبغض,N+EFA1+FXC+Det1+C1=خلل+C0=N+C0=Adj+C0Det1C1
اجتياز,N+EFA1+FXC+C1=طالث+Det2+C2=فوخ+C0=N+C0C1Det2C2
إجراءات,N+EFA1+FXC+C0=N+C0=NP1Obl+C0W
إجهاض,N+EFA1+FXC+C0=N+C0W
أجواء,N+EFA1+FXC+C1=علاصفة+C0=N+C0=NP1Obl+C1=Adj+C0C1
أجواء,N+EFA1+FXC+C1=ودية+C0=N+C0=NP1Obl+C1=Adj+C0C1
إحباط,N+EFA1+FXC+C0=N+C0W
احتضان,N+EFA1+FXC+C0=N+C0W
احتراق,N+EFA1+FXC+Det1+C1=بخور+C0=N+C0Det1C1
أحلام,N+EFA1+FXC+Det1+C1=عصافير+C0=N+C0=NP1Obl+C1=NP1Obl+C0Det1C1
```

Fig. 4. Excerpt from the generated dictionary "EFA1.dic"

The Fig. 4 shows an excerpt from the dictionary "EFA1.dic" generated automatically from the lexicon-grammar table "EFA1" by our previous program generating NooJ dictionaries from lexicon-grammar tables proposed in [1]. The generated dictionary contains all the information coded in the lexicon-grammar table.

The Fig. 5 shows an excerpt from the dictionary "EFA2.dic" generated automatically from the lexicon-grammar table "EFA2".

```
# NooJ V5
# Dictionary
#
# Language is: ar
#
# Alphabetical order is not required.
#
# Use inflectional & derivational paradigms' description files (.nof), e.g.:
# Special Command: #use paradigms.nof
#
# Special Features: +NW (non-word) +FXC (frozen expression component) +UNAMB (unambiguous
#                   +FLX= (inflectional paradigm) +DRV= (derivational paradigm)
#
# Special Characters: '\' '"' ' ' ',' '+' '-' '#'
#
```

اتسع,V+EFA2+FXC+Det0+C0=خرق+Prép1=على+Det1+C1=اتق ر+NONHum+N1Hum+VDet0C0Prép1Det1C1
احتار,V+EFA2+FXC+C0=دليل+NONHum+N1Hum+VC0W
اختل,V+EFA2+FXC+C0=عقل+N0pc+N1Hum+VC0W
اختلط,V+EFA2+FXC+Det0+C0=حبل+Prép1=ب+Det1+C1=بال+N0Hum+N1Hum+VDet0C0Prép1Det1C1
خفر,V+EFA2+FXC+Det0+C0=إذ+Det0+C0=ما+V1=طبل+Det1+C1=جمع+NONHum+N1NHum+Adv0VDet0C0V1Det1C1
ارتندت,V+EFA2+FXC+C0=فرائ+N0pc+N1Hum+VC0W
ارتفع,V+EFA2+FXC+Det0+C0=سنا ر+NONHum+N1NHum+VC0W
استتب,V+EFA2+FXC+Det0+C0=أمر+NONHum+VC0W
استتب,V+EFA2+FXC+Det0+C0=أمن+NONHum+VC0W
استنبط,V+EFA2+FXC+Det0+C0=لطم+NONHum+VC0W
استفحل,V+EFA2+FXC+NONHum+VN0W
استقال,V+EFA2+FXC+N0Hum+VN0W
استقرت,V+EFA2+FXC+Det0+C0=أرض+Adv1=تحت+C1=قدم+NONHum+N1pc+N2Hum+VDet0C0Adv1C1

Fig. 5. Excerpt from the generated dictionary EFA2.dic

6   Conclusion and Perspectives

The Arabic language still suffers until now from the lack of linguistic resources, especially on the frozen expressions. Thus, studying the modern Arabic frozen expressions and creating their lexicon-grammar tables will enrich those resources and simplify the uses of the linguistic data and their modifications.

In this paper, we studied the modern Arabic frozen expressions and presented their classifications. In addition, we created lexicon-grammar tables for the fixed and continuous classes of the modern Arabic frozen expressions. Then, we integrated the proposed tables into the NooJ platform by generating their corresponding NooJ dictionaries.

This study will enrich the linguistic resources of the Arabic language, which will help to solve many problems related to automatic natural language processing (ANLP), such as the problem of automatic translation.

As perspectives, we will extend this work by creating lexicon-grammar tables for the other categories of frozen expressions. Then, we will transform them into NooJ dictionaries and build for them syntactic grammars in the NooJ platform, allowing to detect these expressions in texts and corpora.

References

1. Kourtin, A., Amzali, A., Mourchid, M., Mouloudi, A., Mbarki, S.: The automatic generation of NooJ dictionaries from lexicon-grammar tables. In: Fehri, H., Mesfar, S., Silberz-tein, M. (eds.) Formalizing Natural Languages with NooJ 2019 and Its Natural Language Processing Applications. NooJ 2019. CCIS, vol. 1153, pp. 65–76. Springer, Cham (2020). https://doi.org/10.1007/978-3-030-38833-1_6
2. Silberztein, M.: La formalisation des langues, l'approche de NooJ. ISTE Editions, London (2015)
3. Gross, M.: Les phrases figées en français. L'Inform. Grammat. **59**, 36–41 (1993)
4. Baptista, J.: Compositional vs. frozen sequences. J. Appl. Linguist. Spec. Issue Lexicon-Grammar 81–92 (2004)
5. Baptista, J., Correia, A., Fernandes, G.: Frozen sentences of Portuguese: formal descriptions for NLP. In: Proceedings of the Workshop on Multiword Expressions: Integrating Processing, pp. 72–79 (2004)
6. Alqahtni Hijab, M.: The structure and context of idiomatic expressions in the Saudi press. Ph.D. thesis, University of Leeds (2014)
7. Boulaalam A.: التعابير المسكوكة والترجمة: دراسة معجمية دلالية. Ph.D. thesis, Sidi Mohamed Ben Abdellah University, Fez, Morocco (2017)
8. Yaiche, S.: Figement et prédication en arabe et en français: études linguistiques et psycholinguistiques. Ph.D. thesis, Sfax and Paris 8 universities (2014)
9. Minko-Mi-Nseme, S.A.: Modélisation des expressions figées en arabe en vue de la constitution d'une base de données lexicale. Ph.D. thesis, Lyon 2 (2003)
10. Ali, M.S.: La traduction des expressions figées : langue et culture. Traduire Rev. Française Traduction **235**, 103–123 (2016)
11. Abdelmaksoud, M.: Les expressions idiomatiques dans le Coran et leur traduction française: Étude analytique contrastive de l'arabe vers le français dans trois interprétations françaises du sens du Coran. Ph.D. thesis, Mansoura University, Egypt (2018)
12. Gross, M.: Méthodes en syntaxe: Régimes des constructions complétives. Hermann, Paris (1975)
13. Gross, M.: La construction de dictionnaires électroniques. Ann. Télécommun. **44**(1–2), 4–19 (1989)
14. Gross, M.: Une grammaire locale de l'expression des sentiments. Lang. Française Armand Colin **105**(1), 70–87 (1995)
15. Gross, G.: Les expressions figées en français: noms composés et autres locutions. Editions Ophrys (1996)
16. Dubois, J.: Lexis: Larousse de la langue française (2002)
17. محمد محمد داود. معجم التعبير الإصطلاحي في العربية المعاصرة. دار غريب للطباعة و النشر و التوزيع القاهرة، مصر، (2003).
18. Silberztein, M.: Complex Annotations with NooJ. In: Proceedings of the 2007 International NooJ Conference, Jun 2007, p. 214. Cambridge Scholars Publishing, Barcelone (2008)

NooJ Grammars for Italian Negation System and Sentiment Analysis

Mario Monteleone[1][(✉)] and Ignazio Mauro Mirto[2]

[1] Dipartimento di Scienze Politiche e della Comunicazione, Università di
Salerno, Fisciano, Italy
mmonteleone@unisa.it
[2] Dipartimento di Culture e Società, Università di Palermo, Palermo, Italy
ignaziomauro.mirto@unipa.it

Abstract. The main purpose of this study is the formalization of the Italian
morphosyntactic negation system, in order to assess the relevance of this system
as regards Sentiment Analysis (SA) practices and routines. The study will be
conducted through the construction, application, evaluation, and debugging of
specific NooJ grammars.

Italian Negation may be of three different types, that is: lexical/morphol-
ogical, syntactic, and semantic. Here, we will only deal with those features of
Italian negation that are subject to formalization.

As for sentence negation (SN), Italian employs above all the form *non* (not). It
precedes the predicate inflecting in person and number, and produces sentences
such as *Non piove* (It is false that it is raining), which are in opposition to their
affirmative counterparts, i.e. *Piove* (It is true that it is raining).

Keywords: NooJ · Italian negation system · Formal Italian morphosyntax ·
Multiple negation languages

1 Introduction

The main purpose of this study is the formalization of the Italian morphosyntactic
negation system, in order to assess the relevance of this system as regards Sentiment
Analysis (SA) practices and routines. The study will be conducted through the construction, application, evaluation, and debugging of specific NooJ grammars [1, 2].

Italian Negation may be of three different types [3–12], that is: lexical/morphol-
ogical, syntactic, and semantic. Here, we will only deal with those features of Italian
negation that are subject to formalization.

These, and other syntactic aspects participating in the structuration of Italian
negation, will be dealt with and formalized in our research by means of NooJ tools and
routines. Therefore, we will use specific NooJ FSAs/FSTs and assemble them into an
autonomous morphosyntactic system, based on both labeled electronic dictionaries and
local grammars built ad hoc.

© Springer Nature Switzerland AG 2021
M. Bigey et al. (Eds.): NooJ 2021, CCIS 1520, pp. 39–50, 2021.
https://doi.org/10.1007/978-3-030-92861-2_4

2   Methodological Framework and Linguistic Pragmatic Universals

To define our analysis methodological framework, we must try to answer some specific questions, that is:

- As for General and Contrastive Linguistics:
  - Does a language exist in the world that has not developed Negation (NEG) features/mechanisms/structures?
  - Do we construct NEG obtained only using lexical items?
  - In NEG production, which relationship exists between morphosyntax and lexicon? More precisely, which of the (two sets of) items is most effective in assigning a negative value to sentences/propositions?
- As for NLP, Sentiment Analysis (SA), and NooJ:
  - Is it possible to accurately calculate and classify the negative value of sentences/propositions?
  - Can NEG value calculation method be used also to calculate positivity (POS) values?

Answers to these questions will become explicit in the course of our analysis. However, already at this stage of the research, it is possible to confirm what was stated by [13]: every language has means of producing negative modality and translating negative modality as it is expressed in another language.

This assertion may seem difficult to prove on an abstract theoretical level. Yet, it is a fact that all known languages have means of expressing NEG. Hence, it is possible to affirm that NEG is a pragmatic universal related to the behavioral, psychological, and cognitive functions encountered in every language, produced at the discourse level, as we will see using several morphosyntactic and semantic mechanisms.

3   How Negation is Constructed

Lexicons (probably of every known language) list elements with the highest negation value/function, as negation adverbs, used to express a negative evaluation of the speaker with respect to the information communicated.

However, the negativization function of these adverbs is often inverted in co-occurrence with nouns/adjectives/pronouns that have, in turn, high negative value, in terms of lexical semantics. It always happens in languages (such as Italian) in which a double negation does not produce an affirmation.[1]

Actually, a double negative is a construction occurring when two forms of grammatical negation are used in the same sentence. Multiple negations is the more general term referring to the occurrences of more than one negative in a clause. In some languages, double negatives cancel one another and produce an affirmative; in other

---

[1] See par. 4. for more details on double negation in Italian.

languages, double negatives intensify the negation. Languages where multiple negatives affirm each other are said to have negative concord or emphatic negation.

The analysis of NEG in different languages has led to define that the following are negative concord languages: Portuguese, Persian, French, Russian, Greek, Spanish, Old English, Italian, Afrikaans, Hebrew, many vernacular dialects of modern (also non-British) English. On the contrary, Chinese, Latin, German, Dutch, Japanese, Swedish, modern Standard English are non-negative concord languages. Table 1. gives short examples of different NEG sentences in some Romance and Anglo-Saxon Languages:

Table 1. Negative-concord vs. Non-negative-concord languages (NEG elements in bold)

It	Eng	Ger	Fr	Sp	Por
Non ho **niente** nelle mie tasche	I have **nothing** in my pockets; I **haven't** anything in my pockets	Ich habe **nichts** in meinen Taschen	Je **n'**ai **rien** dans mes poches	No **tengo** **nada** en mis bolsillos	**Não** tenho **nada** nos bolsos
Non sapevo **niente**	I **didn't** know anything; I knew **nothing**	Ich wusste **nichts**	Je **ne** savais **rien**	Yo **no** sabia **nada**	Eu **não** sabia de **nada**

4 Negation in Italian

In Italian, NEG may be of two different types:

- Lexical/morphological, i.e., occurring at word/phrase level;
- SN, i.e., occurring within sentences, by means of negation lexical/morphological elements or based on specific morphosyntactic/semantic constructions (producing semantic/logical NEG).

At the morphological level, NEG is introduced by means of:

- The prefixes *s-* as in *sfiorire* (wither); *dis-* as in *disassemblare* (disassemble), *a-* as in *anormale* (not normal), *in-* as in *incapace* (incapable);
- *Non* (non) placed before single words, as in *non-credente* (non-believer), *non-belligeranza* (non-belligerence), *nonviolenza* (non-violence), or *nonviolento* (nonviolent).

As for SN, Italian employs above all the form *non* (not) before predicates inflecting in person and number, as in:

- *Non piove* (It does not rain, i.e., it is false that it is raining)

and in opposition to affirmative counterparts, i.e.:

– *Piove* (It rains, i.e., it is true that it is raining).

Italian is a multiple-negation language, which means that the addition of a negative element before or after *non* is not interpreted as a double negation equivalent to an affirmation of truth, as in logic. A sentence like:

– **Non** *ha parlato* **nessuno** (Nobody spoke)

is not equivalent to the sentence:

– *Qualcuno ha parlato* (Standard English: Someone spoke/Nobody did not speak).

Hence, the two following sentences have the same meaning:

– *Non c'è tempo per fare* **niente** = *Non c'è tempo per fare* **alcunché**[2] (There is no time to make anything)

In Italian, NEG may be produced also by more than two NEG adverbs, as in:

– *Non c'è* **mai più** *tempo per fare* **niente** (There is never more time to do anything)

Besides, as for this last example, note that any different distribution of *mai* produces unacceptable/dubious sentences:

– *?**Mai** *non c'è* **più** *tempo per fare* **niente**
– *?*Non c'è* **più mai** *tempo per fare* **niente**
– *?*Non c'è* **più** *tempo per fare* **mai niente**

Besides, replacing *mai* with its antonym *always,* we produce an unacceptable sentence:

– **Non c'è* **sempre più** *tempo per fare* **niente** (*? There is not always more time to do anything)

Other restrictions are possible to the co-occurrence of *non* with an additional negative element such as *nessuno* (anyone), *mai* (never), *mica,* (actually, really, not at all):

– *Non* is mandatory if it confers negation value on a predicate, as in *Non sapevo che nessuno fosse venuto* (I didn't know nobody had come) or *Non mi dice mai niente nessuno* (Nobody ever tells me anything);
– *Non* is also mandatory when the NEG sentence is introduced by a double pronoun, as in *Nessuno mi dice mai niente* (Nobody ever tells me anything);
– *Mica* has two different uses: a negative polarity item, e.g., in *Non l'ho visto mica* (Actually I didn't see him), and a negation comparable to *non*, but emphatic, as in *Mica l'ho visto* (I really didn't see him).

---

[2] Note that *alcunché*, with equivalent distribution with respect to *niente*, does not contain a NEG morpheme/element.

Other types of SN concern:

- The series of indefinites:
  - *Nessuno*, as in *Nessuno è venuto* (Nobody came);
  - *Niente*, as in *Niente paura* (No fear);
  - *Mai*, as in *Mai visto niente di simile* (I have never seen anything like this);
- The conjunctions *né/nemmeno/neppure* (either/neither) as in ...*né/nemmeno/ neppure si può accettare una cosa simile* (... neither is possible to accept such a thing);
- The correlative conjunctions *né... né* (either/neither... or/nor), as in *né bianco, né nero* (neither white nor black);
- The forms *no* and *tutt'altro* (not at all), used mainly as a holophrastic answer to polar questions as in *Sei felice? No/Tutt'altro* (Are you happy? No, I'm not/Not at all);
- Autonomous and non-autonomous adverbial phrases such as *tutt'altro che/nient'altro che* (anything but/nothing but), as in *È (tutt'altro + nient'altro) che uno sprovveduto* (He is anything but/nothing more than a fool);

4.1 A Remark on Italian Syntactic Negation

We have already seen that Italian is a multiple-negation language and that NEG may be produced also by more than two NEG adverbs.

However, there may be sentences for which a double negation produces an affirmation. The syntactic/transformational mechanisms responsible for this phenomenon are under investigation [14] but still not completely unveiled. Therefore, here we will only account for its peculiarity, giving some specific sample sentences. For instance:

- *Mai io non ho tempo per leggere* (Never I do not have time to read)

has the same meaning as:

- *Io ho sempre tempo per leggere* (I always have time to read)

In this type of sentence, the distribution of *mai* is constraint by contrastive topicalization [15]. All other acceptable distributions of *mai* produce NEG sentences:

- *Io non ho mai tempo per leggere* (I never have time to read)
- *Io non mai ho tempo per leggere* (I never have time to read)

Replacing *mai* with *sempre* (always) produces a NEG sentence with the opposite meaning:

- *Sempre io non ho tempo per leggere* (I always do not have time to read)
- *Io non sempre ho tempo per leggere* (Not always I have time to read)
- *Io non ho sempre tempo per leggere* (I do not have always time to read)

5   Negation and Sentiment Analysis

As already shown, SN may also occur in the absence of any negation lexical/
morphological elements, therefore being based on specific morphosyntactic/semantic
constructions, hence producing semantic/logical NEG needing to be assessed by SA. It
is the case of sentences like:

- *Questo film è (E + molto + incrediblmente) brutto* (This film is (E + very + in-
  credibly) bad)

In these cases, SN often results from the co-occurrence of (even semantically
neutral or positive) terms with a NEG word, as can be seen from the previous example.
Besides, as shown by the following examples, the occurrence of some adverb/adjective
may change the NEG degree in the sentences:

- *Questo film è (blandamente + tendenzialmente + fantasticamente + meravigliosa-
  mente) brutto* (This movie is (mildly + basically + fantastically + wonderfully)
  bad)

Therefore, these specific sentences must be morphosyntactically "interpreted" to
detect correctly NEG presence and its degree(s), verifying words co-occurrence and
restriction rules.

Besides, and on the contrary, it is worth noting that statistical-based NLP will find
difficulties in accurately calculating NEG degrees in the previous sentences, or in others
such as *Non è bello* (It is not beautiful) vs. *È brutto* (It is ugly), or *Non è affatto bello* (It
is not at all beautiful) vs. *Non è affatto brutto* (It is not at all ugly).

It means that morphosyntactic-based SA is necessary if we want to cope correctly
with using NooJ FSA/FSTs. Hence, our SA will be mainly based on the necessary
correct morphosyntactic reckoning of degree differences. The correct evaluation of
NEG degrees will be achieved by means of a morphosyntactic analysis approach.
Electronic dictionaries will be used to calibrate NEG analysis for SN tagging, mainly
by means of:

- NEG adverbs;
- Manner/quantity adverbs and qualifying adjectives (indicating their gradation of
  intensity);
- NooJ Grammars.

As for these grammars, where necessary (i.e., in the absence of NEG adverbs), we
will use adverbs and adjectives NEG degrees and variables to calculate the NEG/POS
value of sentences or propositions.

6 NooJ Grammars for Italian Negation System and Sentiment Analysis

Before dealing with the construction and use of NooJ grammars for Italian Negation System and Sentiment Analysis, we have to remember that the argument itself, from an exquisitely morphosyntactic point of view, is very vast, and would require a greater number of pages than the one at our disposal. For this reason, and by way of example, we will focus on three types of possible grammars, namely.

- A grammar for sentences with NEG adverbs;
- A grammar for sentences with morphosyntactic (hence semantic/logical) NEG;
- A grammar for sentences with affirmative double negation.

As for sentences with NEG adverbs, the graph in Fig. 1 and its metanodes (Figs. 2 and 3) NEG account for degrees going from mild (MLD) to relatively strong (STR1) and strong (STR2). Degrees are calculated based on adverb typology, strength, and distribution. The sentences debugged are as follows (Fig. 3):

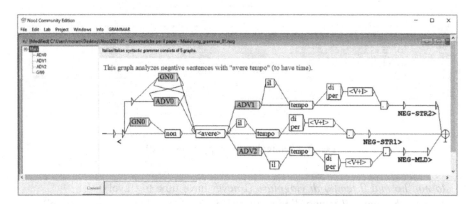

Fig. 1. Neg_grammar_01, main graph

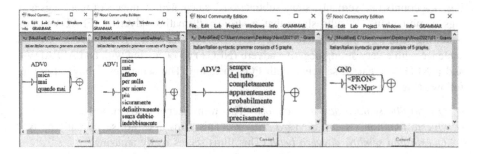

Fig. 2. Neg_grammar_01 metanodes

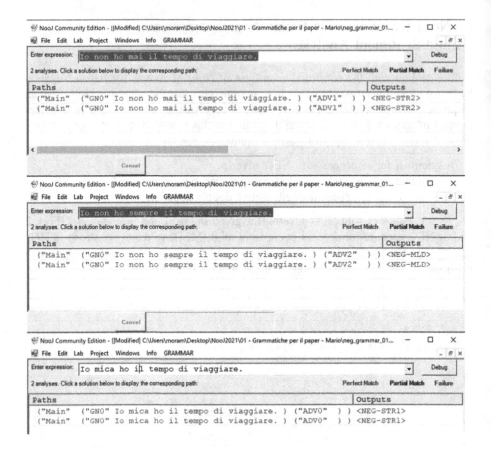

Fig. 3. Debugging for neg_grammar_01

- *Io non ho mai il tempo di viaggiare* (I never have time to travel)
- *Io non ho sempre il tempo di viaggiare* (I do not have always time to travel)
- *Mica io ho il tempo per viaggiare* (Really, I do not have time to travel)

As for sentences with morphosyntactic (hence semantic/logical) NEG, the graph in Fig. 4 accounts for "semantic sums/subtractions" calculated by means of word tags and tags combinations. Results show that a strong affirmative adverb (AFFADV+) co-occurring with a strong negative adjective (NEGA=) creates a NEG sentence, while a sentence with a very strong negative adverb (NEG+) co-occurring with and AFFADV+ and a NEGA= create a sentence with POS meaning. The sentences debugged are as follows (Fig. 5):

- *Questo film sembra davvero schifoso* (This films seems really nasty)
- *Questo film non sembra davvero schifoso* (This films does not seem really nasty)
- *Questo film sembra davvero bello* (This films seems really amazing)
- *Questo film non sembra davvero bello* (This movie does not seem really amazing)

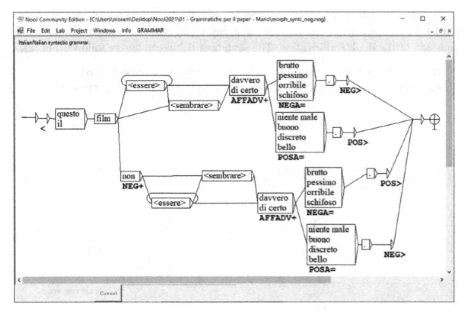

Fig. 4. Morph_syntc_neg Grammar

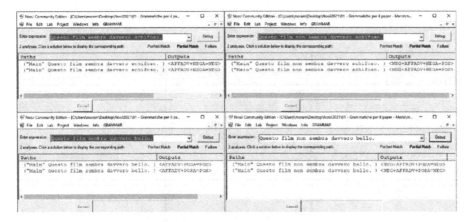

Fig. 5. Debugging for morph_syntc_neg Grammar

As for sentences with affirmative double negation, the graph in Fig. 6 accounts for "semantic sums/subtractions" calculated using words combinations. The results show that the type and degree of the NEG adverbs are crucial for calculating the NEG intensity, which as a mere example has been estimated as very strong affirmation (AFFIR-STR3) and strong affirmation (AFFIR-STR2). The different adverbs used are shown in Fig. 7, with ADV0 being more negative than ADV1. It is important to stress again that as for this type of sentences, the adverbs distribution in the graph is crucial to preserve the affirmative meaning, and that any change in distribution results in the omission of the double affirmation. The sentences debugged are as follows (Fig. 8):

- *Mai io non ho il tempo di leggere* (Never I do not have time to read)
- *Raramente io non ho il tempo di leggere* (Rarely I do not have time to read)

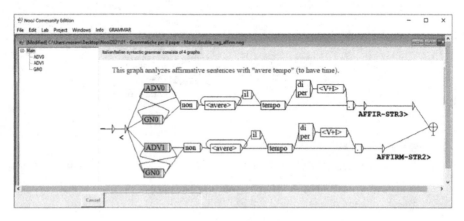

Fig. 6. Double_neg_affirm grammar, main graph

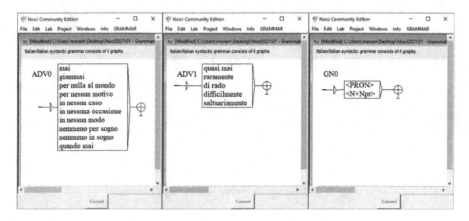

Fig. 7. Double_neg_affirm grammar metanodes

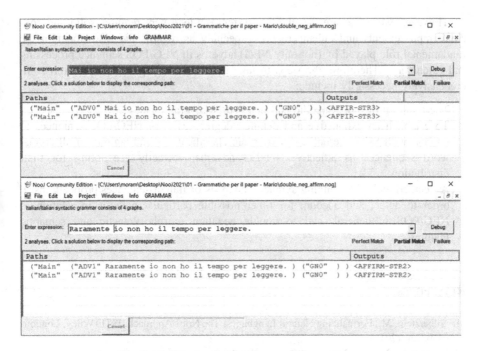

Fig. 8. Debugging for double_neg_affirm grammar

7   Conclusions: Further Possible Enhancements

Although in this study it was not possible to address all the morphosyntactic and formal-semantic aspects of NEG in Italian, we were able to highlight with a few shadows of doubt that it is not possible to renounce to SA if we want to verify accurately the degree of NEG/POS of specific sentences. Above all, we do know by now that this goal cannot be achieved effectively without NooJ and its FSA/FSTs. Note that the statistical approach to these sentences is often fallacious if not completely ineffective, as demonstrated by Fig. 9, the content of which has been taken from Google Translate:

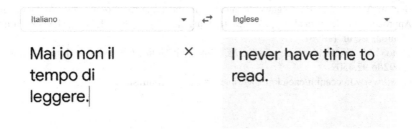

Fig. 9. Google Translate approach to NEG/POS sentences. The meaning (affirmative double negation) of the Italian sentence is overturned in the English sentence translated by means of statistical text analysis.

However, we are aware that the SA system outlined here requires solid and concrete improvements and enhancements, especially as regards the assessment of the fundamental role played by (not only NEG) adverbs in NEG/POS sentence processing and calculation. Therefore, the steps to take in order to complete this research comprehensively necessarily include:

- The building of more specific and detailed NooJ grammars;
- To establish an exhaustive and detailed degree scale for NEG/POS sentences to process with SE, coherent and taxonomic classifications and tagging of all crucial word sequences as adjectives + NEG adverbs, correctly accounting for their distribution;
- A detailed and wide-ranging syntactic analysis of Italian sentences/propositions in order to detect and account for other possible particular patterns in relation to NEG/POS in general, and to double negation morphosyntactic and semantic features.

References

1. Silberztein, M.: Formalizing Natural Languages: The NooJ Approach. ISTE-Wiley, London-Hoboken (2016)
2. Silberztein, M.: The NooJ Manual (2003). http://www.nooj-association.org
3. http://linguaegrammatica.com/avverbi-di-negazione-quali-sono-e-come-utilizzarli
4. http://www.treccani.it/enciclopedia/negazione_%28Enciclopedia-dell%27Italiano%29/
5. https://accademiadellacrusca.it/it/consulenza/sulla-costruzione-della-frase-negativa-in-italiano/169
6. https://aulalingue.scuola.zanichelli.it/benvenuti/2014/12/04/elementi-di-negazione/
7. https://aulalingue.scuola.zanichelli.it/benvenuti/2019/11/21/la-doppia-negazione/
8. https://en.wikipedia.org/wiki/Double_negative
9. https://it.wikipedia.org/wiki/Negazione_(linguistica)
10. https://www.google.com/search?q=la+grammatica+della+negazione+in+italiano&client=firefox-b-d&ei=wmoJYNf1FK-MlwT9iL_QAg&start=20&sa=N&ved=2ahUKEwjX3o-K-6zuAhUvxoUKHX3EDyo4ChDy0wN6BAgBEDw&biw=1344&bih=628
11. https://www.researchgate.net/publication/308208096_La_negazione_di_frase_nell%27italiano_contemporaneo_un%27analisi_sociolinguistica
12. https://www.treccani.it/enciclopedia/avverbi-di-negazione_%28La-grammatica-italiana%29/
13. Bernini, G., Ramat, P.: Negative Sentences in the Languages of Europe. A Typological Approach. In: Empirical Approaches to Language Typology, [EALT], 16. De Gruyter Mouton, Berlin (1996)
14. Mirto, I.M: The hidden side of adverbs. Linguistik Online 92(5) (2018). https://doi.org/10.13092/lo.92.4509
15. https://www.treccani.it/enciclopedia/topicalizzazione-contrastiva/

Syntactic Analysis of Sentences Containing Arabic Psychological Verbs

Asmaa Amzali[1(✉)], Asmaa Kourtin[1], Mohammed Mourchid[1],
Abdelaziz Mouloudi[2], and Samir Mbarki[2]

[1] Computer Science Research Laboratory, Faculty of Science,
Ibn Tofail University, Kenitra, Morocco
[2] EDPAGS Laboratory, Faculty of Science, Ibn Tofail University,
Kenitra, Morocco

Abstract. In the Arabic language, all the structures of simple verbal sentences have the same main components: the predicate (al-mosnad, المسند), the subject (al-mosnad 'ilayh, المسند إليه) that are mandatory in the Arabic sentence, and the complement (al-fodla, الفضلة) to reach the meaning of the sentence. In this paper, we will expand and improve our previous work of identification and classification of Arabic psychological verbs through lexicon-grammar tables [1], to be able to realize a syntactic analyzer of sentences containing Arabic psychological verbs using the NooJ platform. In this regard, we will use the dictionary with about 400 verb entries, containing all the lexical, syntactic, semantic, and transformational information of these verbs, which will facilitate the realization of our analyzer. Then, we will adapt to our needs, the simple sentences analyzer [2, 3], to parse the sentences containing Arabic psychological verbs regardless of the sentence components order. The parser is tested on many texts, and the results were satisfactory.

Keywords: Natural Language Processing (NLP) · NooJ platform · Syntactic analysis · Lexicon-grammar tables · Arabic psychological verbs sentences

1 Introduction

Natural language processing makes our lives easier through question-answering systems, data extraction, machine translation, feeling analysis, etc.

Natural Language Processing (NLP) requires information about the language at different levels: morphological, lexical, syntactical, semantical, and pragmatical, where these levels overly each other, and each level only focuses on a given issue.

One of the crucial steps for NLP, however, involves the automatic recognition of Atomic Linguistic Units (ALUs). Multiword terms, grammatical units, and ambiguous words must be correctly identified in terms of ALUs to assure that the structure of every sentence is accurately analyzed. Otherwise, it will be hard to detect sentences with different word orders, such as "كره زيد أحمد " (Kariha Zaidun Ahmadan; Zaid hates Ahmed) and "كره أحمد زيد" (Kariha ahmadun Zaidan; Ahmed hates Zaid) have a different interpretation, or sentences with different structures, such as "أحبّ زيد هندا"

M. Bigey et al. (Eds.): NooJ 2021, CCIS 1520, pp. 51–61, 2021.
https://doi.org/10.1007/978-3-030-92861-2_5

('Ahabba Zaidun &indan; Zaid loves Hind) and "أكنّ زيد حبّا لهند" ('akanna Zaidun hobban li &indin; Zaid has a love for Hind) have a similar interpretation.

In the NooJ platform, syntactic grammars are very useful to depict the sequence of words that has a meaning. Hence, we can use them to focus on different kinds of sentences containing Arabic psychological verbs.

This work aims to realize a syntactic analyzer of sentences containing Arabic psychological verbs using the NooJ platform [4]. For this reason, we will use the dictionary generated from the lexicon-grammar table of Arabic psychological verbs [1], which will facilitate the realization of our analyzer. Then, we will adapt to our needs, the simple sentences' analyzer allowing us to recognize and denote all the grammatical structures of simple Arabic sentences [2, 3], to analyze the sentences containing Arabic psychological verbs.

This paper is organized as follows: in the second section, we will provide previous related researches. In the third section, we will present a study about the simple sentences containing Arabic psychological verbs, and their grammar structure. In the fourth section, we will present an excerpt of our new lexicon-grammar table for Arabic psychological verbs enriched by adding roots and patterns, and show some implemented NooJ grammar. Then, we will present the tests and results. Finally, in the fifth section, we close our paper with a conclusion and some perspectives.

2 Related Works

In the last years, many approaches have been applied to realize a parser for analyzing the Arabic sentence. Actually, the main approaches are the linguistic and statistical approaches [5].

The linguistic methods require resources: dictionary entries and grammar rules. However, the statistical method is based on the availability of a large corpus of parallel data for learning. The shortcoming of the statistical methods is that this type of corpus is not always available in sufficient quantity for a poorly endowed language such as Arabic, which suffers from the scarcity of linguistic resources. For instance, Arabic grammar does not cover all types of sentences. Subsequently, the linguistic approach proves to be the most adequate.

In [1, 6], Amzali et al. we made a linguistic study for Arabic psychological verbs (see Fig. 1), and we created a lexicon-grammar table [7–10] of Arabic psychological verbs with about 400 verbs entries in three main classes: أفعال الشعور (Negative feeling verbs), أفعال الإحساس (Positive feeling verbs), and أفعال الرأي والتفكير (thought and opinion verbs) then using NooJ platform, we created an automatic tool by transforming the lexicon-grammar tables into the NooJ dictionaries and syntactic grammars.

In [11], Rozwadowska presented an overview of psychological verbs and psychological adjectives. Also, she explained a multidimensional approach to psychological verbs.

Most of the existing researches in Arabic sentence parsing covers simple sentences. The parsing of sentences containing Arabic psychological verb is still in its early stages. However, the shortcoming in these works is in the simple verbal phrase possible grammatical structures, sentences types, and sentences words order.

In [2–4], Bourahma et al. presented a syntactic and semantic classification of Arabic words and created a NooJ parser of simple Arabic verbal sentences with free word order. Also, the authors implemented in the NooJ platform the parser that recognizes and annotates all possible grammatical structures of simple Arabic nominal sentences. In addition, authors enhanced and extended the parser of simple verbal and simple nominal sentences by implementing a set of syntactic grammars modeling Arabic noun phrase structures, which are enriched by the agreement constraints of the noun phrase components to parsing the simple expansive sentences.

<OPT>explication	<OPT>exemple	VN0Prép1N1	VN0N1	VN0	Prép=ل	Prép=إلى	Prép1=ب	Prép=على	Prép=من	Prép=في	N1=Nnr	N1=Nhum	N1=Hum	N0=Nhum	N0=Hum	InTr	Tr	V	
أبذ-عليه-:-غضب	أبذ-عليه-	+	-	-	-	-	-	+	-	-	~	-	+	-	+	~	~	أبذ	أفعال الشعور
أبى-الشيء-:-كرهه-و-لم-يرضه	الشيء-:-كرهه-و-لم-ير	+	+	+	-	-	-	-	-	-	~	+	-	-	+		+	أبى	
أجم-:-كرهه-.	-أجم-الطعام-	-	+	-	-	-	-	-	-	-	~	+	-	-	+	+	~	أجم	
تأجم-: غضب-	تأجم-عليه	+	-	-	-	-	-	+	-	-	~	-	+	-	+	~	~	تأجم	
أرق-:-امتنع-عليه-النوم-ليلا	أرق الرجل	+	+	+	-	-	-	-	-	-	~	+	-	-	+	~	~	أرق	
أزق-:-ضاق-(مأزق)	أزق-على-فلان-, أزق ص	+	~	~	-	-	-	-	-	-	~	-	+	-	+	~	~	أزق	
أزل-الرجل-:-صار-في-ضيق-أو-جدب-أو-شدة	أزل-المكان	-	-	+	-	-	-	-	-	-	~	-	~	+	+	~	~	أزل	
أسف-:-حزن، تألم-و-ندم	ظل-يأسف-لما-شاهده-م	+	-	-	+	-	-	-	-	-	~	+	+	-	+	~	-	أسف	
أسف-:-حزن، تألم-و-ندم	أسف-عليه-	+	-	-	-	-	-	+	-	-	~	+	+	-	+	+	-	أسف	
أسي-:-حزن	على-صديقه-/-أسي-لم	+	~	~	-	-	-	-	-	-	~	-	-	-	+	+	~	أسي	
أسّ-فلانا-:-أغضبه-، فهو أساس	أسّ فلانا-	-	+	-	-	-	-	-	-	-	~	-	+	-	+	+	~	أسّ	
أضم-عليه-:-أضمر-حقده	أضم-عليه-	+	-	-	-	-	-	-	-	-	~	+	+	-	+	~	~	أضم	

Fig. 1. Excerpt of our Arabic psychological verbs lexicon-grammar table created in [1]

3 Syntactic Analysis of Arabic Sentence Containing Psychological Verb

Generally, to parse an Arabic sentence, we must study its grammatical structure. First, we present the structure of the simple Arabic sentence. Then, we study the grammatical structure of simple sentences containing Arabic psychological verbs.

3.1 Simple Sentence Containing Arabic Psychological Verb

The simple Arabic verbal sentence is composed of at most four main elements (see Fig. 2). The first one, the head (al-sadr, الصدر), can be represented by some particles such as negation or interrogation particles, or by incomplete verbs. The kernel of the sentence includes the predicate (al-mosnad, المسند), the subject (al-mosnad 'ilayh, المسند إليه) that are mandatory in the Arabic sentence and the complement (al-fodla, الفضلة) to reach the meaning of the sentence. These four elements have a free order in the Arabic sentence. The following Figs. 3 and 4 shows an example of a sentence containing an Arabic psychological verb:

Fig. 2. The main components of simple Arabic verbal sentence

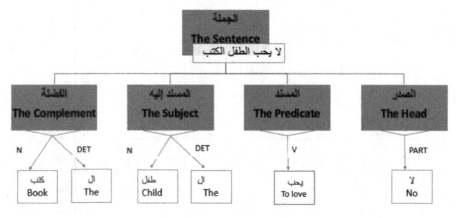

Fig. 3. Example of a sentence containing Arabic psychological verb (a)

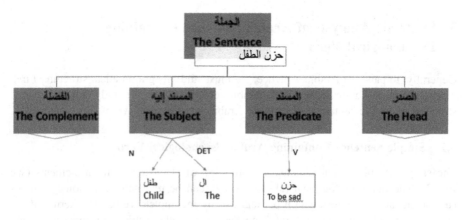

Fig. 4. Example of a sentence containing Arabic psychological verb (b)

3.2 Structure of the Simple Sentence Containing Arabic Psychological Verb

The simple Arabic verbal sentence contains one predicative kernel, and its predicate is a complete verb, whatever its position in the sentence. In the Arabic language, the sentence components order is free.

Concerning the property of transitivity, Arabic psychological verbs are classified into two main subclasses. All the psychological verbs of a given subclass share the same syntactic structure, then we must match these different syntactic structures of the simple Arabic verbal sentence [3]: the first class is based on intransitive verbs 'e.g.: حَزِن (hazina, to sorrow)' and the second class is based on transitive verbs to one object 'e.g.: عَشِق (achiqa, to adore)'.

- **Structure-based on intransitive verbs**

  In this class, the predicate and the subject are obligatory in the structure, such as the sentence:

  حَزِن محمد على صديقه (Mohammed grieves for his friend)
   ↓   ↓   ↓   ↓   ↓
  PRO N Prep S   V

- **Structure-based on transitive verbs to one object**

  The predicate, the subject, and the object are obligatory in the structure; we also must have the three required syntactic positions as illustrated in examples (1), (2), and (3):

(1)
يَعْشَق لوك الطفل (Luc adores the child)
 ↓   ↓   ↓   ↓
N DET S   V

(2)
يَعْشَق الطفل لوك (Luc adores the child)
 ↓   ↓   ↓   ↓
S N DET V

(3)
لوك الطفل يَعْشَق (Luc adores the child)
 ↓   ↓ ↓   ↓
V N DET S

4 Implementation in NooJ

In our previous work [1, 6], we have already created the lexicon grammar table of Arabic psychological verbs, and then we have implemented a NooJ dictionary of Arabic psychological verbs.

In this paper, we have extended our previous work and enrich our lexicon-grammar tables by adding root and pattern [12] for each entry (see Fig. 5), where those two pieces of information serve to build the meaning of most Arabic words and help us in our study. Then, we generated our dictionary from lexicon grammar tables through NooJ [13] (see Fig. 6).

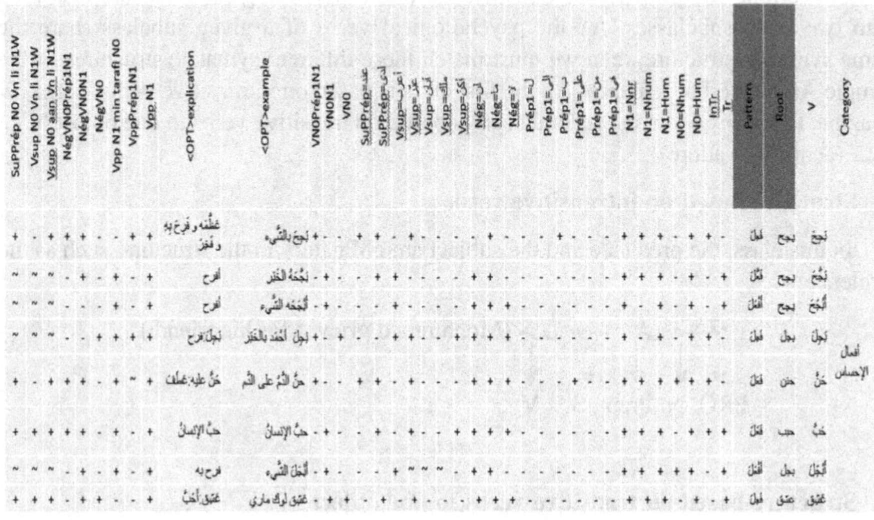

Fig. 5. Excerpt of our lexicon-grammar table

```
# NooJ V5
# Dictionary
#
# Language is: ar
#
# Alphabetical order is not required.
#
# Use inflectional & derivational paradigms' description files (.nof), e.g.:
# Special Command: #use paradigms.nof
#
# Special Features: +NW (non-word) +FXC (frozen expression component) +UNAMB (unambiguous lexical entry)
#                   +FLX= (inflectional paradigm) +DRV= (derivational paradigm)
#
# Special Characters: '\' '"' ' ' ',' '+' '-' '#'
#use qualitatif.nof
#use ex2.nof
بَنجِعَ,بجج,V+InTr+بجج+فَعِل+N0=Hum+N1=Hum+N1=Nhum+Prép1=بـ+Vsup=عبّر+SupPrep=لـدى+SupPrep=عند+Neg=مـا+VN0Prép1N1+VppPrép1N1+FLX=V_jaraha+DRV=I
بَنجَعَ,بجج,V+بجج+فَعَّل+N0=Hum+N1=Hum+N1=Nhum+VN0N1+VppN1MinTarafiN0+NégVN0Prép1N1+SuPPrépN0VnliN1W+Neg=مـا+Neg=لـن+SupPrep=لـدى+Vsup=أعرب+FL
حَنَّ,حنن,V+InTr+حنن+فَعَل+N0=Hum+N0=Nhum+N1=Hum+N1=Nhum+Prép1=على+VN0N1+VN0Prép1N1+Vsup=عبّر+SupPrep=لـدى+FLX=V_habba+DRV=D_habba:FLXDRV
حَنَّ,حنن,V+InTr+حنن+فَعَل+N0=Hum+N1=Hum+N1=Nhum+Prép1=إلى+VN0+VN0Prép1N1+Vsup=عبّر+SupPrep=لـدى+Vsup=عبّر+SupPrep=عند+SupPrep=لـدى+Neg=لا+Neg=
حَنَّ,حنن,V+InTr+حنن+فَعَل+N0=Hum+N1=Hum+N1=Nhum+Prép1=لـ+VN0+VN0Prép1N1+Vsup=عبّر+SupPrep=لـدى+Vsup=عبّر+SupPrep=عند+SupPrep=لـدى+Neg=لا+Neg=
أحَبَّ,حبب,V+InTr+Tr+حبب+فَعَل+N0=Hum+N1=Hum+N1=Nhum+VN0N1+VN0Prep1N1+VppN1+VppN1MinTarafiN0+SuPPrepN0VnliN1W+VsupN0VnliN1W+VsupN0aanVnliN
عَشِقَ,عشق,V+Tr+عشق+فَعِل+N0=Hum+N1=Hum+N1=Nhum+VN0N1+VppN1+VppN1MinTarafiN0+NegVN0N1+SuPPrepN0VnliN1W+VsupN0VnliN1W+VsupN0aanVnliN1W+Sup
أبْجَعَ,بجج,V+Tr+بجج+أفْعَل+N0=Hum+N1=Hum+VN0N1+VppN1MinTarafiN0+NegVN0N1+SuPPrepN0VnliN1W+VsupN0VnliN1W+VsupN0aanVnliN1W+Neg=لا+Neg=مـا+Ne
حَنَّ,حنن,V+InTr+حنن+فَعَل+N0=Hum+N1=Hum+N1=Nhum+Prép1=إلى+VN0+VN0Prép1N1+FLX=V_habba+DRV=D_habba:FLXDRV
حَنَّ,حنن,V+InTr+حنن+فَعَل+N0=Hum+N1=Hum+N1=Nhum+Prép1=لـ+VN0+VN0Prép1N1+FLX=V_habba+DRV=D_habba:FLXDRV
بَجَلَ,بجل,V+InTr+بجل+فَعَل+N0=Hum+N1=Hum+N1=Nhum+VN0+VppN1+VppN1MinTarafiN0+VsupN0VnliN1W+VsupN0aanVnliN1W+Vsup=عبّر+Vsup=أكنّ+Neg=لا+Neg=مـا
بَجَّلَ,بجل,V+InTr+بجل+فَعَّل+N0=Hum+N1=Nhum+VN0N1+VppN1MinTarafiN0+VsupN0VnliN1W+VsupN0aanVnliN1W+Vsup=عبّر+Vsup=أعرب+Neg=لا+Neg=مـا+Neg=لـن+Fl
```

Fig. 6. Excerpt of our dictionary

Then, we created a syntactic grammar based on the grammar of a simple Arabic sentence [3], built by Bourahma et al. Our grammar takes into account the two structures based on intransitive verbs and transitive to one object verbs. The following figure (Fig. 7) describes the first level of our grammar.

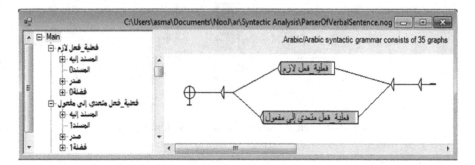

Fig. 7. First level of the syntactic grammar

As shown in Figs. 8 and 9, we present the sub-grammar based on an intransitive verb and a transitive verb to one object of the simple sentence containing the Arabic psychological verb.

Our grammar analyzes and annotates the component of the input sentence, and produces an annotation parse tree. Our grammar can parse any simple sentence containing Arabic psychological verbs.

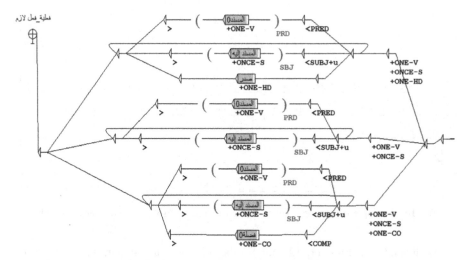

Fig. 8. Sub-grammar based on intransitive verb

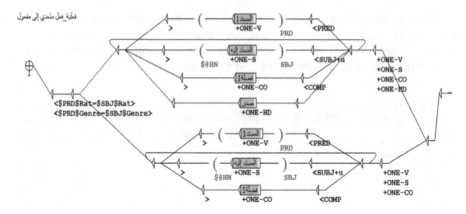

Fig. 9. Sub-grammar based on transitive verb to one object

Finally, we have tested our grammar on texts to verify their efficiency (see Fig. 10). The parser annotates the sentence with intransitive verbs (حزن الطفل, the child was sad) when "حزن" is a predicate, and "الطفل" is a definite noun. In addition, the annotations produced by the parser represent the grammatical structure of the sentence.

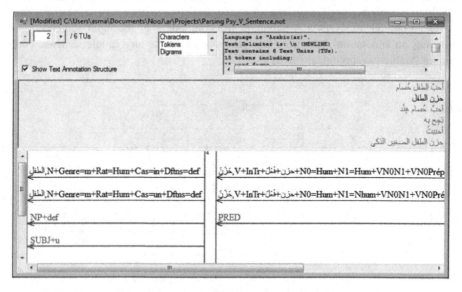

Fig. 10. Example of parsing a simple sentence containing Arabic psychological verb

As illustrated in Figs. 11, 12, and 13, the sentences are similar, but the order of their components is different. The analyzer returns the same annotations in the three examples:

- (زيد يحب هندا , Zaid love Hind) [Subject + Predicate + Object] (SPO)
- (يحب زيد هندا , Zaid love Hind) [Predicate + Subject + Object] (PSO)
- (زيد هندا يحب , Zaid love Hind) [Subject + Object + Predicate] (SOP)

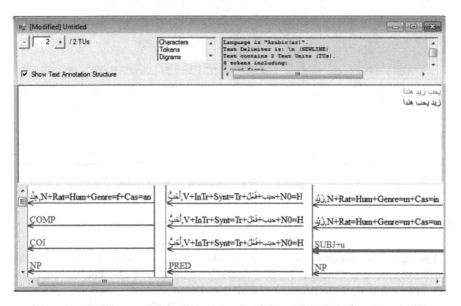

Fig. 11. Annotation of a sentence with SPO structure

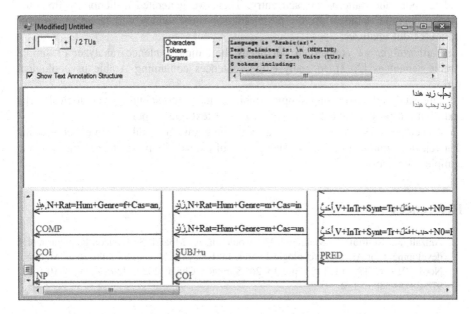

Fig. 12. Annotation of a sentence with PSO structure

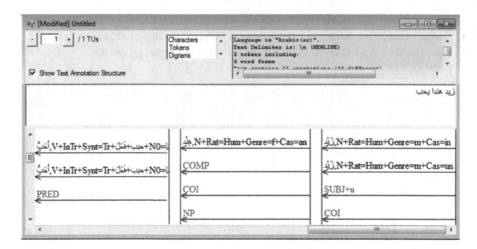

Fig. 13. Annotation of a sentence with SOP structure

5   Conclusion and Perspectives

In this paper, we extended our previous work presented in [1] to create a syntactic analysis of simple sentences containing Arabic psychological verbs. For that, we began with a presentation of the structure of a simple Arabic sentence. Then, we studied the grammatical structure of simple sentences containing Arabic psychological verbs.

In addition, we enriched our lexicon grammar of Arabic psychological verbs by adding roots and patterns to each entry. Then, we generated a dictionary from the lexicon-grammar table of Arabic psychological verbs, which will facilitate the realization of our analyzer.

Furthermore, we adapted to our needs the simple sentences analyzer of simple Arabic sentences [2, 3], to analyze the sentences containing Arabic psychological verbs.

This study allows parsing simple Arabic sentences containing psychological verbs and giving a positive effect on the efficiency of text and corpora.

As perspectives, we will enrich the syntactic grammar by all agreement constraints that reject ungrammatical cases. Then, we will extend the parser to be able to parse complex sentences.

References

1. Amzali, A., Kourtin, A., Mourchid, M., Mouloudi, A., Mbarki, S.: Lexicon-grammar tables development for Arabic psychological verbs. In: Fehri, H., Mesfar, S., Silberztein, M. (eds.) NooJ 2019. CCIS, vol. 1153, pp. 15–26. Springer, Cham (2020). https://doi.org/10.1007/978-3-030-38833-1_2

2. Bourahma, S., Mbarki, S., Mourchid, M., Mouloudi, A.: Syntactic parsing of simple Arabic nominal sentences using NooJ linguistic platform. In: Lachkar, A., Bouzoubaa, K., Mazroui, A., Hamdani, A., Lekhouaja, A. (eds.) Arabic Language Processing: From Theory to Practice, chapter 18. ICALP 2017. Communications in Computer and Information Science, vol. 782, pp 244–25. Springer, Cham (2018). https://doi.org/10.1007/978-3-319-73500-9_18
3. Bourahma, S., Mourchid, M., Mbarki, S., Mouloudi, A.: The parsing of simple Arabic verbal sentences using NooJ platform. In: Mbarki, S., Mourchid, M., Silberztein, M. (eds.) Formalizing Natural Languages with NooJ and Its Natural Language Processing Applications. NooJ 2017. Communications in Computer and Information Science, vol. 811, chapter 7, pp 81–95. Springer, Cham (2018). https://doi.org/10.1007/978-3-319-73420-0_7
4. Silberztein, M.: La formalisation des Langues: l'approche de NooJ. ISTE Editions, London (2015)
5. Taghbalout, I., Atta Allah, F.A., Elmmarraki, M.: Etude comparative des approches de traduction automatique. In: Journée doctorales en technologies de l'information et de la communication. Rabat, Maroc (2014)
6. Amzali, A., Mourchid, M., Mouloudi, A., Mbarki, S.: Arabic psychological verb recognition through NooJ transformational grammars. Bekavac, B., Kocijan, K., Silberztein, M., Šojat, K. (eds.) Formalising Natural Languages: Applications to Natural Language Processing and Digital Humanities. NooJ 2020. Communications in Computer and Information Science, vol. 1389, pp. 74–84. Springer, Cham (2021). https://doi.org/10.1007/978-3-030-70629-6_7
7. Tolone, E.: Analyse syntaxique à l'aide des tables du Lexique-Grammaire du français. Informatique et langage. Université Paris-Est (2011)
8. Tolone, E.: Les tables du lexique-grammaire au format TAL. In: MajecSTIC 2009, Nov 2009, electronic version, p. 8. Avignon, France (2009)
9. Gross, M.: Une grammaire locale de l'expression des sentiments. Langue française 105(1), 70–87. Armand Colin (1995)
10. El Hannach, M.: Syntaxe des verbes psychologiques en arabe. Thèse de Doctorat en linguistique. Université Paris 7, France (1999)
11. Rozwadowska, B.: Psychological verbs and psychological adjectives. In: The Wiley Blackwell Companion to Syntax, Second Edition, pp. 1–26 (2017)
12. Blanchete, I., Mourchid, M., Mbarki, S., Mouloudi, A.: Formalizing Arabic inflectional and derivational verbs based on root and pattern approach using NooJ platform. In: Mbarki, S., Mourchid, M., Silberztein, M. (eds.) Formalizing Natural Languages with NooJ and Its Natural Language Processing Applications. NooJ 2017. Communications in Computer and Information Science, vol. 811, pp. 52–65. Springer, Cham (2018). https://doi.org/10.1007/978-3-319-73420-0_5
13. Kourtin, A., Amzali, A., Mourchid, M., Mouloudi, A., Mbarki, S.: The automatic generation of NooJ dictionaries from lexicon-grammar tables. In: Fehri, H., Mesfar, S., Silberztein, M. (eds.) Formalizing Natural Languages with NooJ 2019 and Its Natural Language Processing Applications. NooJ 2019. Communications in Computer and Information Science, vol. 1153, pp. 65–76. Springer, Cham (2020). https://doi.org/10.1007/978-3-030-38833-1_6

Formalizing Predicates for Discovery Under the Lexicon Grammar Framework

Javiera Jacobsen, Walter Koza[✉], Mirian Muñoz, and Francisca Saiz

Pontificia Universidad Católica de Valparaíso, Valparaíso, Chile
{javiera.jacobsen.m, mirian.munoz.a,
francisca.saiz.n}@mail.pucv.cl, walter.koza@pucv.cl

Abstract. This text proposes a method for automatic analysis of predicates for discovery (PD) in Spanish. A PD is a predicative unit that projects an argument structure (AS) whose meaning alludes to 'something that is found by someone - or something- somewhere' (e.g., 'encontrar', 'hallar'). This type of task is useful in fields such as medicine, since it offers the possibility of automatically identifying findings of interest (diseases, test results, etc.) in large text corpora. The present work is based on Lexicon Grammar (LG), which proposes a formalization from the nature of arguments (object classes) and transformational possibilities. The methodology is carried out as follows: (i) manual identification of PDs from a corpus of gynecology and obstetrics; (ii) elaboration of LG tables for each PD, where object classes are categorized and possible transformations are listed; and (iii) computational modeling. For the last stage, electronic dictionaries and computer-generated grammars were built in NooJ. The algorithm with automatically detected and generated ASs from PDs (325 grammatical sentences) was evaluated against an annotated corpus (1000 manually-annotated sentences, randomly extracted from a corpus of 5 million words). Results gave 98% accuracy, 88% coverage, and 92% F-measure.

Keywords: Predicates for discovery · Lexicon grammar · Automatic analyses

1 Introduction

The present research describes a methodology for automatic analysis of Spanish predicates for discovery (PD). A PD refers to a predicate whose meaning implies the finding of an object in a given place by an agent. An example of this with 'encontrar' is below (1):

(1) El estudiante encontró el billete en la acera (*The student found the ticket on the sidewalk*).

Here, the syntactic structure involves three arguments, with syntactic functions of subject ('the student'), direct complement ('the ticket') and locative argument ('on the sidewalk'), respectively.

Focusing on this type of predication is justified insofar as its computational treatment may be of interest in automatic information extraction tasks in certain areas of knowledge – e.g., in the case of medicine, which requires resources to retrieve

M. Bigey et al. (Eds.): NooJ 2021, CCIS 1520, pp. 62–71, 2021.
https://doi.org/10.1007/978-3-030-92861-2_6

information regarding findings of patient condition, test results, etcetera. Specifically, we demonstrate an algorithm that automatically generates AS for PDs and, in turn, detects such constructions in natural language texts using the Lexicon Grammar (LG) model, developed by Gross [1].

Here, the LG proposes a formal description of natural languages based on simple sentences, on the one hand, as a distributional analysis based on the characterization of the arguments and their location in the AS; and, on the other, as a specification of the transformational possibilities presented by each sentence. The information provided by the linguistic description is then modeled for computational processing. This paper makes use of NooJ [2], a tool with several utilities, such as electronic dictionaries and computer-generated grammars.

The methodology is as follows: (i) manual identification of PDs from a gynecology and obstetrics corpus; (ii) elaboration of LG tables for each PD, where object classes are categorized and possible transformations listed; and (iii) computational modeling, using NooJ to build electronic dictionaries and computer-generated grammars. The algorithm developed to automatically detect and generate AS from PDs (325 grammatical sentences) was evaluated against an annotated corpus (1000 manually annotated sentences, randomly extracted from a corpus of 5 million words).

The results discuss model efficacy (98% accuracy, 88% coverage and 92% F-measure) and how the developed algorithm is useful for this kind of tasks.

The paper is organized as follows. Section 2 gives an account of the LG model and its theoretical underpinnings; Sect. 3, the methodology; and Sect. 4, results.

2 Lexicon Grammar

Developed by Gross [1], Lexicon Grammar (LG) states that natural languages may be described from the set of simple sentences that compose them, and makes use of tables that group lexical items of a grammatical category, i.e., that share properties. This framework is based on three aspects: (i) that syntax is indissoluble from the lexicon; (ii) that the identification of simple sentences (instead of words or phrases) represents the minimal syntactic and semantic contexts of analysis; and (iii) that this offers a formalization and a descriptive method applicable to any language [3]. This theory proposes a combined study of syntactic rules and lexical selection preferences in relation to the transformation possibilities of a given sentence.

In this regard, LG tables are presented in the form of a matrix, where: (i) rows show the elements of the corresponding class; (ii) columns, the syntactic-semantic properties that are not necessarily accepted by all members of the class; and (iii) intersections have a + or − sign depending on whether the lexical entry described by the row accepts the property described by the column. These syntactic-semantic properties refer directly to the base construction associated with the class, to a transformation of the base construction, or to an additional construction. If a word has two distinct senses, then it will have two lexical entries. As an example, Fig. 1 shows a fragment of one of the verb tables presented in Tolone [4].

NO =: Nhum	NO =: N-hum	NO =: Nnr	<ENT>Ppv	Ppv w: se figé	Ppv w: les figé	Ppv w: Neg	<ENT>V	Neg	N0 V	N0 être V-ant	N0 V de N0pc	N1 =: Nhum	N1 =: N-hum	N1 =: le fait Qu P	Ppv w: lui	Ppv w: y	[extrap]	N0idée V Loc N1esprit	<OPT>
+	-	-	les	-	+	-	lâcher Advm	-	+	-	-	+	-	-	-	-	-	-	Max les lâche difficilement à Ida
+	-	-	<E>	-	-	-	renaître	-	+	+	-	-	+	-	-	+	-	+	Max renaît au bonheur de vivre
+	-	-	se	+	-	-	rendre	-	+	-	-	+	+	+	-	-	+	+	Max s'est rendu à mon opinion
+	-	-	se	+	-	-	rendre	-	+	-	-	+	-	-	-	-	-	-	Le caporal s'est rendu à l'ennemi
+	-	-	<E>	-	-	-	renoncer	-	-	-	-	+	+	-	-	+	-	-	Max renonce à son héritage
+	+	+	ne	-	-	+	revenir	+	-	-	-	+	-	-	+	-	-	-	La tête de Luc ne revient pas à Max

Fig. 1. Excerpt of an LG table for distributional analysis [4].

This method thus accounts for polysemy in lexical entries on the basis of the different AS they take. Table 1 shows an example of this method with the verb '*comer*':

Table 1. Excerpt of a LG table of selection preferences for the verb '*comer*'.

Argument 0		Lemma	Argument 1		Example
+ANIM	−ANIM		+FOOD	−FOOD	
+	−	*comer*	+	−	El perro comió un filete *The dog ate a steak*
−	+	*comer*	−	+	El óxido comió el metal *Rust ate the metal*

In this regard, two possible meanings for this verb can be observed: one referring to the action of feeding and the other related to the process of corrosion of a metal.

In addition, the LG proposes a second table for transformations that allow us to go from a sentence O1 to a sentence O2. This is justified by an argument of economy: O1 has certain constraints, quite complex, that also appear in O2, which implies that, if described independently, these constraints would appear twice in the grammar. For this purpose, the transformational solution consists of describing 01 with all its constraints and applying an operation that transforms 01 into 02, without affecting them [5]. However, according to Gross [1], all transformations have exceptions, so it is essential to differentiate the elements of the lexicon, according to whether or not they can undergo a given transformation. Here, in order to determine syntactic classes, it is an indispensable requirement to describe these units and their properties.

Thus, continuing with the example of '*comer*', a table of transformations can be drawn up as follows (Table 2):

Table 2. Example of LG Table of transformations.

Sentence	Passive Voice	Nominalization
El perro comió un filete *The dog ate a steak*	+	+
El óxido comió el metal *Rust ate the metal*	+	−

In this way, the meaning of both sentences can be differentiated on the basis of the transformation possibilities they present:

(9)

    a. 01: El perro comió un filete → 02: The dog's food was a steak.
    b. 01: El óxido comió el metal → 02: *The rust's food was metal.

Furthermore, in relation to disambiguation of meanings generated from AS, when a series of arguments in the same given position give a predicate a constant meaning, they constitute what Gross [6] calls 'object classes'. For the verb '*tomar*', for example, nouns like '*vino*', '*cerveza*', '*agua*' or 'Coca-Cola', insofar as they give the verb the same meaning (equivalent to '*beber*'), form an object class akin to 'beverages'; on the other hand, the object class for nouns such as '*tren*', '*bus*', or '*avión*' ('means of transportation') gives another meaning to the verb. The present work – which seeks to analyze predicates specific to the area of medicine, specifically, gynecology and obstetrics – established the following object classes: 'medical professionals' (ProfMed: + Animate + Human + Medical Professional); 'patients' (+Animate + Human); and 'anatomical area', among others.

3 Methodology

The methodology, presented below, consisted of (i) selection of discovery verbs; (ii) elaboration of LG tables; and (iii) creation of computer resources: (a) electronic dictionaries and (b) computer-generated grammars.

3.1 Verb Selection

This research uses the corpus from the FONDECyT 1171033 Project, which composed over five million words from all Gynecology and Obstetrics texts published in SciELO-indexed journals available online, from the first issue to the last issue of 2017.

First, all verbs present in the corpus (approximately 14,300) were extracted using NooJ. Second, manual analysis identified 42 possible candidates. Finally, and using information from a general language dictionary, the 5 most prototypical verbs of discovery were selected: '*descubrir*', '*detectar*', '*develar*', '*encontrar*' and '*hallar*'. This group is referred to as Verb Class Five (VCV).

3.2   Lexicon Grammar Tables

The second stage elaborated Lexicon Grammar (LG) tables for the distributional and transformational aspects of the VCVs.

Distributional tables identify and classify the arguments selected by each predicate, as well as the ASs projected by each. Thus, information in the tables corresponds to lemmas (predicates), arguments (A0 and A1), object classes, and examples of simple sentences. The different properties of each predicate is expressed with the symbols '+' (admits) and '−' (does not admit) (Table 3).

Table 3. Table of distributional analysis of the predicate '*encontrar*'

A0		Lemma	A1					Prep	A2	Example
			+CC							
+H	+E		+C		+A				+L	
SD	SD		SD	SN	SD	SN	SUB	en		
+	−	*encontrar*	+	−	−	−	−	+	+	Los médicos encontraron un flujo anormal en el DV *Doctors found an abnormal flow in the VD*
+	−	*encontrar*	−	−	+	−	−	+	+	Los especialistas encontraron una incidencia de bajo peso al nacer *The specialists found an incidence of low birth weight*
+	−	*encontrar*	−	−	−	+	−	+	+	El médico encontró mayor frecuencia de distrés transitorio e hipoxia *The physician found increased frequency of transient distress and hypoxia*
+	−	*encontrar*	−	−	−	−	+	−	−	Los investigadores encontraron que la prevalencia de la infección fue de 42.2% *The researchers found that the prevalence of infection was 42.2%*
−	+	*encontrar*	−	−	−	+	−	−	−	El análisis encontró una mayor probabilidad para el desarrollo de DPP *The analysis found an increased likelihood for the development of PPD*
−	+	*encontrar*	−	−	−	−	+	−	−	El estudio encontró diferencias clínica y estadísticamente significativas *The study found clinically and statistically significant differences*

Next, transformational tables use corpus identification methods – i.e., following G. Gross [6] and Silberztein [2] – and native speaker self-knowledge – i.e., from manual analysis of discovery predicates – as a reference for transformational analyses. This resulted in eleven possible transformations: periphrastic passive, reflexive passive, pronominalization of A0, pronominalization of A1, negation, nominalization, locative adverb, elision of A0, elision of A2, relative A0, and relative A1 (Table 4).

Table 4. Transformational possibilities for discovery predicates.

N°	Transformation	Example: '*El médico encontró el tumor en el estómago*'
1	Periphrastic passive	The tumor was found by the doctor in the stomach
2	Reflexive passive	The tumor was found in the stomach
3	Pronominalization of A0	He found the tumor in the stomach
4	Pronominalization of A1	The doctor found it in the stomach
5	Negation	The physician did not find the tumor in the stomach
6	Nominalization	The tumor was found
7	Adverb Locative	The physician found the tumor there
8	Elision A0	He found the tumor in the stomach
9	Elision A2	The physician found the tumor
10	Relative A0	It was the physician who found the tumor in the stomach
11	Relative A1	That's what the doctor found in the stomach

Subsequently, a number was assigned to each of the transformations to simplify the review. This creates another type of table with all argument structures from distributional analysis, and their possible transformations as identified with the symbols ' +' (admits) or '−' (does not admit) (Table 5).

Table 5. Transformational analysis of predicate '*encontrar*'

Encontrar	T1	T2	T3	T4	T5	T6	T7	T8	T9	T10	T11
Los médicos encontraron un flujo anormal en el DV *Doctors found an abnormal flow in the VD*	+	+	+	+	+	−	+	+	+	+	+
Los especialistas encontraron una incidencia de bajo peso al nacer *The specialists found an incidence of low birth weight*	+	+	+	+	+	−	+	+	+	+	+
El médico encontró mayor frecuencia de distrés transitorio e hipoxia *The physician found increased frequency of transient distress and hypoxia*	+	+	+	+	+	−	+	+	+	+	+

(*continued*)

Table 5. (*continued*)

Encontrar	T1	T2	T3	T4	T5	T6	T7	T8	T9	T10	T11
Los investigadores encontraron que la prevalencia de la infección fue de 42.2% *The researchers found that the prevalence of infection was 42.2%*	−	+	+	+	+	−	+	+	+	+	+
El análisis encontró una mayor probabilidad para el desarrollo de DPP *The analysis found an increased likelihood for the development of PPD*	+	+	−	+	+	−	−	+	−	+	+
El estudio encontró diferencias clínica y estadísticamente significativas *The study found clinically and statistically significant differences*	+	+	−	+	+	−	−	+	−	+	+

The information obtained at this stage was the basis for the creation of computer resources, described as follows.

3.3   Developing Electronic Dictionaries

We verified our theoretical descriptions against an electronic dictionary for each VCV with morphosyntactic features, i.e., grammatical category (V = verb), the class to which it belongs (Class V), the derivational model for nominalization (e.g., '*encontrar*', nominalized as '*encuentro*' and inflected as 'COYOTE'), and the predicate inflectional model (e.g., '*encontrar*', inflected as 'ACERTAR') (Fig. 2).

```
Entry       S-Lemma     Category clase DRV                FLX
descubrir   descubrir   V        CV    MIENTO:COYOTE      ABRIR
detectar    detectar    V        CV    CCIÓN:ILUSIÓN      AMAR
develar     develar     V        CV    CIÓN:ILUSIÓN       AMAR
encontrar   encontrar   V        CV    NTRO:COYOTE        ACERTAR
hallar      hallar      V        CV    AZGO:COYOTE        AMAR
```

Fig. 2. Dictionary for each VCV.

Next, grammar models for nominalizing the predicates were elaborated to establish the rules of derivation. Thus, predicate '*encontrar*' derives to its noun '*encuentro*' by replacing the final 'o' with 'ue'; and its ending 'ar', with 'o' (Fig. 3).

```
AZGO = <B>zgo/N+nomin;
NTRO = <U><N><B2>o/N+nomin;
MIENTO = <B>miento/N+nomin;
CCIÓN = <B3>ción/N+nomin;
CIÓN = <B>ción/N+nomin;
```

Fig. 3. Derivational grammar for predicate nominalization.

3.4   Elaborating Computer-Generated Grammars

The next step is to elaborate grammars for the generation and recognition of PDs. For the first case, we start from a declarative, active voice sentence that has the structure shown in Fig. 4:

(─SNHUM─ ─) ──── (<V+CV+3a+sg+ind>) ──────── (─SNCONC─) ─PLOC─ (SNLOC ─)
AO   <$THIS$número=$NHUM$número>   A1   A2
                  PRED

Fig. 4. Argument structure for a PD

Red text indicates the predicate and its arguments. For practical purposes, we exemplify this with the verb in the third person singular, indicative. Here, $PRED consists of a verb of class V ('V + CV') and has an A0 that corresponds to a noun phrase (SN) whose head has the +human feature ('SNHUM'), as shown in Fig. 5; an A1, also nominal, but with +concrete head ('SNCONC'); an associated preposition ('PLOC'); and an A2, with a structure similar to 'SNCONC'.

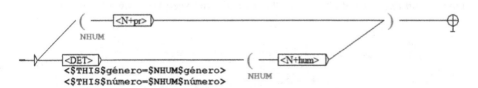

Fig. 5. Structure for SNHUM

The $THIS command is used to establish the rules of concordance and agreement. In this case, the determiner (<DET>) agrees in gender and number with the head of the SN; while concordance with $NHUM is in number.

With this structure, it is possible to generate simple sentences (e.g., '*Juan encontró el cheque en el armario*' [*Juan found the check in the closet*]), and to subsequently formalize possible transformations, such as passive voice, negation, nominalization, etcetera, as shown in Fig. 6.

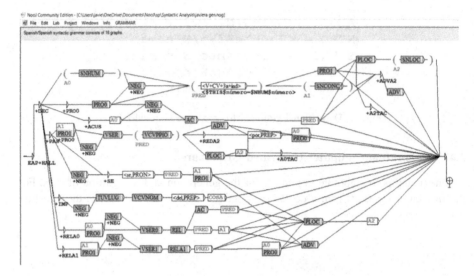

Fig. 6. Transformational generative grammar in NooJ. Starting point ASP + HALL (predicative argument structure of the discovery predicate class). Variables, arguments (A0, A1 and A2), and predicate shown in parentheses.

The above grammar was used to develop another for natural language text recognition, whose results are presented below.

4   Results and Conclusions

Transformational analysis took 325 automatically generated structures from the sentence '*Juan encontró el cheque en el armario*'. An excerpt is shown below, in Fig. 7.

```
File  Edit  Lab  Project  Windows  Info  DICTIONARY
Dictionary contains 325 entries

Juan lo encontró aquí,EAP+HALL+DEC+ACUS+ADVA2
Juan lo encontró allí,EAP+HALL+DEC+ACUS+ADVA2
Juan lo encontró ahí,EAP+HALL+DEC+ACUS+ADVA2
Juan no lo encontró,EAP+HALL+DEC+ACUS+NEG
Juan no lo encontró en el armario,EAP+HALL+DEC+ACUS+NEG
Juan no lo encontró aquí,EAP+HALL+DEC+ACUS+NEG+ADVA2
Juan no lo encontró allí,EAP+HALL+DEC+ACUS+NEG+ADVA2
Juan no lo encontró ahí,EAP+HALL+DEC+ACUS+NEG+ADVA2
eso fue lo que encontró,EAP+HALL+DEC+RELA1+LEJ
eso fue lo que encontró Juan,EAP+HALL+DEC+RELA1+LEJ
eso fue lo que encontró en el armario,EAP+HALL+DEC+RELA1+LEJ
eso fue lo que encontró él,EAP+HALL+DEC+RELA1+LEJ
eso fue lo que encontró él en el armario,EAP+HALL+DEC+RELA1+LEJ
eso fue lo que encontró él aquí,EAP+HALL+DEC+RELA1+LEJ
eso fue lo que encontró él allí,EAP+HALL+DEC+RELA1+LEJ
eso fue lo que encontró él ahí,EAP+HALL+DEC+RELA1+LEJ
eso fue lo que encontró Juan en el armario,EAP+HALL+DEC+RELA1+LEJ
eso fue lo que encontró Juan aquí,EAP+HALL+DEC+RELA1+LEJ
eso fue lo que encontró Juan allí,EAP+HALL+DEC+RELA1+LEJ
```

Fig. 7. Transformations include passive voice, nominalization, negation, replacement by pronouns and adverbs, and possible combinations.

Automatic detection took a random sample of 1000 VCV entries from the entire corpus. Excluding verboids, there were a total of 647 PD entries. An extract of these is shown in Fig. 8.

Fig. 8. Recognition of PDAS from VCV.

Of that total, the grammar algorithm managed to correctly detect 381 PDs, as can be seen in the image above, and incorrectly detected fifteen (mainly due to hyperbaton and ambiguities). This yielded a coverage of 88%, an accuracy of 96%, and an F-measure of 92%.

Our methodology thus showed adequate generation and detection for this type of task. We expect to continue future work with other classes of predicates in Spanish.

References

1. Gross, M.: Méthodes en syntaxe, 1st edn. Hermann, Paris (1996)
2. Silberztein, M.: Formalizing Natural Languages. The NooJ Approach. 1st. edn. ISTE, London (2016)
3. Messina, S., Langella, A.: Paraphrases V<-> in one class of psychological predicates. In: Monti, J., Monteleone, M., di Buono, M. (eds.) Formalizing Natural Languages with NooJ 2014, pp. 140–149. Newcastle, Cambridge (2015)
4. Tolone, E.: Conversión de las tablas del Léxico-Gramática del francés en el léxico LGLex. In: 2nd Argentinian Workshop on Natural Language Processing. Universidad de Córdoba, Córdoba (2012)
5. Palma, S.: Hacia un enfoque semántico de las expresiones idiomáticas. In: Coursera, J., Dijan, M., Gaspara, A. (eds.) La lingüística francesa. Situación y perspectivas a finales del siglo XX, pp. 313–321. Prensas de la Universidad de Zaragoza, Zaragoza (1994)
6. Gross, G.: Manual de análisis lingüístico. Aproximación sintáctico-semántica al léxico. 1st. edn. Editorial UOC, Barcelona (2014)

Digital Humanities and Teaching

Who is to Blame for What?
An Insight Within the French Yellow Vests'
Movement Through Dole's Books
of Grievances

Marion Bendinelli[(✉)]

Université Bourgogne Franche-Comté/ELLIADD (UR 4661), Paris, France
marion.bendinelli@univ-fcomte.fr

Abstract. In the occasion of the Yellow Vests' Movement, people expressed their distress and hopes in demonstrations, debates, letters, online social media or platforms, and books of grievances. This latter form of written expression interests us for its communicative and discursive characteristics. We seize the opportunity of the NooJ Conference held in Besançon to challenge ourselves and this corpus with NLP methods and tools. The present paper deals with the expression of blame in the book of grievances of Dole (Jura, France). It is a quest for the identification and collection of the utterances in which writers blame someone for doing something. To this aim, we use NooJ software to design a grammar able to describe a three-slot pattern involving the designation of (1) a demand for action; (2) the motives for the writers' troubles; (3) the culprits. The paper describes our method that follows both inductive and deductive paths, and that relies on the DM dictionary provided with the software and on the handling of the nouns' concordance lines.

Keywords: NooJ grammar · Speech act of blame · Inductive and deductive method · Concordance lines

1 Introduction

Our research deals with the written texts that are present in the books of grievances opened during the French Yellow Vests' Movement as an answer to this troubled period. A first research [1] focused on describing the physical characteristics and communication functions of the book available in Dole (Jura, France) taken as a case study. It also led to portray the different registers writers have used to express themselves, adopting either a more intimate voice or a formal and rhetorical tone. In the present paper, we will briefly summarize this data. The issue at hand is yet different: we want to focus on a particular speech act, the expression of blame. It implies to identify who the culprits are, what they are responsible of, and the kind of demand aimed at putting an end to the (moral, financial…) sufferings. Therefore, we look for a semantic and syntactic pattern.

To identify this pattern, we rely on the software Nooj [6] in order to write a grammar that will be able to list all relevant utterances. This is quite a challenge for us

© Springer Nature Switzerland AG 2021
M. Bigey et al. (Eds.): NooJ 2021, CCIS 1520, pp. 75–86, 2021.
https://doi.org/10.1007/978-3-030-92861-2_7

since, as a computer-based discourse analyst, we are rather accustomed to other software environments and methodologies. As a consequence, the present paper exposes our path of thoughts, in a step-by-step presentation that would hopefully led us to a more general discussion of computer-based methods for discourse and text analysis.

2   France and Its Sociopolitical Context in 2018: The Yellow Vests' Movement and the Books of Grievances

2.1   A Brief Introduction to French Yellow Vests' Movement

The Yellow Vests' Movement [from now on YVM] is a popular movement that has emerged in November 2018 in France, in reaction to the decision made by the government to raise the level of taxes on gas prices. Its name derives from the type of vest people decided to wear in order to pass from invisibility to visibility[1]. Rural population as well as workers depending on their cars on a daily basis rallied first on social networks (mainly *Facebook*) and then on streets and roads, to express their anger and claim their rights to be treated with respect. Massive demonstrations (Fig. 1a) took place all over the country, and gathered as soon as December tens of thousands of people each Saturday, above all in Paris. The city of Dole (Jura) and its 25,000 inhabitants (Fig. 1b) is a milestone to the history of this social movement; there, the first demonstration took place on November 2nd with people, cars and trucks blocking the main road and bridge of the city. Yellow Vest's demonstrators, whether official members of the movement or not, are not the usual types of persons that would participate to demonstrations in France: they scarcely belong to a political party or a given Union, and have rarely joined previous social movements.

The YVM was born as a spontaneous, unstructured and apolitical movement. Therefore, academics as well as politicians have considered the movement as unexpected and unprecedented in its format and length. By spring 2019, the visibility of the movement lowered even though, for more than two years now, each popular rally still is the occasion for whoever claiming to be a Yellow Vests' member to demonstrate in the streets and asks for more equity – among other grievances.

a.   b.

Fig. 1. a. The French Yellow Vests' Movement as seen in the streets. **b.** France and Dole (*Google map*, 2021.05.31).

---

[1] This is precisely the original function of this jacket, usually employed on construction sites or in case of emergencies on roads.

Apart from giving nationally broadcasted speeches, Emmanuel Macron (the current French President of the Republic) and his government (of which Edouard Philippe was Prime Minister in 2019) answered the country's social situation by organizing a *Grand Débat* (Great Debate). Its goal was to provide everyone (pro and anti YVM) with a space to express his or her wishes, demands, hopes, distress, etc. It offered four modalities of expression, opened roughly from mid-December to the end of February (with the exception of regional conferences that took place in March). While the online platform and the live debates were topic-oriented, mails (whether electronic or not) and Books of Grievances were not. People could write on whatever topics they wished to address, and adopt whatever format and register they enjoyed. Private agencies (*Roland Berger, Blue Nove, Cognito, Opinion Way, Missions publiques* and *Res Publica*) specialized in automatic massive data processing and civic technologies compiled the (online, oral and paper-made) texts and summarized their content and tone so that E. Macron and his government could adopt policies directly inspired by the popular contributions.

2.2   The Characteristics of Dole's Book of Grievances

The Book's Physical Characteristics and Communication Functions. We have studied the book of grievances of Dole for three reasons. First, the city is important to the YVM, as we have already mentioned; second, it displays an interesting sociodemographic, geographic and political profile. Indeed, it's an aging city that have tended to vote for right-wing and extreme (either left and right) representatives for the past decade; also, it appears as a not-so-much attractive territory in terms of employment and its population relies quite heavily on their cars to reach biggest cities (Besançon, Dijon). Therefore, we expect topics such as purchasing power, job insecurity, welfare and taxes to be addressed by the people writing in the. The third reason is a practical one: we have asked by emails sent to the Communication Staff of various cities in Franche-Comté an access to their books; the Head of Dole's Mayor Cabinet, Karine Métivier, has been the only one to answer immediately and positively to our request.

Dole's book of grievances was freely accessible and available to anyone entering the town hall [1] from mid-December to February 18th. We digitized[2] it on February 4th: by that time, 64 texts had been written, reaching a total number of 18,026 tokens. To count the number of texts, we have established that one type of writing and/or one signature equals one voice, hence one writer[3]. A first look at the book reveals the existence of 56 handwritten texts and 8 computer-typed ones (Fig. 2). Some writers have adopted a

---

[2] The on-site digitization of the book was made possible thanks to the portable scanner borrowed from Besançon federative research structure in human and social sciences, Maison des Sciences de l'Homme et de l'Environnement Claude Nicolas Ledoux (UAR 3124, université Bourgogne Franche-Comté/CNRS).

[3] One person signed three different texts under three different identities (Head of the weather station, Brother-in-law of a disabled woman, Forester); yet we could not know whether he or she would write on behalf of different persons or if he or she would intentionally display different voices. From a discourse analysis perspective, what matters is the expression of points of view; therefore, in that particular case, we have decided to count three different texts and writers.

very personal and conversational tone, beginning their contribution with *"Bonjour"* (Hello) or ending it with *"Bonne chance"*, *"Merci"* (Good luck, Thank you); others on the contrary have preferred a much more formal tone as well as a very structured speech, wording their message just like a letter or a (political) platform. Though handwritten texts outnumber typed ones, the length of each set is roughly the same: 9,226 tokens for handwritten texts, 8,800 tokens for typed ones.

Fig. 2. Text 26 (typed) and text 27 (handwritten).

Texts fulfill three communicative functions:

- first, they enable writers to claim their existence and their legitimate right to have their voice heard;
- second, writing in the book helps people to organize their thoughts and opinions whose archival and transmission to present and future generations [4] are then guaranteed;
- third, writers use the book as a space of free expression to explicitly denounce the unfair and undeserved situations they are victim of [2].

Preprocessing the Texts. To proceed with the analyses of the book, we had to transcribe all texts manually because OCR techniques[4] could not yield satisfying

---

[4] We have used Abbyy FineReader to try the OCR (Optical Character Reading) technique. For lack of time, we could not experiment HTR (Handwritten Text Recognition) techniques, such as the one developed by the platforms Transkribus (https://readcoop.eu/transkribus/) or e-Scriptorium (https://escripta.hypotheses.org/).

results: indeed, softwares prove to be useless when confronted to various types of writing whose level of quality and clarity may vary from writer to writer. We also had to replace all personal indications (names, addresses, signatures) by adequate tags to guarantee the writers' anonymity. Besides, we chose to normalize incorrect spellings and grammar mistakes, though keeping the record of the original forms with TEI-conformant tags[5]. Finally; we also used this language to document texts' layouts as well as the discourse function of given segments or paragraphs (rhetorical questions, formulaic, opening or closing expression, argument, conclusion...), hence reaching a fine-grained transcription of Dole's original book of grievances[6].

Note that the pieces of information documenting spelling and grammatical mistakes as well as the texts' layout and discourse structure are not taken into consideration in this paper, since it is not relevant to answer our present research issue.

3   An Attempt to Model Blaming Someone for Something

3.1   Wanted! Who Are the Culprits?

Before considering the possibility to design into a grammar the way writers identify culprits and blames, we need to identify who the culprits are. To carry out this step, we import our corpus in NooJ software, and apply to it the DM dictionary [5] provided with the software for the analysis of French texts. This linguistic resource contains 67,997 entries describing adjectives, adverbs, conjunctions, determiners, interjections, nouns, numerals, prepositions, pronouns and verbs. The dictionary provides morphological and syntactical information to each lexical unit in order to correctly (1) parse a given text (i.e., word forms are associated to their parts of speech and lemmas); (2) generate word forms out of lemmas.

Then, we call the *Locate a pattern* function to draw an exhaustive list of the nouns that are present in the corpus (Fig. 3a). Finally, we visualize them in the concordancer (Fig. 3b), i.e. the index of sequences that shows each word form (the pivot of the sequence) in its context (roughly 10 word forms on the left and on the right of the pivot word).

---

[5] TEI stands for Text Encoding Initiative. It is "is a consortium which collectively develops and maintains a standard for the representation of texts in digital form [and] specify encoding methods for machine-readable texts, chiefly in the humanities, social sciences and linguistics" (https://tei-c. org/).

[6] We thank Anaïs Rico–Perrier, our Master student in Discourse Analysis (year 2018–2019), who carried out all technical tasks with us during her 2 month training as a member of this research action: she helped with the transcription, the normalization, the anonymization and the TEI structuration of the data.

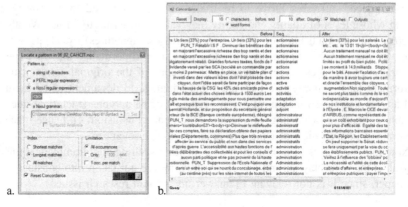

Fig. 3. Screenshots of Nooj functionalities and results: **a.** The *Locate a pattern* function; **b.** Nouns' concordance lines ordered alphabetically (first 26 results).

NooJ identifies 6,181 word forms among which we select 58 tokens because writers tend to use them to designate the actors, companies or institutions they see as responsible for their distress and their financial and/or social troubles. We have to admit here that not all writers use these tokens to blame someone or something: for example, depending on their size, enterprises are considered as positive (example 1) or negative (example 2) actors of our modern world.

Example 1. Contribution 7

"Suppression du CICE et trouver une vraie solution pour épauler les très petites, petites et moyennes entreprises"
Suppression of the tax credit and find a real solution to back up very small, small and medium-sized enterprises

Example 2. Contribution 24

"Vous [E. Macron] l'octroyez [=notre argent] à votre guise à des grosses entreprises qui ne jouent pas le jeu pour réduire le chômage mais qui engraissent leurs actionnaires."

You grant it at your will to big companies that do not play the game of reducing unemployment but line its shareholders' pockets.

The 7th writer asks the State a policy to support the enterprises while the 24th writer blames them for sharing their benefits with their shareholders rather than spending it to hire new employees. Tagging entreprises as a culprit somehow blurs the interpretation of the token with positive results (cases in which *entreprises* does refer to culprits) and false results (cases in which *entreprises* does not refer to culprits). However, at this stage of the research, we have decided not to be restrictive by distinguishing each particular occurrence. The next step of the method (Subsect. 3.2) should indeed help eliminate false positives by taking into consideration the occurrence environment (or context).

We then range all 58 nouns into categories as indicated in Table 1 (labels are ours).

Table 1. The designation of the culprits: categories and word forms.[7]

Category	Word forms
Miscellaneous	*bénéficiaire, CICE, conseiller, classe préparatoire, dirigeant, elite, entreprise (public), journaliste, psychopathe, récidiviste, société* (beneficiary, Tax credit to lower the cost of labor on wages and help companies gain market shares, councilor, competitive-entry higher education establishment, leader, elite, (public) enterprise, journalist, psychopath, recidivist, society)
Political institution and their members	*administration, Assemblée nationale, CESE, conseil constitutionnel, commune, collectivité, collectivité territoriale, corps, département, ENA, énarque, État, fonctionnaire, garde républicaine, préfecture, préfet, région, secrétaire (d'État), sous-préfecture* (administration, national Assembly, Economical, Social and Environmental Council, constitutional council, town, local authorities, partially autonomous region, body, department, prestigious grande école training future government officials, holder of ENA diploma, State, civil servants, Republican Guard, prefecture, prefect, region, (State) secretary, subprefecture)
Political representatives	*député, élu, Emmanuel Macron, gouvernant, gouvernement, maires, Ministres, parlementaire, Président de la République, sénateur* (deputy, elected representative, Emmanuel Macron, people in power, government, mayor, Minister, member of Parliament, President of the Republic, senator)
Symbols of the modern (capitalistic) society	*actionnaire, banque, bus Macron, camions, casseurs, constructeur automobile, (grandes) enseignes, étrangers, garagistes, immigration, immigrés, patrons, poids-lourds, privilégiés, propriétaire, riche, routier, terrorisme* (shareholder, bank, long-distance bus, rioters, car manufacturer, trucks, (large) stores, immigration, aliens, garage owner/mechanic, immigrants, CEO, heavy-weight, privileged people, owner, rich, long-distance transporter, terrorism)

We finally add a specific semantic tag (*Responsable*) to these nouns in the DM dictionary, adopting the required syntax as showed in (1) in the case of the noun *actionnaire* (shareholder). Such operations are indeed permitted precisely because this dictionary is one "on which the NooJ community will have control" [5].

$$\text{actionnaire}: \ N + FLX = S\_0 + Sem = Responsable \tag{1}$$

[7] In the table, word forms in French are ordered alphabetically; translations follow the same order as in French. Translations were produced with the help of online Larousse bilingual dictionary (https://www.larousse.fr/dictionnaires/francais-anglais/); when the exact translation could not be found, we defined the word to help understanding.

3.2   What Are the Culprits Responsible for? Looking for a Pattern

To find what the culprits are responsible for, we follow the same method as in Subsect. 3.1: first, we call the *Locate a pattern* functionality of the software in order to produce a list of utterances containing an occurrence of any noun bearing the semantic label <Responsable>.

The operation yields a table of 391 sequences; going through these concordance lines, we notice a recurring syntactical pattern standing for a three-slot construction:

- a request for action, and in particular, the partial or total limitation of something felt as unfair or harmful;
- the indication of the level or the domain where the action is to take place, in particular the policy or behavior qualified as negative;
- the indication of who/what causes this unfair or harmful situation (the culprits).

Also, the pattern utterances may be recursive: indeed, one nominal group or one clause may be extended by a second nominal group or a second clause, and so on, with or without an ellipsis, as illustrated in examples 3 to 5.

Example 3. Contribution 57

"*Limitation des traitements des hauts-fonctionnaires, députés, sénateurs.*"
Limitation of the senior civil servants' wages, deputies, senators.

Example 4. Contribution 58

"*Abolir les privilèges des anciens présidents, des sénateurs, députés, etc.*"
Abolish the privileges of former presidents, senators, deputies, etc.

Example 5. Contribution 29

Table 2. The pattern and its paradigms of lexicalization.

Action	Level/Domain	Culprit
[verb] *abolir, baisser, dissoudre, diviser, interdire, limiter réduire, remettre (en question), supprimer* (abolish, decrease/lower, dissolve, divide/split, forbid, limit, reduce, suppress) [noun] *abolition, arrêt, baisse, désengagement, diminution, dissolution, fin, limitation, réduction, révision, stop, suppression, transformation* (abolition, stop, decrease, desengagement, diminution, dissolution, end, limitation, reduction, reappraisal, suppression, transformation) [adverb] *moins, seulement, pas, plus, trop* (less, only, no, no more, too much/many)	*nombre, expression d'une quantité donnée* (number, expression of a given quantity) *avantage, bénéfice, charge, contrôle, dépense, émolument, emprise, taxe, prélèvement, insolence, invasion, paiement, privilège, pouvoir, salaire, submersion, train de vie* (advantages, benefit, cost, control, spending, wage, grip, tax, contribution, arrogance, invasion, payment, privilege, power, salary, submersion, standard of living)	*députés, entreprises, actionnaires, État...* (deputies, enterprises, shareholders, State...) (see 58 culprits as listed in Table 1)

"l'Assemblée Nationale, diviser par 2 le nombre de députés et leur supprimer des avantages"
the National Assembly, split in two the number of deputies and suppress them some advantages

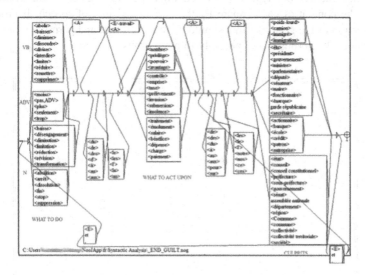

Fig. 4. The grammar for the speech act of blame (with lexical units' paradigms).

Each slot of the sequence corresponds to a given paradigm of lexical units: in Table 2, we have listed these units, ordering them alphabetically and according to their grammatical category (column Action) or to their meaning (column Level/Domain).

We are now able to design the grammar for the pattern, its various slots (indicated as mandatory or facultative) and forms of lexicalization (Fig. 4).

Following NooJ constraints [6], the grammar reads from left to right, from one square to another, until the software no longer finds matching sequences and stops (as symbolized by the crossed circle situated at the far-right of the figure); each arrow indicates the existence of a node, i.e. opens an alternative between two or more paths.

Each square gathers lemmas displaying the same distributional properties and, as often as possible, a close meaning: for example, in the first column (Action/What to do), nouns are divided into two squares, separating those implying a total suppression from those indicating a diminution. Such an ordering also eases the reading of the grammar. Lexical units are written as lemmas so that the grammar may find all corresponding morphosyntactic word forms; when necessary, the part-of-speech tag is indicated to disambiguate it (see the case of *"pas"* as an adverb).

To verify the grammar well-formedness, we apply it to the corpus: not only the grammar finds the utterances we had considered to build the patter, thus verifying its validity, but it also identifies new utterances that we had missed in the previous phase. Eventually, the grammar collects 38 utterances.

84   M. Bendinelli

3.3 An Attempt to Design the Speech Act of Blame in Dole's Book of Grievances

The very last step of our research is to simplify the first version of the grammar by replacing the content of each square by the paradigms' part of speech. It produces a second version of the grammar that should be more abstract and permit a more general application to the corpus – and possibly to any corpus.

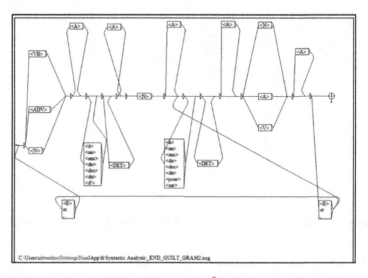

Fig. 5. The second version of the grammar[8] (with grammatical categories).

This second version is reproduced in Fig. 5. Grammatical tags are the following: A – Adjectives, ADV – Adverbs, DET – Determiners, N – Nouns, VB – Verbs; E stands for Empty which means that the slot may be lexicalized or not. Its application to our corpus yields many results, maybe too many; still, we think this step is necessary to notice possible candidates for the pattern.

The application of the more abstract grammar leads to the discovery of new utterances instantiating the pattern with lexical units that are different than the ones we previously identified (examples 6 to 11).

Example 6. Contribution 3

"L'abandon de la prime au changement de véhicule"
The abandonment of the incentive to change one's vehicle

Example 7. Contribution 3

"Le rétablissement de l'ISF"
The restoration of wealth tax

---

[8] The second version of our grammar may not be fully satisfying since it still indicates prepositions' lexicalizations: this is caused by a technical problem we could not fix before submitting the paper.

Example 8. Contribution 2

"Demande de contrôle sur tous les élus et révocation en cas de faute préjudiciable au Peuple"
Request for some control over the elected representatives and dismissal in case of prejudiciable offence to the People

Example 9. Contribution 2

"Demande d'une autorité très compétente sous contrôle pour la planète"
Request for a very skillful authority under control for the planet sake

Example 10. Contribution 2

"Demande d'une Police et d'une justice pour les animaux"
Request for a Police and for justice personel for animals' protection

Example 11. Contribution 2

"Demande URGENTE D'un Référendum d'initiative citoyenne en toutes matières"
URGING request of a Referendum initiated by citizen in all issues

4 Conclusion

The organization of the NooJ Conference held in Besançon in June 2021 was the occasion for us to handle NooJ software and test it on our material – here, the texts written in Dole's book of grievances during the YVM. More familiar of computer-based methods for the analysis of textual data (in particular the textometric method [3]), we positively consider using NooJ in our future research. Indeed, it provides another way to look to the data at hand and to describe them; by handling linguistic resources (the DM dictionary) and writing ad-hoc grammars, we may study patterns – in the case of this paper, the speech act of blame – and carry out a fine-grained semantic and syntactic annotation of the corpus. In doing so, the possibility to articulate top-down and bottom-up approaches was highly appreciated: our paper shows that it is not only possible but also essential to overcome initial intuitions and hypotheses.

In terms of perspectives, we wish to follow the current path and insert the present grammar into a more global one: the objective would be to design the various kinds of narration and argumentation that unfold in the corpus depending on the type of writings (intimate vs formal register) and on the topics.

Also, we believe that designing grievances as expressed in Dole's book offers the possibility to study them at a more general level – in all books of grievances – but also, and especially, to any given type of corpus concerned by such a speech act. Indeed, the present grammar may be easily adapted and implemented for the study of customer services and hotlines, or public consultations and debates, i.e. any kind of textual data where people are invited to express their opinions on the situation they are enduring as well as to suggest solutions to improve their everyday life.

Finally, our research leads us to look positively toward the possibility to gather NLP/NooJ specialists and TXM/Textometric specialists: the university Bourgogne

Franche-Comté may be best positioned to realize this perspective, with the collaboration of the members of NLP and Computer-based Discourse analysis research teams.

References

1. Bendinelli, M., Rico–Perrier, A.: Sens et matérialités des contributions citoyennes. Analyse textométrique et discursive du cahier citoyen de Dole (Jura), Communication, JE Quels outils d'analyse pour les gilets jaunes?. Sciences Po, Mate-SHS, METSEM, Paris (2020)
2. Genestier, Ph.: Les « Gilets Jaunes » : Une question d'autonomie autant que d'automobile. Le Débat (204), 16–34 (2019). https://www.cairn.info/revue-le-debat-2019-2-page-16.htm. Accessed 10 Oct 2021
3. Heiden, S., Magué, J-P., Pincemin, B.: TXM: Une plateforme logicielle open-source pour la textométrie – conception et développement. In: Bolasco, S., Chiari, I., Giuliano, L. (eds.) Proceedings of 10th International Conference on the Statistical Analysis of Textual Data - JADT 2010, pp. 1021–1032. Edizioni Universitarie di Lettere Economia Diritto, Roma (2010)
4. Klock-Fontanille, I.: Des supports pour écrire d'Uruk à Internet. Le français aujourd'hui (170), 13–30 (2010). https://www.cairn.info/revue-le-francais-aujourd-hui-2010-3-page-13.htm. Accessed 10 Oct 2021
5. Trouilleux, F.: Le DM, a French dictionary for NooJ. In: Vučković, K., Bekavac, B., Silberztein, M. (eds.) Automatic Processing of Various Levels of Linguistic Phenomena: Selected Papers from the NooJ 2011 International Conference, pp. 16–28. Cambridge Scholars Publishing, Cambridge (2012). https://hal.archives-ouvertes.fr/hal-00702348/document. Accessed 10 Oct 2021
6. Silberztein, M.: La formalisation des langues: l'approche de NooJ. ISTE, Londres (2015)

Sensitivity to Fake News: Reception Analysis with NooJ

Magali Bigey[✉] and Justine Simon

ELLIADD (UR 4661), University of Franche-Comté, Besançon, France
{magali.bigey,justine.simon}@univ-fcomte.fr

Abstract. The power of the image is to touch the deepest feelings of the audience (indignation, compassion, sublimation, fear, hatred, astonishment, etc.). Internet users, who are often drowned in a permanent flow of information, are not led to analyze an image. They are simply touched, affected by the content. This appeal to emotion is a favorable ground for the deployment of post-truth. Post-truth is a situation where the reality of facts influences public opinion less than the appeal to emotions and personal beliefs. It is the emotion that prevails, the truth has become secondary. We decided to undertake a reception study with students of the Information-Communication OTC, aiming to understand their (in-)capacity to discern infox in a digital context, their verbalization of personal emotions and the forms of self-involvement in the discourse. After having collected over two consecutive years the reactions of about 80 students to several kinds of pictures in context and out of context, we will show how NooJ allows us to bring out the personal involvement in discourse, and the differences in student's permeability once they have been a bit sensitized to this issue. We will use lexicon analysis, concordances analysis, but also semantic information analysis (on expressed feelings for example). We have been interested in ethos in discourse, and we will see that it is often associated with emotional reactions, making a clear link with the emotional web that has been strongly emerging in recent years.

Keywords: Infox by image · Reception · Digital networks · Image education · Ethos · Postures

1 Introduction

The challenges of the digital transition are everywhere and are particularly important when it comes to media literacy. With the multiplication of screens and the easy access to all kinds of information, a major challenge arises from the incessant circulation of information through images. While the vast majority of media information passes through social and digital networks, we notice that a significant part of it is diverted towards false information, or even that it is completely made up of false information, feeding conspiracy theories or other attempts at de(sin)formation.

This article is at the crossroads of fact checking and new digital skills. Within the framework of a research linked to media education, it is a question of training students in critical thinking from a work of reception of infox by the image. An experiment was

© Springer Nature Switzerland AG 2021
M. Bigey et al. (Eds.): NooJ 2021, CCIS 1520, pp. 87–100, 2021.
https://doi.org/10.1007/978-3-030-92861-2_8

conducted in October 2020 to understand how students interpret images. Why do some perceive them as forms of de(sin)formation and others not? What personal, socio-cultural, psychological, etc. filters do they mobilize when faced with an image? What are the significant areas in their eyes? But also, how do students inscribe their ethos in the discourse? And in what way do these markers of self reveal different forms of postures: critical, aesthetic, emotional... ?

The first part aims at clarifying the theoretical concepts used and the method-ological approach adopted, which combines discourse analysis and lexicometry with reception analysis, through the use of NooJ [15], concordance analysis, co-occurring contexts and the lexicon of expressed emotions for example. The second part syn-thesizes the first results of the analysis. The aim of this research work is to help fight infoxes by proposing an image education that allows to take a step back and to sharpen a sense of relevant analysis while developing skills adapted to this new digital challenge.

2 Theoretical and Methodological Framework

2.1 Fake News and Media Literacy

This research work responds to both societal and scientific issues.

Educating about images [7–9, 13] and raising awareness about the different forms of fake news - or infox, according to the French acception - is a way to fight them. The proliferation of information is not always ethically acceptable, and it is important to make students understand that manipulation is often underlying depending on the objective sought by the "infoxer" (political, economic, etc.). The objective is to ensure that they adopt an analytical perspective[1] when faced with information that is deemed dubious or malicious and, in the latter case, especially that they do not share it[2]. The more general interest is thus to defend the ethics of journalistic work in order to give back confidence to the citizens, while giving them the means to identify the points of vigilance as for their reception for a perennial media education.

From a scientific point of view, this article is an extension of research on the circulation of false information via socionumeric networks, and more specifically on the sharing of infoxes through images [4, 14] - an interrogation that crosses with the question of reception [3]. Beginning in August 2018, an informational watch of the Twitter accounts of four news verification sites was set up. The analysis was based on the publications made on Twitter and Facebook that generated the most reactions (on the total retweets/shares, replies/comments, likes). This first work allowed us to identify

---

[1] There are many fact-checking initiatives to adopt this analytical hindsight. See [5]. On fake news, more globally, see [6, 10, 12].

[2] According to a survey conducted by BVA-La villa numeris in 2018 by the Ministry of Europe and Foreign Affairs, more than half of French people who share information have already done so when they knew it was unreliable: 34% wanted to arouse the interest of their friends and 31% admit that they had absolutely not checked the source. Access: https://www.lavillanumeris.com/180404-fake_news-analyse.

a classification of four types of image manipulation. The project was then enriched by the study of the reception of these manipulated images, which is the subject of this article.

2.2 Ethos in Discourse

The scientific approach adopted is at the crossroads of Information and Communication Sciences and Language Sciences. For the methodological part, which we will present below, the analysis is done using lexicometric software. And from a theoretical point of view, the question of self-inscription is central to the analysis.

The interpretation of manipulated images questions, of course, the question of discerning doctored information, but it also engages the subjectivity of the person who appropriates its content. By exploiting the concept of ethos [2, 3, 11], i.e. the inscription of oneself in the discourse, we open new perspectives of analysis. The image itself is no longer the focus of concern, but its interpretation becomes essential. With the appearance of the "I", one can identify personal, emotional, etc. filters of interpretation. The "I", whether explicit or not, allows us to speak about ourselves and to position ourselves. In this way, the reception of infox by the image by students brings into play: the putting forward of their cultural background, their mastery of analysis (image analysis and social digital networks), the claim of their group of belonging, or the attempt to highlight themselves in a desire to be appreciated. The study of ethos in discourse is thus coupled with a social issue of "expressive individualism" [1]. On the question of truth, we can see that it becomes secondary. At the time of the self culture, each one sees in these doctored images his own truth. We know that the power of the image in general is to touch the deepest feelings of the public. Internet users, who are often drowned in a permanent flow of information, are not led to analyze an image. They are simply touched, affected by the content. This appeal to emotion is a favorable ground for the deployment of "post-truth". By making students aware of this problem, where, when faced with an infox, it is emotion that takes precedence, the challenge is to introduce and explain this notion of post-truth[3].

2.3 Constitution of the Corpus and the Sub-corpus

The experiment was carried out with nearly 160 students beginning their first year of university in the Information-Communication field. We subjected all the students to the same series of images (presented in context and out of context consecutively) with exactly the same instructions, which were to write in three minutes maximum what they perceived in front of each of the images presented, without telling them that they were infoxes. We would like to emphasize that although the students are all in their first year and first semester of training for the DUT Information-Communication, they are divided into three different options (Digital Information in Organizations "IN",

---

[3] Post-truth is a situation of reception where the reality of facts influences public opinion less than the appeal to emotions and personal beliefs.

Communication of Organizations "COM" and Advertising "PUB"), which, as we shall see, has its importance in the reception of infoxes.

Once collected, the answers in word format were exported individually into an excel spreadsheet to which some kind of metadata were added, in order to be able to process them in a global way but also differentiated: the answers to each visualized image (13 in number, 6 of which out of context and then in context), the group of students, their gender, in order to be able to carry out very fine analyses afterwards, which are now possible in the sorting and processing of the data. This is a tedious and time-consuming task, but it saves considerable processing time. A methodological point to note: the lexicometric analyses of the answers are systematically done after deleting the questions.

Once the corpus was constituted, it was studied by calling upon the language sciences and, in the first phase of analysis, lexicometry as well as the theories of reception, while always keeping in mind the observation of the inscription of the self in the discourse. This last point is fundamental to identify individual reactionary postures, each person expressing his or her opinion and emotions accompanied by one of the markers of self-expression discourse (I, me, my..., nouns with a full semantic scope, negative or, on the contrary, very positive adjectives, verbs of feelings used), all of this participates in the study of self-inscription in discourse and of the person's posture in front of the information received, in this case, images.

3 Reception Analysis

3.1 Methodology and Lexicometric Discourse Analysis

We proceeded in an orderly fashion to define what unites students from different options in the reception of infox through images, and what distinguishes them in this posture. Among the students of the three options, we first identified personal postures and markers of ethos in their reactions to images. We then worked on the appearance of semantically strong words (horror, fear, panic) and their correlation with one or more options. Next, we separated the three types of images according to the following typology, derived from a classification of four forms of image manipulation [4]:

– "fabricated images," which are iconic realizations that constitute false evidence;
– "doctored images", which are modified, embellished, and aestheticized in order to influence an audience (recolored images, cropped images, additions through copy-pasting, etc.);
– "decontextualized images", which consist in using an image from a previous context;
– finally, "over-interpreted images" (images that have not been doctored or decon-textualized), where it is the commentary of the enunciator. The person will impose his point of view, strategically overinterpreting what is shown

Here again, we have identified the postures of the students, depending on their option, and also on their gender.

3.2 General Analysis of the Corpus

We proceeded on the total corpus from which were subtracted the questions as well as all the elements that did not come from the raw response of the students. This makes it possible to identify the most frequent words, and terms that emerge immediately and in greater number in front of the images. This first corpus, close to the total corpus, is made up of all the answers, without distinction.

The first remarkable thing about this corpus is the very important proportion of personal pronouns in the first 50 most frequent occurrences: we, us, he, I, she, then we notice the appearance of person and persons. These first markers of the inscription of the self in the discourse are very present, they give us a good indication of the manifest impact of the modified image on the students. With each mention of a marker of ethos, it is the inscription of oneself in discourse, the projection of one's self and one's belonging to the mentioned environment that is signified. This question of the ethos in discourse on the general corpus deserves a deepening, it is particularly from the ethos that we can measure the intellectual engagement of the receiver on the infox by the image. In this perspective, we have first extracted and then analyzed the occurrences of the pronoun I as well as its co-occurring context.

To do this, in the total corpus of 1257 occurrences of I on the 2002 argued responses, we chose a span of 5 words before and after. The first results concerning the most common words show the terms: think, find, know, thought; they clearly show an introspective positioning in relation to the images (Fig. 1).

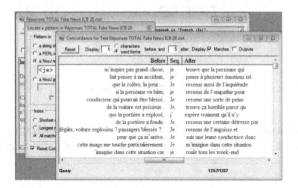

Fig. 1. Concordance of <I> on the total corpus

The close lexicon shows well the competence of the students to speak about their impressions, of their distance with what is visualized and understood. The lexicon of the visual appears here very strongly, some positioning themselves on the pure description of the images. What is interesting, in the light of this word cloud repre- sentative of the co-occurring context of the pronoun I, is to bring out the verbs that are closest to it. Indeed, the use of verbs in discourse generates a perceptible analysis of the postures (the verbs of state or of action bring again the analysis on different tracks of reception, and reveal the feeling in front of the image).

The following query, on the verbs of the sub-corpus I, has allowed to emerge 4822 verbs that it is necessary to classify, by number of occurrence but also by aspect (Fig. 3).

The illustration of the verbs that were most often used (Fig. 2) shows a majority of I think, I imagine, I find, I don't know… we always show reflection and expectation.

Fig. 2. Cooccurring context of "I", representation after extraction of the concordance pasted then in Tagcrowd

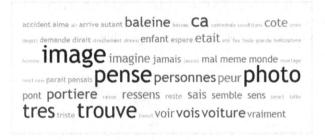

Fig. 3. Most common co-occurring verbs

In the close vocabulary, we see fear appear; it will be interesting to analyze the lexicon around the idea of uneasiness, of the impression of oppression quoted several times (Fig. 4):

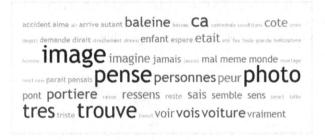

Fig. 4. Most common lexicon in the verb sub-corpus

In the same way, by cross-checking the data of the total corpus with the data of the sub-corpus made up of sentences mentioning I, we see the same terms appearing. The ethos is present in these expressed feelings of anxiety, fear, sadness... (Fig. 5)

Fig. 5. The most common lexicon around *I*

The main thing that stands out is the identification of many words that express a physical sensation or sensations; some of these images have a real physical impact on the students who look at them.

The question is now to try to define if profiles emerge among the students, and if they react in the same way whatever the option they are enrolled in.

4   Contrastive Analysis of the Corpus

The second corpus differs from the first in that it separates the students' options into three distinct groups. Once again, the most frequently expressed vocabulary was observed. We proceeded in the same way as in the first analysis. We analysed the words that are overused and those that are underused compared to the rest of the corpus appear. This makes it possible to bring out the differences in reception that appear between the students according to their option. Once again, a remarkable thing concerns the lexicon of fear, through the same word: although the groups are not balanced in terms of the number of students, we were able to notice that, compared to the other two, one group used this term significantly more (3 times for the IN group, 9 times for the COM group, 45 times for the PUB group[4]). Comparatively, the figures shed light on this first result in a clear manner: 9.67% for the IN group, 18% for the COM group, 61.64% for the PUB group.

Examples regarding the Yolocaust photomontage[5]:

– The photo immediately made me "scared" and shocked (2020 - COM)

---

[4] Respectively, there are 31 responses for Digital Information (IN) students, 50 for Organizational Communication (COM) students and 73 for Advertising (PUB) students.

[5] This is a special case because it comes from a work of the Israeli artist Shahak Shapira, who in his project "Yolocaust" questions our culture of commemoration by bringing together on his site current selfies in the camps with old photographs that show the horror that inhabited these places.

- However, when I looked at it better I was immediately surprised and a feeling of fear or I don't know how to explain it but I was suddenly horrified, destabilized, unhealthy feelings (2020 - PUB)

Examples concerning the photomontage of the whale:

- I have a very big fear of anything on the sea floor this image makes me very anxious. (2020 - IN)
- This image scares me, crossing a bridge and the sea floor naturally scare me. But the two combined I am anxious, I panic. (...) This is an anxiety-provoking image. (2020 - PUB)
- It makes me extremely afraid. (2020 - COM)

This result of the expression of the emotional is confirmed with other terms such as *anguish, distressing, sad, awful, terrible...*

- *anguish*: 1 time for the IN, 2 times for the COM and 12 times for the PUB
- *sad*: 10 times for the INs, 4 times for the COMs, 61 times for the PUBs (we can add 15 occurrences of *sadness* whereas for the other groups the occurrences of the word *sadness* are anecdotal)

In general, among Advertising students, self-expression words come in the most frequent occurrences, with here over 515 values of "I" in this subcorpus (Fig. 6).

Fig. 6. Co-occurring words of ethos markers

We found from the previous results and from the exploration of the corpus that the words of feeling arrive very quickly in the writings and in the reactions. The identified terms are mainly anguish, anxious, shock, evil, death, and we also notice an important proportion of sadness and fear.

In the sequence of terms we have just mentioned, we have identified the verb to love, which arrives quickly in context. More than a third of its total occurrences are in the formula "I" + negation (I do not like for example) (Fig. 7).

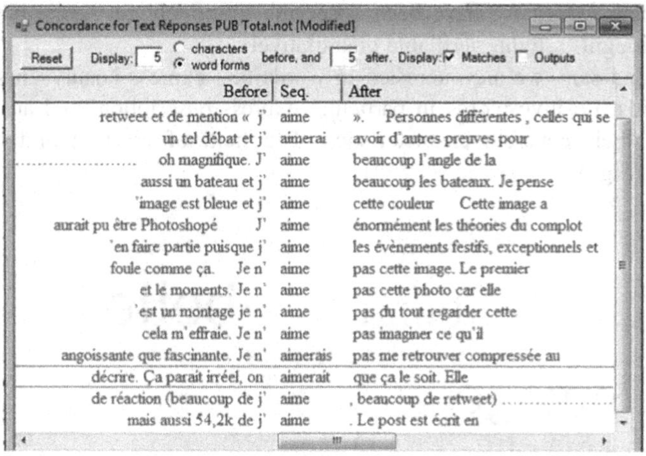

Fig. 7. Illustration of the occurrences of "love" in context

The negation immediately enters in resonance with the image, with the visual. The other occurrences mainly mention the "Like" function of Facebook, which it is necessary not to confuse with expressed feelings.

By focusing on this posture of appreciation, and on the lexicon of the emotional, which as we have seen is very present, we have noticed that out of 161 mentions of negative terms of the emotional (that is to say on average more than one per student), we systematically notice a strong lexicon (Fig. 8):

Fig. 8. Illustration of the emotional lexicon around the verb "to love"

In light of these results and the precision of the lexicometric analysis of the responses, we can clearly deduce that the vocabulary of emotion and feelings is strongly overused by students in the Advertising option, compared to students in Digital Information. This goes so far as to denote distinct student profiles, within the same discipline, which we have been observing intuitively for years, but which has now been brought to light, verifiable quantitatively[6].

In a second step, we are interested in words that express beauty, in semantically positive words. Positive words in particular express description, and are focused on images and their concrete characteristics. The field of creation and creativity is emphasized (Fig. 9).

Fig. 9. Illustration of the words of "beauty" present in the corpus

If we analyze them closely, we can see that they are used for descriptive purposes, and that they drain with them other words of *beauty* just as the words of *fear* did.

If we separate the corpus in two, with the boys' responses and the girls' responses, we clearly see an identical lexical posture. They react to the same elements, use the same terms among the most common in the total corpus (Fig. 10).

Fig. 10. Most common words in the boys' corpus

Here, it is the terms of putting at a distance of what is seen (with think, think, seems…) that is interesting to note (Fig. 11).

---

[6] The analyses and the experiment that we have carried out here show results with these students and under these circumstances, but we can add that the experiment was carried out the previous year, under the same conditions, with the same groups of students, we obtained approximately the same results for self-expression.

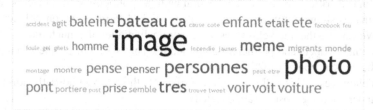

Fig. 11. Most common words in the girls' corpus

The same thing is observed on both corpora. It will be interesting to check the students' reactions according to the different typologies of infox by image, through new lexicometric analyses and other sub-corpora.

4.1   The Different Postures Integrated by the Students

Beyond these linguistic differences in expressing themselves in front of misleading images, we have noticed that in their speeches, the students present different ways of reacting to these forms of manipulation, and we have identified and thus been able to underline several postures:

- "fake news alert" posture: which will discern doctored information and criticize the dangers of manipulation:
  - The person posting the photo on Facebook evokes a conspiracy theory, insinuating that the man is responsible for the fire, I have a feeling of annoyance because I do not appreciate that we look for the small beast and think that this fire is purely accidental. (2020 - PUB)
  - The caption supports the conspiracy theory when we are not even given any proof that this is a real photo or even really a man in it. The name of the account, Facebook again, is also an element that pushes to say that the picture is fake. (2020 - COM)
  - Shared by a Facebook page with a political objective ("Social Front"), I think that the image is taken out of context and this, with the objective to give energy to the Yellow Vests movement and to set fire to the powder keg (all this to oppose the then and current president, Emmanuel Macron). Indeed, people are in majority in yellow but we see very clearly that it is not fluorescent vests which are however the trademark of this movement. Moreover, the movement is very organized and does not take the usual form of a demonstration. (2020 - PUB)

We see several times that when Facebook comes back into the context, the students, whatever their option, have more distance from the infox.

- aesthetic critical posture: in relation to the beauty of the image and the object of its representation;
  - I feel a lot of things with this image. (....) this gigantic whale provokes me incredible emotions. (...) I find this image magnificent! I think that it is not a false photo, but I cannot be sure. (2020 - NUM)

– ideological critical posture: in connection with the politico-social subjects evoked in the images shown (environmental problems, linked to immigration policies, etc.)
  • We can see that the yellow vests are extremely numerous, much more than what the newspapers and politicians could tell us. That's a lot of people unhappy with the current policy (2020 - PUB)
  • Yellow vest? This still existed in February? Is this irony? I honestly don't think I understood the post… (2020 - PUB)
– writing of oneself: in connection with the inscription of oneself in the discourse (See footnote 2);
  • I love this image, I have seen it before but I think it is out of proportion to the bridge (2020 - COM)
  • I feel a lot with this image (2020 - NUM)
– emotional posture related to a feeling: from astonishment to disgust or anger, even if the students are sometimes aware of the fallacy of the images (See footnote 3).
  • Personally this image shocks me, although it is probably a montage. (2020 - PUB)
  • At first we feel sorrow and empathy and then anger (2020 - COM)
  • This image disgusts me, it is horrible, 2 eras, 2 worlds are mixed (2020-PUB)
  • (…) when you look at this picture it is natural to be disgusted (2020 - NUM)
  • Even if it's not true I feel discomfort and disgust (2020 - PUB)

All these postures and the students' reactions clearly show us that they feel emotions when they come into contact with the images, and even more so when they come into contact with the infoxes through images that are created in order to make people react.

5   Conclusion

In this research we were interested in the process of reception of infoxes through images by first year students, not yet aware of the phenomenon. We first noticed, in their speeches, different ways of reacting to these forms of manipulation of publications; we were thus able to highlight several postures on their part:

– posture of "fake news alert"; aesthetic critical posture; ideological critical posture; self-writing; emotional posture in connection with a feeling.

Beyond these postures, we also analyzed their propensity to inscribe themselves in the discourse they produced upon seeing these infoxes. We found that the implication of oneself in the reception discourse is often strong, even very strong (overuse of the pronoun "I" for example), even when the students are aware of the manipulation and in the latter cases, this does not prevent them from expressing their feelings and from considering the image, even in its fake character, as a real image… It is an astonishing and paradoxical posture, and we also noticed that the writing of oneself in the process of disinformation passes much by the emotion, and it is this same emotion which is the engine of the circulation of the infox…

We also noticed that in 2019, students in one of the three options who alone had at the time of the experiment received in class elements of reflection about infox through images, had greater hindsight and a slightly sharper critical sense than students in other options. Similarly, in 2020, students in the same option, without having received any course or reflection on infoxes, again seemed more inclined to detect them, and in any case put less pathos and ethos in their answers.

Image education can be done at the beginning of university, it would allow students to understand these mechanisms that work on emotions, and would make them less permeable to what they see almost permanently on social networks. The goal of this research work is to help combat infoxes by proposing an education in images that allows students to take a step back and sharpen a sense of relevant analysis, while developing skills adapted to this new digital challenge.

References

1. Allard, L., Vandenberghe, F.: Express Yourself! Les pages perso entre légitimation techno-politique de l'individualisme expressif et authenticité réflexive peer-to-peer. In : Réseaux, vol. 117, pp. 191–219 (2003)
2. Amossy, R.: La présentation de soi. Ethos et identité verbale. Presses universitaires de France, Paris (2010)
3. Bigey, M.: Twitter et l'inscription de soi dans le discours. L'ethos pris au piège (ou pas) de la frontière sphère privée/sphère publique. In: Les Cahiers du numérique, vol. 14, pp. 55–75 (2018)
4. Bigey, M., Simon, J.: Désinfoxiquer les images sur les réseaux socionumériques. Vers une démarche empirique d'éducation à l'image. In: Bonfils, Ph., Dumas, Ph., Remond, É., Stassin, B., Vovou, I. (dirs) L'éducation aux médias tout au long de la vie: des nouveaux enjeux pédagogiques à l'accompagnement du citoyen, Conférence TICEMED 12, Athènes, 7–9 Avril 2020, pp. 198–206 (2021)
5. Bigot, L.: Le fact checking en France en une chronologie. In: La Revue des Médias (2019). https://larevuedesmedias.ina.fr/le-fact-checking-en-france-en-une-chronologie
6. Charaudeau, P.: La Manipulation de la vérité. Du triomphe de la négation aux brouillages de la post-vérité. Lambert-Lucas, Limoges (2020)
7. Gervereau, L.: Un siècle de manipulations par l'image. Somogy-BDIC, Paris (2000)
8. Gunthert, A.: L'image partagée: la photographie numérique. Textuel, Paris (2015)
9. Jehel, S.: L'image dans l'éducation aux médias et à l'information. In: Ihadjadene, M., Saemmer, A., Baltz, Cl. (dirs) Culture informationnelle. Vers une Propédeutique du numérique, Hermann, Paris, pp. 133–155 (2015)
10. Le Bras, S.: Les fausses nouvelles: une histoire vieille de 2 500 ans. In: The Conversation France (2018). http://theconversation.com/les-fausses-nouvelles-une-histoire-vieille-de-2-500-ans-101715
11. Meizoz, J.: La Fabrique des singularités. In: Postures littéraires II. Slatkine, Genève (2011)
12. Mercier, A. (dir).: Fake news et post-vérité: tous une part de responsabilité! In: Fake news et post-vérité, E-book The Conversation France (2018). https://theconversation.com/fake-news-et-post-verite-20-textes-pour-comprendre-et-combattre-la-menace-97807
13. Sassoon, V.: Éduquer les jeunes aux images, un enjeu de citoyenneté. In: La Revue des Médias (2018). https://larevuedesmedias.ina.fr/eduquer-les-jeunes-aux-images-unenjeu-de-citoyennete

14. Simon, J.: L'infox par l'image sur les réseaux socionumériques. Détournements, Circulation et Mises en récit. In: Interstudia, vol. 25, pp. 41–52 (2019)
15. Silberztein, M.: La formalisation des langues: l'approche de NooJ. ISTE, Londres (2015)

Negation Usage in the Croatian Parliament

Kristina Kocijan[1]([✉]) 🆔 and Krešimir Šojat[2] 🆔

[1] Department of Information and Communication Sciences, Faculty of
Humanities and Social Sciences, University of Zagreb, Zagreb, Croatia
krkocijan@ffzg.hr
[2] Department of Linguistics, Faculty of Humanities and Social Sciences,
University of Zagreb, Zagreb, Croatia
ksojat@ffzg.hr

Abstract. At the center of this research is an analysis of negation usage in the
Croatian Parliament. Research shows that psychologically speaking, it is much
harder to process a negative word followed by a positive adjective (e.g., *he is not
happy*) than an adjective with a negative prefix (e.g., *he is unhappy*). We
investigate how negation is used among Croatian politicians during parliamentary sessions and whether its usage is dependent on the speaker's gender
and party preference, but also the time when the session was held.

Transcripts of the Croatian Parliament's sessions have been available since
2003. Each transcript includes information on the date of the session, the
speaker, and his/her party followed by the speech. We have made a selection of
4 points in time per each year since 2003 (January, May, September, December)
for which the data exists in order to test if the time period of the session (just
before and after the recess) has an impact on the usage of negation. This corpus
is over 9 million tokens in size. Additionally, from this data, we were able to sort
out different sub-corpora according to the gender of each speaker and their party.

For this experiment, a syntactic grammar was designed to annotate different
types of negation on the sentence level: (a) negative verb + positive adjective;
(b) positive verb + negative adjective; and (c) negative verb + negative adjective.

Keywords: Negation · Negative verb · Negative adjective · Syntactic
grammar · Political discourse · PDA · Croatian · NooJ

1 Introduction

Our language changes as we grow older, but also depends on who we are talking to and
what message we are trying to convey. We use different communication styles when
talking to younger *vs.* older members of our near family, or when talking to colleagues
at work as compared to our peers during an informal gathering. If we identify more
closely with particular members of our society, whether at home or at work, we will try
to mimic their communication style so we can feel more connected to that
person/group. Our mental models of social, cultural, or other situations, which van Dijk
refers to as *context models* [13], help us use more or less appropriate language constructions for a given situation.

© Springer Nature Switzerland AG 2021
M. Bigey et al. (Eds.): NooJ 2021, CCIS 1520, pp. 101–113, 2021.
https://doi.org/10.1007/978-3-030-92861-2_9

The same can be observed within the realm of political discourse, where the power of language use can make a difference between trust and distrust, and ultimately, losing or winning votes in an election. When talking about the macro-level of parliamentary context, Calzada-Perez [4] points out that "overall cultural rules (e.g., of politeness, preference for concrete or abstract language, forms of political representations, the relative strength of political parties, etc.)" will have an impact on the form of language utilized in parliamentary communication. This is aligned with Bayley's belief that the "social norms, institutional norms, and history of a culture" all influence the language of parliament speakers. By selecting a word to use and how the selected words are put together, the speaker is thus using language to shape the politics of a certain group or time period – something which can be observed in political speeches ever since the era of the ancient Greeks and Romans [5, 8].

Wilson [15], among others [2–4, 14], points out that the area of political discourse analysis has lately attracted interest from different research perspectives (critical, descriptive, psychological, sociological), and rightly so. Still, the central point of interest in this paper will be linguistic rather than solely political analysis. Since we cannot observe these two approaches as alternatives but rather as different pieces of the puzzle, we will consider some political context when interpreting the language patterns we detect.

Agnes W. He gives a very clear illustration of the role of discourse analysis within the field of linguistics as a domain that "seeks to describe and explain linguistic phenomena in terms of the affective, cognitive, situational, and cultural contexts of their use and to identify linguistic resources through which we (re)construct our life (our identity, role, activity, community, emotion, stance, knowledge, belief, ideology, and so forth). Essentially, it asks why we use language the way we do and how we live lives linguistically" [7:429]. The approach we take here can thus be positioned within the domain of political discourse analysis (PDA) or, more precisely, that of political linguistics as defined by Okulska and Cap in 2010 as the "study of language and language practices mainly (but not exclusively) within political contexts" (as cited in Dunimre [6:736]). Dunmire [6] also gives a rich overview and description of other interpretations and trends of PDA.

More on theories of gender-related language differences are found in Bucholtz [3], with special attention given to research from 1974 by Keenan, who observes that a different discourse style "provides a distinct form of power" in the speech of the men and women of Malagasy. At the same time, Bucholtz points out the importance of tile tracking of language and its analysis through time, stressing that "gender identities and power relations cannot be determined from a reading of social structures alone, or an ahistorical investigation of a given bit of discourse, for every text has a history of previous contexts in which those identities and relations may have operated very differently, and may continue to carry a trace of their prior effects" [3].

In order to show the differences in rhetoric styles regarding the usage of negation among speakers in the Croatian Parliament, in Sect. 2, we will first explain the usage of negation in the Croatian language in general. This will be followed (Sect. 3) by a more detailed description of the specialized political corpus used for this research. In Sects. 4 and 5, we will show the design of our algorithm and its results with respect to each corpus perspective – gender, party orientation, and time. We will conclude with some final remarks and future plans.

2 Negation in Croatian

In this paper, we present a continuation of previous research on negation and antonyms in Croatian within the NooJ platform. In Žanpera et al. [16] and Žanpera [17], the negation of Croatian lexemes by means of particular affixes is discussed and analyzed. Negation is observed as a means for the formation of antonyms by adding derivational affixes primarily to Croatian nouns, but also to verbs and adjectives. The authors present a set of rules based on a list of affixes with negative meaning, as well as procedures for their automatic detection. In this work, we expand our research of negation in Croatian to the level of syntax.

The prototypical element used to form negation in the Croatian language is *ne*, which can be translated to English as *not* or *un*. This negative particle can be applied at the level of derivational morphology as well as at the syntactic level. When used in derivation, it is attached as a prefix to all major parts of speech: nouns, verbs, adjectives, and adverbs. This kind of derivation is mainly used for the formation of antonyms with the same morphological root (see examples 1–4).

$$\textbf{nouns}: \textit{sreća} \text{ [happiness]} - \textit{nesreća} \text{ [misfortune, accident]} \tag{1}$$

$$\textbf{adjectives}: \textit{sretan} \text{ [happy]} - \textit{nesretan} \text{ [unhappy]} \tag{2}$$

$$\textbf{adverbs}: \textit{sretno} \text{ [happily]} - \textit{nesretno} \text{ [unhappily]} \tag{3}$$

$$\textbf{verbs}: \textit{usrećiti} \text{ [to make happy]} - \textit{unesrećiti} \text{ [to make unhappy]}. \tag{4}$$

As in the cases above (examples 1–4), the addition of the prefix *ne* to the lexemes on the right side produces complementary antonyms – i.e., absolute opposites characterized by a mutual *either-or* relation. However, the semantics of derivatives is frequently idiosyncratic and unpredictable, as in examples 5–7:

$$\textit{zgodan} \text{ [handsome]} - \textit{nezgodan} \text{ [inconvenient, troublesome, unfavourable]} \tag{5}$$

$$\textit{dužan} \text{ [handsome]} - \textit{nedužan} \text{ [innocent]} \tag{6}$$

$$\textit{stati} \text{ [to stand]} - \textit{nestati} \text{ [to disappear]}. \tag{7}$$

As mentioned above, in this paper we expand our focus since our objective is to detect negation at the syntactic level. More precisely, we combine affixal negation of single lexemes, as described in the examples above, with the negation of verbs in sentences. In other words, we focus on the negation of adjectives and auxiliary verbs in sentences like (8) and (9).

$$On \; nije \; bio \; sretan. \; - \; \text{He } \textbf{was not} \text{ happy.} \tag{8}$$

$$On \; je \; bio \; nesretan. \; - \; \text{He was } \textbf{un}\text{happy.} \tag{9}$$

The expression of negation is language-dependent – i.e., it varies from language to language. As in other Slavic languages, double negatives are common and frequent in Croatian, as shown in examples (10) and (11).

$$On \; \textbf{\textit{nije}} \; vidio \; \textbf{\textit{ništa}}. \; \text{[literally: He did } \textbf{not} \text{ see } \textbf{nothing}.] \tag{10}$$

$$Vidio \; je \; \textbf{\textit{ništa}}. \; \text{[He saw } \textbf{nothing}.] \text{ (empathic usage)} \tag{11}$$

Moreover, multiple negatives at the sentence level are possible, as demonstrated in examples (12), (13), and (14).

$$On \; \textbf{\textit{nije ništa}} \; učinio. \; \text{[literally: He has } \textbf{not} \text{ done } \textbf{nothing}.] \tag{12}$$

$$On \; \textbf{\textit{nikada nije}} \; bio \; \textbf{\textit{nesretan}}. \; \text{[literally: He has } \textbf{not never} \text{ been } \textbf{un}\text{happy.]} \tag{13}$$

$$\textbf{\textit{Nitko nije nikada nigdje ništa}} \; \textit{učinio}.$$

$$\text{[literally: } \textbf{Nobody} \text{ has } \textbf{not never nowhere nothing} \text{ done.]} \tag{14}$$

Thus, next to a positive verb + a negative adjective (example 9) and a negative verb + a positive adjective (example 8), combinations of a negative verb + a negative adjective are possible as well (*nije nesretan* [**isn't un**happy]). To sum up, targeted constructions that we use for the design of rules in NooJ look like the following:

1. *On je nesretan* – He is **un**happy

   – consists of the verb *biti* [to be] (copula) + negated adjective.

2. *On nije sretan* – He **is not** happy

   – consists of the negated verb *biti* [to be] (copula) + positive adjective.

3. *On nije nesretan* – He **is not un**happy

   – consists of the negated verb *biti* [to be] (copula) + negated adjective.

Syntactically, these constructions consist of the copula (*biti*) + predicate nominative (*adjective*). Both elements can be either negated or not. The whole procedure aims to detect the frequency of various combinations and distributions according to different parameters from collected transcripts of parliamentary discussions. In this research, we focus on negation and its usage according to various parameters: gender, time, and political party. Such parameters are difficult to capture in general corpora. Therefore, a corpus of parliamentary discussions was collected (transcribed from recordings). The collection and preparation of the corpus are described in more detail in Sect. 3 below. Before that, it is important to define what we consider under the term 'negative adjective'. As in other languages, it is easy for Croatian to express a negative characteristic in two ways:

A. The prefix *ne* is found at the beginning of an adjective: *nesretan* [**un**happy]
B. in numerous cases, no morpheme marker would help detect a negative adjective, as in: *dobar* [good] – *loš* [bad]; *lijep* [beautiful] – *ružan* [ugly].

At first glance, the first expression may seem easy to recognize via simple regular expression [find all adjectives that begin with the string 'ne': <A+ MP ="^ne">]. However, things are not as straightforward as they may appear, since the prefix 'ne' is found in words like *nesebičan* [unselfish] or *nepobjediv* [invincible].

The second way to express a negative characteristic is hard to detect just by looking at its morphology. Thus, we turn to semantics, and by adding the tag **+neg** to NooJ dictionary entries, our semantic grammar can recognize such adjectives. However, at this time, we will confine our research project to detecting negative adjectives that start with a suffix '*ne*' or '*najne*' if the adjective is in its superlative form.

3   Corpus Preparations

Many will attest that building a specialized corpus is not a trivial process (for different challenges dealing with corpus preparations, cf. [9]) even in the era of electronic documents and big data. Besides being a time-consuming process, it is also difficult to obtain a balanced collection relevant to research questions that are at the same time available for use. The same is true for our corpus preparation steps, since the male speakers have always considerably outnumbered the female speakers, and speakers from larger political parties have always outnumbered representatives of smaller parties.

It is important to note that our corpus is made of transcriptions of parliamentary debates, which implies a degree of incompleteness [1], since pauses, intonation, and other discourse elements are not included in the text. Although data such as the education, occupation, or geographical region of each speaker is available, at this time, we have added only the gender and party information to our dataset to obtain subsets suitable for our research.

For the purpose of our research, we have prepared a specialized corpus that has a selection of texts from different time periods within the political register. Since the text is produced during parliamentary discussions and by politicians, we can say that it satisfies Van Dijk's definition of political discourse [13]. According to Bayley [2], "parliamentary talk is a sub-genre of political language and it represents its most formal and institutionalized variety."

The following analytical steps have been taken (the first two of which were conducted by Parliament personnel): (1) the recording of debates; (2) transcription; (3) the compilation of transcripts; (4) the reorganization of corpora by designated criteria; (5) data gazing; (6) hypothesis; (7) algorithm design; (8) data analysis; (9) hypothesis verification. We will proceed with descriptions of steps (3) and (4) in this section, and give more details on steps (5) through (9) in the following sections.

The corpus was collected manually from the official Croatian Parliament web site.[1] Regardless of its dominantly political content, when discussing political discourse and its analysis, we will be referring to it within the context of an example discourse type "without explicit reference to political content or political context," as defined by Wilson [15:398].

Each document has a list of speakers, including their party affiliation, and the transcription of their discourse. Passages of inaudible speech are also marked by the transcriber and have not been removed from the corpus. We have moved the data to the staging area, adding columns for each speaker's gender and the time frame of their speech, including session and section numbers, as well as the year and month when the session was held. This arrangement allowed us to swiftly extract different types of corpora in order to facilitate our research questions: is the usage of negation dependent upon gender, party, or time.

At this time, to our knowledge, there has been no research on negation usage in a more general corpus of Croatian texts. Although it would be interesting to compare results, it would be hard to rearrange a general corpus from the perspectives of gender and party preferences. However, we may learn how to predict these features if we can detect the patterns that typify them. This is something we plan to tackle in the future.

3.1   Gender-Oriented Corpus

The gender-oriented corpus uses data on *speaker's name, political party,* and *discourse,* and includes a total of 5 555 909 tokens. It has a masculine [CRO_Parliament_M.noc] and a feminine [CRO_Parliament_F.noc] section. Each section holds 16 documents, but the size of each document differs in favor of the masculine speakers: the masculine section has 4 456 476 tokens in total, which is over four times larger than the feminine section, which has 1 099 433 tokens (Fig. 1). Such a disparity in results has been reported for other domains as well [10].

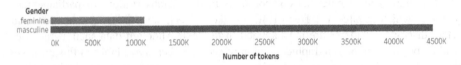

Fig. 1. Distribution of tokens per gender

---

[1] The archive of Parliamentary sessions is maintained by the Information and Documentation Department and the Parliamentary transcripts are freely available at https://edoc.sabor.hr/ Fonogrami.aspx.

3.2   Party-Oriented Corpus

The party-oriented corpus consists of 42 sections, each bearing the name of a party (41 parties; 1 section with no party preferences) and is 6 133 160 tokens in size (Fig. 2). The top 5 sections include the two largest parties in Croatia (HDZ: 2 119 576 tokens; SDP: 1 211 294 tokens) followed by MOST (583 778 tokens), the "No party preferences" section (315 096 tokens), and the *Nezavisni* [independent] section (302 398 tokens). The remaining sections range from 239 910 down to 1 235 tokens (Fig. 2).

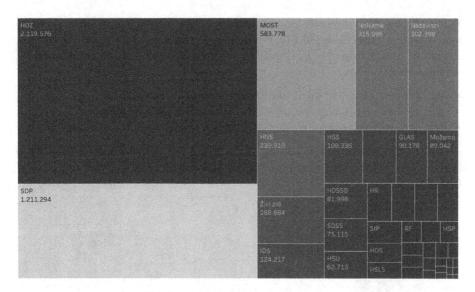

Fig. 2.   Distribution of tokens per party

3.3   Time-Oriented Corpus

The time-oriented corpus is made out of 4 sections coinciding with different time periods, two of which are months before the summer/winter recess (May and December) and two of which are just after the recess (September and January). The total size of this corpus is 6 138 386 tokens that are distributed over each section in the following manner: January - 1 056 397 tokens; May - 1 309 019 tokens; September - 1 535 818 tokens; December - 2 237 152 tokens (Fig. 3).

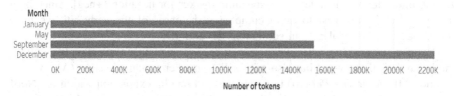

Fig. 3.   Distribution of tokens per month

The discrepancies in total size between the different corpora are due to the number of columns that were used in building them. And while all three corpora include the speaker's name, political party, and discourse, the time-oriented corpus also includes the columns on gender, the session and section numbers, and the date when the session was held.

4 Grammar

We have opted for a computer-assisted analysis of our corpora that will be based on a finite-state transducer designed with the NooJ linguistic tool [12]. For this experiment, a syntactic grammar has been designed to annotate different types of negation on the sentence level:

- N1: negative verb + positive adjective [*nije sretan* – en. **isn't** happy];
- N2: positive verb + negative adjective [*je nesretan* – en. is **un**happy];
- N3: negative verb + negative adjective [*nije nesretan* – en. **isn't un**happy].

The main graph (Fig. 4.A) consists of 3 sub-graphs, each of which is designed to annotate specific negation type: type N1 (Fig. 4.B), type N2 (Fig. 4.C), and type N3 (Fig. 4.D).

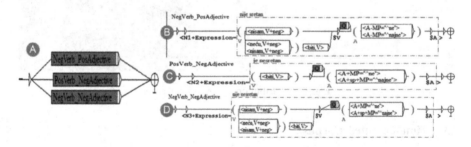

Fig. 4. Main graph and sub-graphs describing negation models

Sub-graphs consist of a verb (placed in the variable $V) and an adjective (placed in the variable $A), with the difference being presence or absence of negation in both variables, depending on the negation type the sub-graph is describing. The positive verb *biti* [to be] in Fig. 4.C has only a POS marker, while its negative form (*nisam*) [not to be] in Fig. 4B and 4D and negative form of the verb (*neću*) ['not to want' used for the future tense], include also a semantic marker for negation [+neg]. Since both *nisam* and *neću* are used to build complex verb tenses of the verb *biti*, we have introduced an additional path in sub-graphs 4B and 4D.

Positive and negative adjectives are described with a regular expression that defines the beginning of the word but also with a POS marker for an adjective (A). We use notation MP (*Matching Pattern*) to define the Perl regular expression within the NooJ syntax grammar. Here, in particular, the expression [+MP = ^ne] in Fig. 4C recognizes only adjectives that start with the prefix *ne-*, while the expression [-MP = ^ne] in

Fig. 4B and 4D recognizes adjectives that must not start with prefix *ne-*. For the recognition of superlative forms of negative adjectives, we use attribute notation [+sp], but also the expression [+MP = ^najne], since the negative prefix of superlative adjectives is found between the prefix *naj-* and the adjective (e.g. *najnesretniji* – the most **un**happy).

In some occurrences, an additional word (most commonly an intensifier) is found between the two variables. This is described within the sub-sub-graph named **Q**. The grammar is applied to each corpus set, and the results are discussed in the following section.

5 Results

Throughout much sociolinguistic research (Sweden, Netherlands, USA, UK) as discussed in Romaine [11], female speakers are reported to speak closer to the standard, and tend to use more prestigious variants of the language, especially in more formal situations. We notice that usage patterns change over time for both genders. Additional research is needed to understand the reasons behind these changes.

Difference and similarities in negation usage considering the speaker's gender is best seen in Figs. 5 and 6 for male and female speakers, respectively. We observe that both male and female communities use negation a certain percentage of the time but also that their usage patterns differ. This is in line with observations by Romaine [11] concerning the variability of speech forms in a person of a particular gender. Usage of negation thus seems to be conditioned by gender as a social factor.

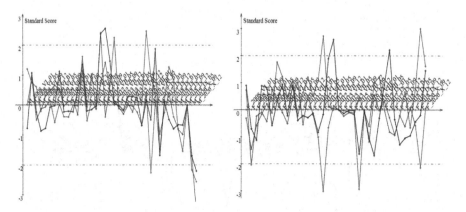

Fig. 5. Distribution of negation usage in male Speakers of Parlament from 2008 to 2020

Fig. 6. Distribution of negation usage in female Speakers of Parlament from 2008 to 2020

It is important to notice that this difference is rather quantitative since both groups use all three models of negation but in various degrees throughout the time span we covered. When we compare the percentages between these two groups, there is a very slim difference between them (Table 1). These results show that male speakers overall

Table 1. Distribution of three types of negation usage in gender-oriented corpora vs full corpus

Gender	N1	N2	N3
M	79.10%	**19.80%**	**1.10%**
F	**79.68%**	19.65%	0.68%
In full corpus	79.22%	19.77%	1.01%

prefer N2 and N3 negation types slightly more than their female colleagues, while female speakers tend to use more N1 negation than their male colleagues. However, when we compare the distribution across the time span (Fig. 5 and Fig. 6), we can observe changes happening in both corpora, and we conclude, therefore, that usage of a particular negation type is not consistently dependent on the speaker's gender.

Next, we observe the negation usage patterns among the speakers from different parties (Fig. 7). Here also we detect different usage patterns: three out of 42 Parties use only pattern N1, while 18 use only patterns N1 and N2. Still, all of the Parties use predominantly the N1 pattern (between 63% and 100% of the time), while the N2 pattern is used 0% to 37% of the time and the N3 is used 0% to 4% of the time.

It is important to note that most of the speech analyzed came from members of the two largest parties: 29% of the detected negations in the corpus were uttered by members of HDZ and 25% by members of SDP. Third in line, with only 7% of the overall detected negations, were members of MOST. Twenty-two parties participated with less than 1% of the detected negations, while the remaining seventeen participated within the range of 1% to 6% of the detected negations. These results were to be expected due to the nature of the corpus as described in Sect. 3.2.

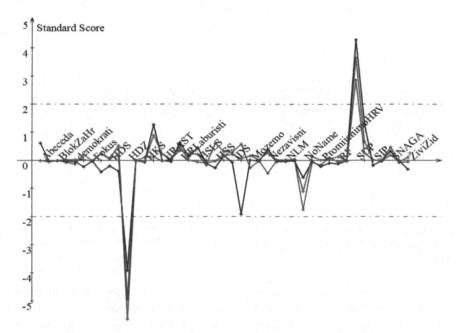

Fig. 7. Distribution of negation usage in Speakers belonging to different parties (entire corpus)

Lastly, we present the results of negation usage patterns in the time-oriented corpus. The Croatian Parliament is in session from 15 January to 15 July, and from 15 September to 15 December. We consider the periods May–September, and December–January as the months preceding and following the time of a recess. Table 2 provides tabular information on the percentage of each negation type used in the two months prior to recess (May and December) and two months just after it (January and September).

We can observe that Speakers, in general, tend to use more N1 negation type and fewer N2 and N3 types in the months following the time-off in the Parliament, while the share of N2 and N3 slightly increases in the months prior to it.

Table 2. Distribution of negation usage patterns in time-oriented corpus

	1	2	3
5 – May	77.88%	**20.94%**	**1.17%**
9 – September	79.45%	19.64%	0.91%
12 - December	80.16%	18.82%	1.03%
1 – January	**80.62%**	18.56%	0.82%

In Table 3, we observe the dissimilitude of the top 5 negation types used in the entire corpus and compare them to the top 5 used in the two gender corpora. The list of the 5 most frequently used type N1 negations in the masculine section is an exact copy of the top 5 examples in the whole corpus. However, the feminine section uses the expression *nije moguće* [isn't possible'] more often, which places this expression in the third position. Their list also introduces the expression *nije potrebno* [isn't necessary] as the 5th most used N1 negation. They also use the expression *nije jasno* [isn't clear] less often than is the case for the other two groups (i.e., the masculine section and the whole corpus).

Again, the masculine section list matches the xhole corpus list for the N2 negation type, but this time only in the list members and not entirely in the same order. Similarly, the feminine section introduces a different order in addition to three more expressions (*je nedavno, smo nedavno* and *je nespojiva*). The most frequently used N2 negation in full and masculine corpora is *je netočno* [is incorrect], while *je nedopustivo* [is unacceptable] is most common in the feminine section.

The last type - N3 - presents the most differences between the lists, with one new entry in the masculine section: *nije neobično* [isn't unusual], and four in the feminine section: *nije nemoguće* [isn't impossible], *nije neshvatljivo* [isn't incomprehensible], *nisu nejasni* [aren't unclear'], and *nismo bili jako neuspješni* 'we weren't very unsuccessful'.

Table 3. Top 5 negations for each negation type used in full corpus vs masculine and feminine sections

Neg. type	Full corpus	M	F
N1	*nije dobro*	*nije dobro*	*nije dobro*
	nije točno	*nije točno*	*nije točno*
	nije jasno	*nije jasno*	***nije moguće***
	nije samo	*nije samo*	*nije samo*
	nije moguće	*nije moguće*	***nije potrebno***
N2	*je netočno*	*je netočno*	***je nedopustivo***
	je nedopustivo	***je nemoguće***	***je netočno***
	je nemoguće	***je nedopustivo***	***je nedavno***
	je nevjerojatno	*je nevjerojatno*	***smo nedavno***
	je neprihvatljivo	*je neprihvatljivo*	***je nespojiva***
N3	*nije nevažno*	*nije nevažno*	*nije nevažno*
	nije neugodno	*nije neugodno*	***nije nemoguće***
	nije neobično	***nije neposredno***	***nije neshvatljivo***
	nije neposredno	***nije neobično***	***nisu nejasni***
	nije nebitno	***nije nelogično***	***nismo bili jako neuspješni***

6   Conclusion

In this paper, we have demonstrated a procedure for the detection of frequency of various combinations of negation usage and their distribution according to different parameters from collected parliamentary discussions. The parameters taken into consideration are gender, time, and political party.

Further research will include more informative-communicative characteristics of political discourse – namely, whether there is a difference in negation usage during the more stereotypical talks (opening and closing sessions) or more emotional-expressive talks (during election time). More in-depth research is planned in the future, at which time we will include speeches from the remaining time periods. In order to facilitate a domain-comparative analysis, the designed algorithms will be applied to other types of texts ranging from general corpora to specific corpora (for example, corpora of patients with Alzheimer's disease) in order to learn about preferred context models.

Acknowledgements. The research reported here was supported by the European Commission in the CEF Telecom Programme: Action No. 2019-EU-IA-0034, CURLICAT.

References

1. Amador-Moreno, C.P.: How can corpora be used to explore literary speech representation? In: O'Keeffe, A., McCarthy, M. (eds.) The Routledge Handbook of Corpus Linguistics, pp. 531–544. Routldge Taylor & Francis Group, London (2010)
2. Bayley, P.: Introduction: the whys and wherefores of analyzing parliamentary discourse. In: Bayley, P. (ed.) Cross-Cultural Perspectives on Parliamentary Discourse, pp. 1–44. John Benjamins, Amsterdam/Philadelphia (2004)

3. Bucholtz, M.: Theories of discourse as theories of gender: discourse analysis in language and gender studies. In: Holmes, J., Meyerhoff, M. (eds.) The Handbook of Language and Gender, pp. 43–68. UC Santa Barbara (2003). https://escholarship.org/uc/item/583711gp. Accessed 01 July 2021

4. Calzada-Perez, M.: Researching the European parliament with corpus-assisted studies: institutional dimensions. In: Specialised Translation in Spain, vol. 30, no. 2, pp. 465–490 (2017)

5. Chilton, P.: Analysing Political Discourse: Theory and Practice. Routledge, London (2004)

6. Dunmire, P.L.: Political discourse analysis: exploring the language of politics and the politics of language. Lang. Linguist. Compass 6(11), 735–751 (2012). https://doi.org/10.1002/lnc3.365

7. He, A.W.: Discourse analysis. In: Aronoff, M., Rees-Miller, J. (eds.) The Handbook of Linguistics, pp. 445–462. Wiley, Hoboken (2017)

8. Kirvalidze, N., Samnidze, N.: Political discourse as a subject of interdisciplinary studies. J. Teach. Educ. 05(01), 161–170 (2016)

9. Levshina, N.: Corpus-based typology: applications, challenges and some solutions. In: Linguistic Typology, Advance online publication (2021). https://doi.org/10.1515/lingty-2020-0118

10. Rao, P., Taboada, M.: Gender bias in the news: a scalable topic modelling and visualization framework. Front. Artif. Intell.: Lang. Comput. 4, 664737 (2021). https://doi.org/10.3389/frai.2021.664737

11. Romaine, S.: Variation in language and gender. In: Holmes, J., Meyerhoff, M. (eds.) The Handbook of Language and Gender, pp. 98–119. Blackwell, Oxford (2003)

12. Silberztein, M.: Formalizing Natural Languages: The NooJ Approach. Cognitive Science Series, Wiley-ISTE, London (2016)

13. Van Dijk, T.A.: What is political discourse analysis? In: Bloomaert, J., Bulcaen, Ch. (eds.) Political Linguistics, pp. 11–52, Amsterdam (1997)

14. Van Dijk, T.A.: Discourse, context and cognition. Discourse Stud. 8(1), 159–177 (2006). Special Issue: Discourse interaction and cognition

15. Wilson, J.: Political discourse. In: Tannen, D., Hamilton, H.E., Schiffrin, D. (eds.) The Handbook of Discourse Analysis, pp. 398–415. Blackwel, Oxford (2015). https://doi.org/10.1002/9781118584194.ch36

16. Žanpera, N., Kocijan, K., Šojat, K.: Negation of Croatian nouns. In: Fehri, H., Mesfar, S., Silberztein, M. (eds.) NooJ 2019. CCIS, vol. 1153, pp. 52–64. Springer, Cham (2020). https://doi.org/10.1007/978-3-030-38833-1_5

17. Žanpera, N.: Računalno prepoznavanje i označavanje negacije u hrvatskom. MA thesis, Sveučilište u Zagrebu, Filozofski fakultet (2020). https://urn.nsk.hr/urn:nbn:hr:131:050307. Accessed 07 July 2021

Locating Traces of Subjectivity in Diplomatic Discourse: The Example of the French Ministry of Foreign Affairs

Annabel Richeton[(✉)]

ELLIADD, Bourgogne Franche-Comté University, Besançon, France

Abstract. Our project, following studies on institutional discourse analysis [3, 6], considers the discourse of the French Ministry of Foreign Affairs. Our corpus (circa 20 million words) gathers a sample of text data from the diplomatic communication outer face, including various monological and dialogical situations of communication and involving Ministers' or State Secretaries' speeches, interviews, press releases, etc. Diplomatic discourse is characterized by its normalization, neutrality, and standardization [4, 17]. As a consequence, a Minister of Foreign Affairs' speech shouldn't include any subjective unit, may it be affective or evaluative. Yet, subjectivity may show up with the creation of words used to express biases and opinions since prefixes and/or suffixes do change the original root meaning. We focus our interest on the word "Europe" and its derivations. Using NooJ [7], we first built a grammar able to develop all the occurrences derived from the French name "Europe" so as to include single word forms and multi-word units: adjectives (européen, anti(-)européens, europhobe, etc.); nouns or names (européanisation, alter-euroépanisme, eurocratie, etc.); verbs (européiser, déseuropéaniser, etc.). NooJ assisted us in locating each word form in the corpus and determining its context(s) of use thanks to the concordance. It allows us to identify the types of sentences in which each word appears and their syntactic functions and roles. We eventually confront this data with the corpus parameters so as to look at a possible evolution of the institutional discourse driven by, or depending on, among other variables, presidential mandates, ministers and their political party, Government of the day.

Keywords: Discourse analysis · Diplomatic discourse · French Ministry of Foreign Affairs · Europe · Subjectivity · NooJ

1 Introduction

French Ministry of Foreign Affairs discourse is known to be a very normalized type of discourse [6], with many rules and standards to be followed. Many studies can be led on this kind of discourse, especially on its evolution over time: on one hand, the formal markers indicating a change in the functions of the institution, depending on the presidential mandates, the ministers, the emergence of new technologies and digital social networks, etc.; on another hand, the evolution of the French power representations as well as those of the other countries. In order to study the French Ministry of Foreign Affairs under the 5th Republic, we built a two-sided observation system:

© Springer Nature Switzerland AG 2021
M. Bigey et al. (Eds.): NooJ 2021, CCIS 1520, pp. 114–123, 2021.
https://doi.org/10.1007/978-3-030-92861-2_10

- An XML-TEI corpora gathering a sample of text data from the diplomatic communication inner face (between those involved in French diplomacy) and outer face (targeting the media and the general public), including various communication situations (speech, telegram, interview, press release, communication on social networks, etc.);
- Background data, to reveal the interdiscourse and interpret the diplomatic discourse (prescriptive documents, guideline books, metadiscourse, etc., from diplomatic archives and investigative work of the actors).

This study focuses on the first corpus, which is made of exactly 12,654 texts and 19,779,122 words. 39 ministers, delegated ministers, and State secretaries, speaking from 1997 to 2020 are represented in this corpus, in 23 communication situations. Table 1 shows the French political situation during this time period:

Table 1. French political situation (presidents and Foreign Affairs ministers) from 1997 until today.

1997–2002	Right-wing president, left-wing minister
2002–2007	Right-wing president, left-wing minister
2007–2010	Right-wing president, left-wing minister
2010–2012	Right-wing president, right-wing minister
2012–2017	Left-wing president, left-wing ministers
2017–today	Centrist president, left-wing minister, right-wing and centrists State secretaries

Our work follows studies on institutional discourse analysis [3, 6] through the diplomatic communication outer face, which has already been studied in other fields (history, sociology, or political sciences). These previous works show that diplomatic discourse can be considered as a standardized discourse, which must be neutral.

In this study, we aim to find out whether subjectivity can be detected in such a uniform kind of discourse, and if so, how it could manifest. We focus here on the forms derived from "Europe": Who says what? Do these terms describe a feeling toward Europe, European citizens, politicians? Do the speakers use them to refer to themselves? Are they used in a positive or negative way? How does their use imply an opinion?

2 The NooJ Approach

To find the word forms we are interested in, we built a morphological grammar in order not to miss any out. We selected these terms thanks to our knowledge about our corpus and visiting online dictionaries. Some forms do not actually do exist in dictionaries: they are accepted, understood, but are quite recent neologisms, so their spelling is has not yet been made permanent. Moreover, speeches transcripts are not written by a single person; that is why we can find words written in at least two ways.

We found that we wanted to get word forms such as *européaniser, européanisation, eurobéat* ("euro blissfully naïve"), *euro-hostilité, euro-pessimisme, pro-européen*, etc., with or without a hyphen, with every inflection: masculine or feminine, plural or singular, but we do not want *européen, euro* (the currency), *euro-any country* ("euro-russe") or websites, programs, etc. Therefore, we built the following morphological grammar (Fig. 1):

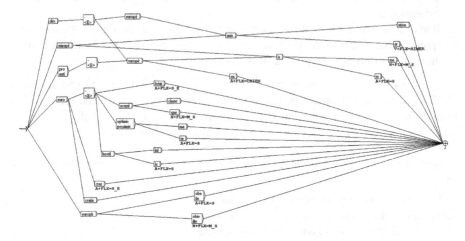

Fig. 1. Morphological grammar of the word forms derived from Europe

Then, we generated a dictionary (Table 2) in order to build a small syntactical grammar (Fig. 3) to find all these terms in our corpus (Fig. 2).

Table 2. 71 word forms recognized in the corpus

dés-européanisation,TERME+Europe	pro-européennes,TERME+Europe	euro-hostiles,TERME+Europe
dés-européaniser,TERME+Europe	proeuropéiste,TERME+Europe	euro-hostilité,TERME+Europe
déséuropéanisation,TERME+Europe	proeuropéistes,TERME+Europe	euro-sceptique,TERME+Europe
déséuropéaniser,TERME+Europe	proeuropéisme,TERME+Europe	euro-sceptiques,TERME+Europe
anti-européiste,TERME+Europe	proeuropéen,TERME+Europe	euro-scepticisme,TERME+Europe
anti-européistes,TERME+Europe	proeuropéens,TERME+Europe	euro-pessimiste,TERME+Europe
anti-européisme,TERME+Europe	proeuropéenne,TERME+Europe	euro-pessimistes,TERME+Europe
anti-européen,TERME+Europe	proeuropéennes,TERME+Europe	euro-pessimisme,TERME+Europe
anti-européens,TERME+Europe	eurobéat,TERME+Europe	euro-optimiste,TERME+Europe
anti-européenne,TERME+Europe	eurobéate,TERME+Europe	euro-optimistes,TERME+Europe
anti-européennes,TERME+Europe	eurobéats,TERME+Europe	euro-optimisme,TERME+Europe
antieuropéiste,TERME+Europe	eurobéates,TERME+Europe	eurosceptique,TERME+Europe
antieuropéistes,TERME+Europe	eurohostille,TERME+Europe	eurosceptiques,TERME+Europe
antieuropéisme,TERME+Europe	eurohostilles,TERME+Europe	euroscepticisme,TERME+Europe
antieuropéen,TERME+Europe	eurohostilité,TERME+Europe	europhile,TERME+Europe
antieuropéens,TERME+Europe	eurocrate,TERME+Europe	europhilie,TERME+Europe
antieuropéenne,TERME+Europe	eurocratie,TERME+Europe	europhiles,TERME+Europe
antieuropéennes,TERME+Europe	eurocraties,TERME+Europe	europhobe,TERME+Europe
pro-européiste,TERME+Europe	eurocrates,TERME+Europe	europhobie,TERME+Europe
pro-européistes,TERME+Europe	euro-béat,TERME+Europe	europhobes,TERME+Europe
pro-européisme,TERME+Europe	euro-béate,TERME+Europe	europessimiste,TERME+Europe
pro-européen,TERME+Europe	euro-béats,TERME+Europe	europessimistes,TERME+Europe
pro-européens,TERME+Europe	euro-béates,TERME+Europe	europessimisme,TERME+Europe
pro-européenne,TERME+Europe	euro-hostile,TERME+Europe	

Fig. 2. Syntactical grammar recognizing the word forms in our corpus

Thanks to this grammar, we extracted the concordances to obtain 521 occurrences of the words we are interested in (Fig. 3).

Before	Seq.	After
réalité, il y a les partis démocratiques, que j'appellerais	pro-européens	, et les partis non démocratiques, que j'appellerais non-européens
les Français, qu'ils soient d'ailleurs europhiles voire parfois	eurosceptiques	, savent bien que de plus en plus de solutions à
dans la plupart des pays, et la montée de partis	eurosceptiques	qui vont compliquer l'émergence de majorités claires au Parlement
un certain nombre de constantes comme la montée des partis	eurosceptiques	ou même franchement antieuropéens, voire parfois d'extrême droite, une
ne se déplaçant pas, soit en votant pour des partis	anti-européens	, ont lancé une alerte : ils nous font porter l'exigence
aux dernières élections européennes, tout comme les scores des partis	pro-européens	, dont celui de la liste Renaissance porté par notre majorité
encore une demande, y compris de la part des partis	pro-européens	, que l'Europe change, qu'elle soit plus proche des
Allemagne aujourd'hui, c'est l'extrême droite, les partis	anti-européens	rencontrent un grand succès en Italie. L'extrême droite est
vague populiste annoncée n'a pas eu lieu. Les partis	pro-européens	se sont mobilisés et ont globalement bien résisté. La hausse
des souverainistes (voire nationalistes) pour les élections de 2014 ? Les partis	europhiles	s'engageront-ils pleinement dans la campagne, si proche des
on ne retrouve pas cette confiance, alors effectivement les partis	eurosceptiques	, ceux qui exploitent les peurs, vont continuer de progresser. C
dit de la politique industrielle européenne. Comme lui, je suis	pro-européen	et partisan d'une Europe ouverte ; pas d'une Europe
saines et solides. C'est précisément parce que je suis	pro-européen	que je ne veux plus de cette fuite en avant
simple, il n'était pas question de laisser aux seuls	eurosceptiques	ou aux anciens partisans du 'non' le soin de débattre
précisément, si nous allions dans la direction proposée par certains	eurosceptiques	, nous affaiblirions cette coordination plus importante que nous recherchons, a
européenne, à la commission, contrairement à ce qu'affirment certains	eurosceptiques	ou certains «euro-hostiles» n'est pas destiné à alimenter
-ce une erreur de perception, nous ne sommes pas moins	pro-européens	ou intégrateurs que d'autres, pas du tout ; simplement nous
la Commission. Les citoyens européens ont exprimé des choix moins	antieuropéens	que ce qu'on pouvait craindre. Nous avons également réussi
bulletins de vote nationalistes et extrémistes et imposeront des régressions	anti-européennes	. Nous voici engagés dans un scénario grinçant, transformé en piège
part des grandes formations politiques européennes face à des formations	eurosceptiques	voire extrémistes qui, en tournant le dos lors de l
du projet européen. Et quand il y a des tentations	europhobes	- et il y en a nous réaffirmons ce principe. Cela
des nations sceptiques si ce n'est sensibles aux tentations	anti-européennes	, voire xénophobes et populistes : regardez certains résultats électoraux récents
mettant en avant, du premier au dernier jour, ses convictions	pro-européennes	- ce qu'aucun de ces prédécesseurs n'avait fait aussi
c'est que l'Italie a quand même des traditions	pro-européennes	. Quelles que soient les tentations de tel ou tel membre
rendue compte que les Français, qu'ils soient d'ailleurs	europhiles	voire parfois eurosceptiques, savent bien que de plus en plus
à Londres, vous avez allumé D. Cameron et les conservateurs	eurosceptiques	, en les traitant, dit le Guardian, de 'pathétiques'. Je sais
faire un discours sur l'Europe qui était un discours	pro-européen	. Il est important que soit affirmé par le président sortant
de l'austérité, on observe une montée d'un discours	eurosceptique	. Les partis populistes sont ceux qui se font le plus
qui, à l'élection présidentielle, ont voté pour des candidats	eurosceptiques	, voire europhobes ou ne pas voir, scrutin après scrutin, s
nombre de suffrages qui se sont portés sur des candidats	eurosceptiques	. Disons les choses : l'Europe est perçue comme trop lointaine
regarde les scores au premier tour de tous les candidats	europhobes	, comme vous dites, ou eurosceptiques, on est pas loin de
l'éclatement, il y a des courants nationalistes, des courants	europhobes	. Nous préférerions que le Royaume-Uni reste dans l'Union
gouvernement. C'est une bonne nouvelle, parce que les engagements	pro-européens	de ce futur gouvernement sont forts, et nous allons pouvoir
'est même la première phrase du livre : «Longtemps, je fus	pro-européen	». Vous l'expliquiez notamment par la méfiance de beaucoup d
entende Emmanuel Macron, il a fait la campagne la plus	pro-européenne	qu'un candidat aux présidentielles pouvait faire, c'est d
puisque c'est là où les citoyens sont le plus	pro-européens	, en tous cas d'après les derniers sondages. L'Irlande
voir les marins pêcheurs ; c'est peut être les plus	anti-européens	de la liste notamment sur le fonds d'aide qui
naît, dans les pays qui traditionnellement ont été les plus	europhiles	, cet euroscepticisme, voire ce populisme, capable de détruire à la
Bourlanges ou aux communistes, qui sont paraît-il les plus	pro-européens	du Parlement européen, d'après ce que j'entends de

Fig. 3. Concordancer: 521 word forms

Some of the speakers from our corpus are not involved in the use of the ***Europ-word*** forms. 24 are concerned: 11 speakers from the left-wing political parties (socialists and ecologists), 3 from centrists political parties ("neither left nor right", from LREM-part), 7 from the right-wing political parties (belonging to Gaullism stance), and 3 unlabeled speakers.

From now on, we will use canonical forms (lemmas) to consider a set of forms. For example, *euro-skepticism* will mean it with or without an hyphen, but also *euro-skeptic* and *euro-skeptics*, with or without an hyphen. Here is the complete list of forms:

européaniser; européanisation; européisme (européisme, européiste, européistes)**; pro-européen** (pro-européen, pro-européens, pro-européenne, pro-européennes, proeuropéen, proeuropéens, proeuropéenne, proeuropéennes)**; anti-européen** (anti-européen, anti-européens, anti-européenne, anti-européennes, antieuropéen, antieuropéens, antieuropéenne, antieuropéennes)**; euro-scepticisme** (euro-scepticisme, euro-sceptique, euro-sceptiques, euroscepticisme, eurosceptique, eurosceptiques)**; euro-optimisme** (euro-optimisme, euro-optimiste, euro-optimistes)**; eurocrate** (eurocratie, eurocrate, eurocrates)**; euro-pessimisme** (euro-pessimisme, euro-pessimiste, euro-pessimistes, europessimisme, europessimiste, europessimistes)**; euro-hostilité** (euro-hostilité, euro-hostile, euro-hostiles, eurohostilité, eurohostile, eurohostiles)**; eurobéat** (eurobéat, eurobéate, eurobéats, eurobéates, euro-béat, euro-béate, euro-béats, euro-béates)**; europhobe** (europhobe, europhobes, europhobie)**; europhile** (europhile, europhiles, europhilie).

We then built two histograms in order to better understand the occurrences I collected (Fig. 3.). On the first one, we can see first that *euro-scepticisme*, *pro-européen*, and *anti-européen* are the most present forms in the corpus. Moreover, left-wing ministers are overrepresented especially for *anti-europeén*, *européanisation*, *européaniser*, and *euro-scepticisme*, which is due to the number of speakers in the

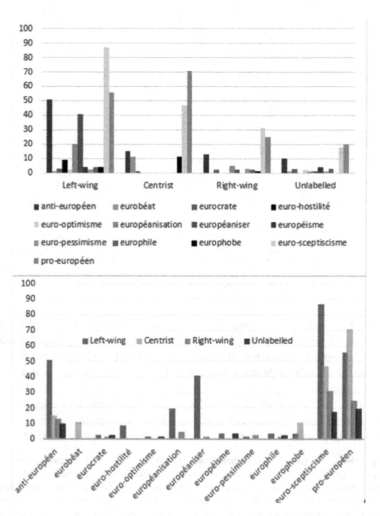

Fig. 4. Use of word forms with relation to the different political parties

sample. On the second one, we can confirm the previous observations, but also note that centrists stand out by their use of *eurobéat* and *europhobe*. We have therefore chosen to focus on a few observations and try to understand these uses (Fig. 4).

3 Analyzing the Uses of "Euro-Words"

3.1 Euroscepticisme vs. Anti-Européen

Firstly, we turned our attention to the use of *euroscepticisme* et *anti-européen* (which could be considered as quasi-synonyms) with relation to political affiliations and periods.

On one hand, both words are used by every political party to name other European countries like UK and Brexit, Czech Republic, Italy, Ireland, Poland, and so on, but also politicians (Nigel Farage, David Cameron, Andrej Babis, etc.):

> "le Premier ministre britannique, M. Cameron, à la fois parce qu'il pense sincèrement qu'il y a des choses à réformer en Europe et aussi parce que son parti était assez **anti-européen** et parce qu'il avait la concurrence d'un autre **parti anti-européen** Ukip"
> "British Prime Minister, Mr. Cameron, due to the facts that he genuinely believes that there are things to reform in Europe, that his party was quite anti-European, and that he faced competition from another **anti-European** party Ukip"
> *Laurent Fabius, June 2nd, 2015, press release* [9].

Other uses differentiate ministers. For instance, Centrists (who have all been appointed since the start of Emmanuel Macron's presidential term in May 2017) use both *euro-scepticisme* and *anti-européen* to refer to the National Rally (the French far right-wing party), or to show that, since French people elected Emmanuel Macron (and, by extension, voted against Marine Le Pen), they cannot be euroskeptics.

For the right-wing parties, *euro-scepticisme* is used to talk about French people (after the 2014 elections to the European Parliament and the National Rally's victory), while *anti-européen* is also used when attempting to separate from the far right-wing ("We are not *anti-European*" means "We are not far right-wing").

Regarding the left-wing politicians, *anti-européen* is used to express that "The *French anti-European feeling* does not exist":

> "d'une part, un intérêt général pour les questions européennes et une perception globale plutôt positive : ce tableau, corroboré par toute une série d'enquêtes, infirme l'idée communément répandue de la montée du sentiment **anti-européen** en France."
> "on the one hand, a general interest in European issues and a rather positive overall perception: this picture, corroborated by a whole series of surveys, invalidates the commonly held idea of the rise of **anti-European** sentiment in France"
> *Pierre Moscovici, April 9th, 1998, statement for the launch of an information campaign on Europe* [10].

but also to explain that it is necessary to fight anti-Europeanism by listening to French citizens' concerns:

> "une élection marquée par une très forte abstention dans toute l'Europe et par un vote populiste **anti-européen** extrêmement important"

"an election marked by a very high abstention rate all across Europe and an extremely high anti-European populist vote"
Harlem Désir, National Assembly, May 27, 2014, right after the European elections [5].

3.2   *Eurobéat* ("Euro-Blissfully Naïve") and *Europhobie* in Centrists' Speeches

In our corpus, centrists are all part of the same period, under the same president: the current one, Emmanuel Macron. His party, *La République en marche!* (*The Republic on the move!*, LREM) is a new political party that was born in 2016 for the 2017 French presidential election.

Until Emmanuel Macron, the French political scene was divided between left-wing and right-wing. E. Macron claimed that he was *neither left- nor right-wing* at the launch of his political party in April 2016 [2], and then affirmed that he was *both right- and left-wing*. He wanted to relegate this concept (Left vs. Right) to the status of an *old political world* [7]. Ever since the beginning of his mandate, E. Macron has stood as a defender of the European Union, and has delivered speeches about it, and calls for "a sovereign, united and democratic Europe" [1].

Our corpus shows that centrists always use *eurobéat* in the negative form, in order to show that Emmanuel Macron and his government are **not** euro-blissfully naive, and that believing in Europe or being very pro-European does not equate to being *eurobéat* or being blind to Europe's failings. This argument goes against criticisms raised from the National Rally and other far right-wing political parties.

Regarding the term *europhobic*, it is used first to refer to the far right-wing candidate, Marine Le Pen:

"Cela a d'abord été une très grande inquiétude pendant la campagne électorale française, entendre des voix eurosceptiques et même clairement **europhobes**"
"It was first of all a great concern during the French election campaign to hear eurosceptic and even outright **Europhobic** voices"
Nathalie Loiseau, October 6th, 2017, France info [11].

The National Rally party is considered by LREM members to be the most anti-European party, and this was one of the biggest disagreements between the two candidates in the second round of the election.

The adjective is also used in the negative form to explain that French and European citizens, should they express doubts about European Union, are in fact waiting for another kind of European governance:

"Je ne crois pas que ces citoyens-là soient [...] **europhobes**. Ils attendent parfois plus, mieux, ou autre chose de l'Europe"
"I don't believe these citizens to be [...] **europhobic**. They are waiting for something more, better, or different from Europe"
Nathalie Loiseau, July, 25th, National Assembly, about dissatisfied French and European citizens [12].

4 *Européaniser* and *Européanisation* in Left-Wing Ministers' Speeches

Finally, we focused our interest on the use of *européaniser* and *européanisation* in left-wing ministers' speeches due to their substantial use in that part of our corpus.

We can observe that the highest number of occurrences of these two words is delivered by only two ministers, in two different contexts.

The first one, Hubert Védrine, was the Foreign Affairs minister from June 1997 to May 2002 in the administration of Prime Minister Lionel Jospin (Socialist Party, Left-wing), under the presidency of Jacques Chirac (Rally for the Republic, right-wing). When H. Védrine uses *européaniser* ou *européanisation*, it is always to refer to the Balkans. This can be explained by the fact that his term had been scarred by the Kosovo war:

> "Il s'agit de conforter l'arrimage des Balkans occidentaux à l'Europe, qui est la clé de leur stabilisation, de leur démocratisation, de leur développement, de la coopération entre eux, en somme de leur **européanisation**."
> "It is a question of strengthening the Western Balkans' ties to Europe, which is the key to their stabilization, democratization, development, and cooperation with each other, in short, to their Europeanisation."
> *Hubert Védrine, July 10th, Brussels* [13].
> "J'ai confiance dans le processus engagé d'aide à l'**européanisation** des Balkans."
> "I have confidence in the process of aiding Balkans to Europeanise."
> *Hubert Védrine, November 20th, interview in Libération* [14].

The second minister is Bernard Kouchner, Minister of Foreign and European Affairs between May 2007 and November 2010, 2002 in the administration of François Fillon (Rally for the Republic) under the presidency of Jacques Chirac (Rally for the Republic). In his speeches, NATO *must* europeanize. We can explain his words with two facts. Firstly, he was a United Nations Representative in Kosovo from 1999 to 2001, so this is a subject he is interested in. Secondly, in 2009, France came back into NATO's integrated military commandment.

> "Vingt et un pays européens font partie de l'OTAN. Il s'agit donc d'européaniser l'OTAN et c'est ce que nous faisons."
> "Twenty-one European countries are part of NATO. So it is a question of Europeanizing NATO and that is what we are doing."
> *Bernard Kouchner, June 18th, 2008, Paris* [15].
> "Aujourd'hui, les deux postes de commandement dit "suprême" de l'Alliance [...] sont détenus par des Américains. Si l'un était confié à la France, je confirme que cela serait un grand pas en avant pour l'européanisation de l'Alliance."
> "Today, the two so-called "supreme" command posts of the Alliance [...] are held by Americans. If one were to be entrusted to France, I can confirm that this would be a great step forward for the Europeanization of the Alliance."
> *Bernard Kouchner, February 18th, 2009, National Assembly* [16].

Here, the use of *eurobéat* and *Europhobe* doesn't depend on the political affiliation of the speakers, but on the political and historical context.

5   Conclusions

This study teaches us that it is possible to find subjectivity even in a very normalized type of discourse.

Thanks to NooJ, this type of lexical study shows that the use of any potential controversial word has to be observed in its context to understand its meaning: the situation and the conditions of the speech must also be taken into consideration (who is talking, to whom, from where and when, and so on).

Ambiguity needs to be removed by examining the co-text (text surrounding the word) of each form we are interested in.

Our example of "euro-words" can be extended to other lexical fields, since linguistic creativity has no limits, especially in an area where discourse is the main way to act. Diplomatic action is essentially a matter of discourse: speeches from its representatives are the starting point to understand global relationships.

References

1. Elysée Website: Initiative pour l'Europe - Emmanuel Macron, pour une Europe souveraine, unie, démocratique. https://www.elysee.fr/emmanuel-macron/2017/09/26/initiative-pour-l-europe-discours-d-emmanuel-macron-pour-une-europe-souveraine-unie-democratique. Accessed 21 May 2021
2. Fougère, M., Barthold, C.: Onwards to the new political frontier: Macron's electoral populism. Organization 27(3), 419–430 (2020)
3. Monte, M., Oger, C.: La construction de l'autorité en contexte. L'effacement du dissensus dans les discours institutionnels. Mots. Les langages du politique (107), 5–18 (2015)
4. Nagimovna, Y.V., Viktorovna, A.J., Adamka, P.: Verbal politeness as an important tool of diplomacy. J. Polit. Law 12(5), 57–61 (2019)
5. National Assembly website: Deuxième séance du mardi 27 mai 2014. https://www.assemblee-nationale.fr/14/cri/2013-2014/20140217.asp. Accessed 21 May 2021
6. Oger, C., Ollivier-Yaniv, C.: Conjurer le désordre discursif. Les procédés de «lissage» dans la fabrication du discours institutionnel. Mots. Les langages du politique (81), 63–77 (2006)
7. Silberztein, M.: La formalisation des langues: l'approche de NooJ. ISTE, Londres (2015)
8. Tiberj, V., Cadenza Academic Translations: Running to stand still: the left-right divide in France in 2017. Revue Française de Science Politique 67(6), I–XXIV (2017)
9. Vie Publique website: Déclaration de M. Laurent Fabius, ministre des affaires étrangères et du développement international, sur la politique étrangère de la France, à Paris le 2 juin 2015. https://www.vie-publique.fr/discours/194978-declaration-de-m-laurent-fabius-ministre-des-affaires-etrangeres-et-du. Accessed 21 May 2021
10. Vie Publique website: Déclaration de M. Pierre Moscovici, ministre délégué aux affaires européennes, sur les grands rendez-vous de l'actualité européenne, à la Grande Arche de la Défense le 9 avril 1998. https://www.vie-publique.fr/discours/138729-declaration-de-m-pierre-moscovici-ministre-delegue-aux-affaires-europe. Accessed 21 May 2021
11. Vie Publique website: Extraits d'un entretien de Mme Nathalie Loiseau, ministre des affaires européennes, à la Radio chrétienne francophone le 29 septembre 2017, sur la construction européenne. https://www.vie-publique.fr/discours/203741-extraits-dun-entretien-de-mme-nathalie-loiseau-ministre-des-affaires-e. Accessed 21 May 2021

12. Vie Publique website: Déclaration de Mme Nathalie Loiseau, ministre des affaires européennes, sur les défis et priorités de la construction européenne, à l'Assemblée nationale le 25 juillet 2017. https://www.vie-publique.fr/discours/203358-nathalie-loiseau-25072017-priorites-de-la-construction-europeenne. Accessed 21 May 2021
13. Vie Publique website: Déclaration de M. Hubert Védrine, ministre des affaires étrangères, sur la situation dans les Balkans occidentaux et leur arrimage à l'Europe, Bruxelles le 10 juillet 2000. https://www.vie-publique.fr/discours/137572-declaration-de-m-hubert-vedrine-ministre-des-affaires-etrangeres-sur. Accessed 21 May 2021
14. Vie Publique website: Interview de M. Dominique Galouzeau de Villepin, ministre des affaires étrangères, de la coopération et de la francophonie, au quotidien "Oslobodjenje" à Sarajevo le 19 septembre 2002, sur l'appui de la France à la reconstruction démocratique des Balkans. https://www.vie-publique.fr/discours/134434-dominique-de-villepin-19092002-reconstruction-democratique-balkans. Accessed 21 May 2021
15. Vie Publique website: Déclaration de M. Bernard Kouchner, ministre des affaires étrangères et européennes, sur les incidences du rejet irlandais du traité de Lisbonne sur la poursuite de la ratification et les priorités de la présidence française de l'Union européenne, Paris le 18 juin 2008. https://www.vie-publique.fr/discours/171328-declaration-de-m-bernard-kouchner-ministre-des-affaires-etrangeres-et. Accessed 21 May 2021
16. Vie Publique website: Audition conjointe de MM. Bernard Kouchner, ministre des affaires étrangères et européennes, et Hervé Morin, ministre de la défense, sur le retour de la France dans les structures intégrées de l'OTAN et l'évolution des missions de l'OTAN, Paris le 18 février 2009. https://www.vie-publique.fr/discours/174439-audition-conjointe-de-mm-bernard-kouchner-ministre-des-affaires-etrang. Accessed 21 May 2021
17. Villar, C.: Le discours diplomatique. L'Harmattan, Paris (2006)

Construction of an Educational Game "VocabNooJ"

Héla Fehri[1]([⊠]), Lazhar Arroum[2], and Sameh Ben Aoun[2]

[1] MIRACL Laboratory, University of Sfax, Sfax, Tunisia
[2] University of Gabes, Gabes, Tunisia

Abstract. The rapid evolution of computer technology has created an upsurge interest in various activities, especially educational games. By introducing the notion of games, Educational Learning takes a new dimensional approach. Both the teaching of educators and the learning of students have benefited from the new world of interactive games and applied sciences within the learning environment. To obtain improved strategies for both learning and teaching, the principle of game-based learning (GBL) can be effectively used. Obviously, it means integrating games into instructional medium. Game-based education involves training and entertainment. Thus, the objective of educational games is to immerse children in educational activities while playing. Indeed, children learn best when their learning is combined with fun play. This entails that Strategy-based games increase the brain's functioning process, encourage kids to learn new things, enhance their talents, and create an emotional bond to learn the subject matter. The aim of this paper is to propose a game developed with NooJ platform. This game is a monolingual educational game that consists of developing the abilities of children and even adults in French language in a simple and fun way through a set of exercises.

Keywords: Educational games · Modern education · NooJ · Dictionary · Transducer · Learning

1 Introduction

According to the progress of technology, we are making sure that it increased rapidly in all different fields. Educational games are considered as important part of it. Nowadays, modern education requires new means to facilitate learning. It is not only a source of entertainment [1] but also a tool of knowledge [2, 3]. The objective of this paper is explaining the benefits of educational games. These types of games encourage children not only entertaining themselves but also discovering new vocabulary. Throughout them, kids can improve their skills because they practice their knowledge and refresh their memories. These games improve players' skills by permitting them learning and discovering new words in different languages [4]. Educational gaming is good opportunity to help kids getting information rapidly and efficiently. It is considered as one of the best gaming improving new words. Children can deal with both new vocabulary and synonyms and antonyms. Furthermore, children become more exited to know more antonyms and synonyms for many French words. Instead of playing violent

M. Bigey et al. (Eds.): NooJ 2021, CCIS 1520, pp. 124–134, 2021.
https://doi.org/10.1007/978-3-030-92861-2_11

e-games, electronic educational games are the appropriate choice for children. The gamer can build essential skills in reading, writing and more. The purpose of this paper is to propose an educational game developed with NooJ platform [5, 6]. This game is named "VocabNooJ" it consist of finding Synonyms and antonyms of French words.

VocabNooJ is based on _dm dictionary [7] and transducers. The next parts of this paper explain this game and its different steps.

2 Proposed Method

VocabNooJ is educational monolingual game. It improves skills of both children and even adults in French language. Indeed, gamer can deal with it easily because it does not require computer skills. He is required to respond to exercises with a degree of difficulty that varies from one level to another.

The proposed approach for the educational game VocabNooJ is composed of three phases called (a) *Identification of Resources,* (b) *Building of Resources* and (c) *Playing Steps*. Figure 1 depicts this approach.

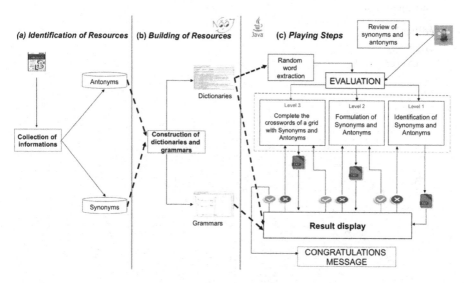

Fig. 1. VocabNooJ proposed game

2.1 Identification of Resources

The phase *identification of resources* (Fig. 1a) consists of collecting synonyms and antonyms of French words. It is based on e-dictionaries such as REVERSO[1] and

---

[1] www.reverso.net.

LAROUSSE[2]. This phase is important to identify and add the necessary semantic features to the dictionaries. These features will be used by the grammars in the process of recognizing synonyms and antonyms of words. In our work, three dictionaries are identified: dictionary of verbs, dictionary of nouns and dictionary of adjectives.

2.2 Building of Resources

The phase *Building of Resources* (Fig. 1b) is going to build the identified resources. _dm dictionary is the only resource in this paper because it covers an important number of words of the French language. In fact, this dictionary contains 67983 entries with derivational and inflectional paradigms. It is already built in the linguistic platform NooJ.

Our contribution in this step consists in adding synonyms and antonyms for each word to obtain new dictionary. For each word, three synonyms and three antonyms are added using "SYN" and "ANT" features. Figure 2 gives an idea of added features for the category of verbs. For example, the verb "abolir" has three synonyms:

- "détruire"
- "supprimer"
- "résilier"

And three antonyms:

- "édifier"
- "ériger"
- "consacrer"

Fig. 2. Extract of the dictionary of the verbs

---

[2] www.larousse.fr.

Figure 3 gives an idea about added synonyms and antonyms for the adjective category. As an example, the adjective "malheureux" has three synonyms:

- "triste"
- "déplorable"
- "misérable"

And three antonyms:

- "heureux"
- "bienheureux"
- "bon"

Fig. 3. Extract of the dictionary of adjectives

Figure 4 represents the category of nouns. For example, the noun "besoin" has three synonyms:

- "répultion"
- "nécissité"
- "privation"

And three antonyms:

- "abundance"
- "repugnance"
- "soif"

128   H. Fehri et al.

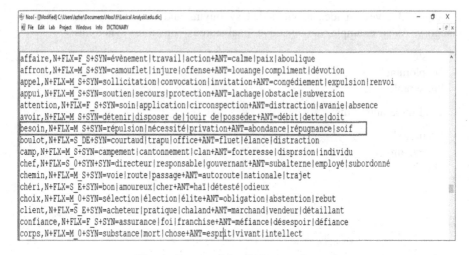

Fig. 4. Extract of the dictionary of nouns

The construction of grammars (i.e., transducers) allows the extraction of the synonyms and antonyms of every word putting in the dictionary. In our game, two grammars are built: a grammar for extraction synonyms and another for antonyms. Each grammar is characterized by initial and final node. Figure 5 represents the grammar for extraction synonyms.

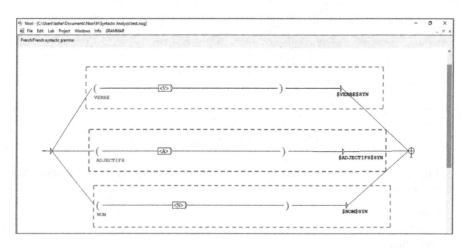

Fig. 5. Grammar of synonyms

As shown in Fig. 5, the grammar of synonyms contains three paths which represent respectively verbs, nouns and adjectives.

- First path:
  - <V> represents the category: verb.
  - "VERBE": variable that contains the appropriate verb.
  - "$VERBE$SYN" returns the synonyms of the verb.

- Second path:
  - `<A>` represents the category: adjective.
  - "ADJECTIFS" variable that contains the appropriate adjective.
  - "$ADJECTIFS$SYN" returns the synonyms of the adjective.
- Third path:
  - `<N>` represents the category: Noun.
  - "NOM": variable that contains the appropriate noun.
  - "NOMSYN" returns the synonyms of the noun.

The transducer represented in Fig. 6 gives the list of antonyms of the given word. It has the same principle of the transducer of the Fig. 5.

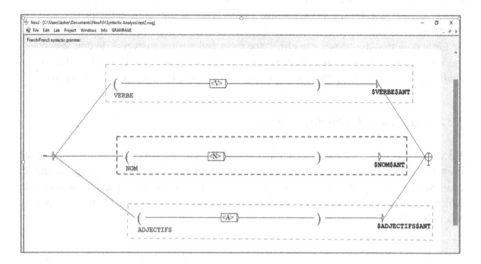

Fig. 6. Grammar of antonyms

2.3   Playing Steps

The phase *Playing steps* (Fig. 1c) has too main steps: Review and Evaluation. They are separated but complete each other. In fact, the first step helps the player winning the second step.

The first step, labelled "Review," is to recognize the synonyms and antonyms of appropriate words. This step is named "Review" because it can help the gamer remember the synonyms and antonyms of a few words before beginning the "Evaluation" part. This can help enrich his or her vocabulary and succeed in the second step.

The second step, labelled "Evaluation", is composed of three exercises the difference being the level of difficulty. A user can only move from one level to the other when he succeeds the current level.

Level 1

In this level, the gamer has to choose the appropriate synonyms and antonyms of some words, which are taken from the built dictionary. This part is the easiest. Furthermore, the gamer can deal with both true and false responses. This level is very important because the player cannot move to the next level without winning it. If he fails, he needs to repeat the same level with new random vocabulary.

Level 2

In this level, the gamer is invited to reformulate the synonyms and antonyms of some words, which are presented randomly. They are taken from the built dictionaries. In fact, in this part the synonyms and antonyms are composed of letters, which are scrambled. Therefore, the gamer needs to reorder and formulates them. He should deal with some formulation in the previous level.

Level 3

In this step, the gamer is going to deal with crosswords. The words are choosing randomly in a grid. The player has to fill in this grid. He gives the correct synonyms and antonyms for the proposed words. This level is the most difficult level in the "Evaluation" part.

Let's note that the gamer can check the right and wrong answers. He can also check the correction of crosswords. However, if the player fails in this level he has to try again in order to win the "Evaluation" part. He deals also with new crosswords.

3 VocabNooJ Experimentation

VocabNooJ is designed for children and even adults to improve their knowledge in the French vocabulary: it is based on synonyms and antonyms. At the beginning, the gamer deals with review part to refresh his skills. Then, he moves on to the Evaluation part, which is composed of three levels. Figure 7 depicts an example of the first part in VocabNooJ.

Fig. 7. Review part

Figure 7 consists of a list bottoms facilitating the game. It contains a text zone to write the word. It has also two bottoms for synonyms and antonyms.

According to the evaluation part, the first level consists of both a list of synonyms and a list of antonyms containing three words. Each word has five proposals in which only three words are correct. This level lists other words randomly in every attempt.

Furthermore, the following figures show the different steps of level 1: the first one (Fig. 8a) presents the interface, the second (Fig. 8b) presents the validation of the attempt and the last one (Fig. 8c) presents the correction.

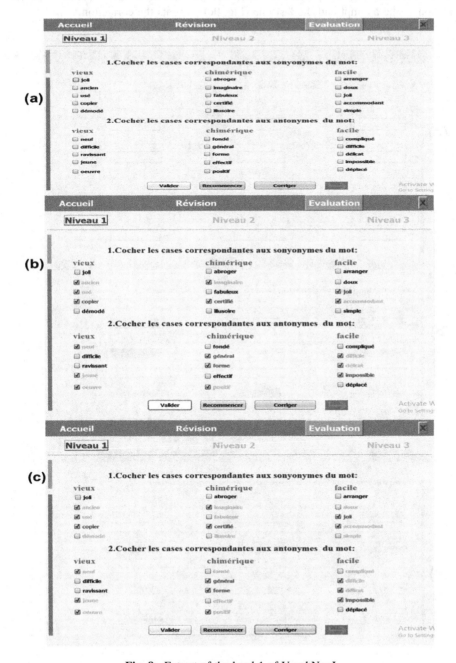

Fig. 8. Extract of the level 1 of VocabNooJ

After winning the previous level, the gamer can move to the next level. Throughout this level, the gamer forms synonyms and antonyms with scrambled letters. He reorders the letters to get correct answers. The following figures show the different steps of level 2: the first one (Fig. 9a) presents the interface, the second (Fig. 9b) presents the validation of the attempt and the last one (Fig. 9c) presents the correction.

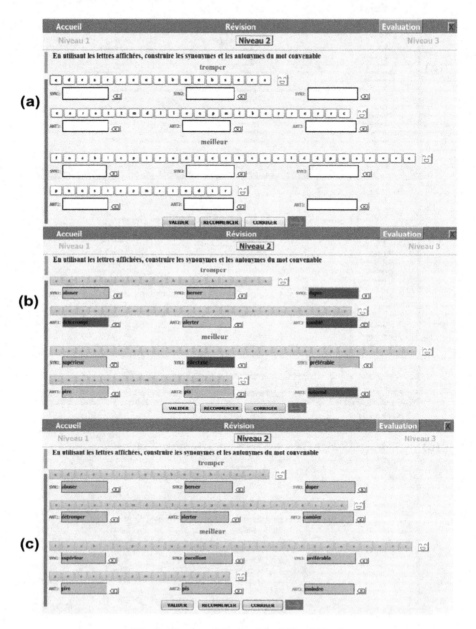

Fig. 9. Extract of the level 2 of VocabNooJ

The third level consists of crosswords in which the player discovers the missing word through the synonyms or the antonyms. The following figures show the different steps of level 3: the first one (Fig. 10a) presents the interface, the second (Fig. 10b) presents the validation of the attempt and the last one (Fig. 10c) presents the correction.

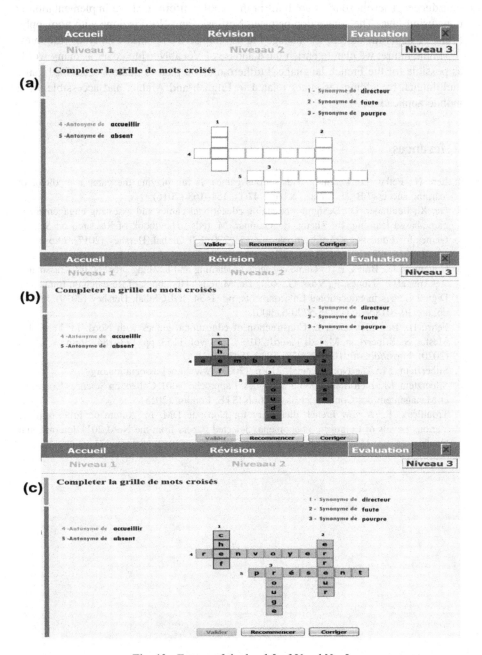

Fig. 10. Extract of the level 3 of VocabNooJ

4 Conclusion

In this paper, we have proposed an educational game named "VocabNooJ". The development of this game is based on a linguistic approach using dictionaries and transducers. These resources are built in the NooJ platform and the implementation is done using Java. The connection between NetBeans and NooJ is done with noojapply. From the experimentation, we managed to develop serious games with NooJ resources.

In the future, we plan to enrich the database of VocabNooJ to cover as many words as possible for the French language. Furthermore, we plan to make VocabNooJ game multilingual by adding resources related to English and Arabic, and accessible via a mobile application.

References

1. Iten, N., Petko, D.: Learning with serious games: is fun playing the game a predictor of learning success? Br. J. Educ. Technol. **47**(1), 151–163 (2016)
2. Ge, X., Ifenthaler, D.: Designing engaging educational games and assessing engagement in game-based learning. In: Zheng, R., Gardner, M. (eds.) Handbook of Research on Serious Games for Educational Applications, pp. 253–270. IGI Global, Hershey (2017). https://doi.org/10.4018/978-1-5225-0513-6.ch012
3. Concilio, I.D., Braga, P.H.: Game concepts in learning and teaching process. In: Krassmann, A., Amaral, É., Nunes, F., Voss, G., Zunguze, M. (eds.) Handbook of Research on Immersive Digital Games in Educational Environments, pp. 1–34. IGI Global, Hershey (2019). https://doi.org/10.4018/978-1-5225-5790-6.ch001
4. Fehri, H., Ben Messaoud, I.: Construction of educational games with NooJ. In: Fehri, H., Mesfar, S., Silberztein, M. (eds.) NooJ 2019. CCIS, vol. 1153, pp. 173–184. Springer, Cham (2020). https://doi.org/10.1007/978-3-030-38833-1_15
5. Silberztein, M.: The NooJ manual, 213 p. (2003). www.nooj-association.org
6. Silberztein, M.: La formalisation des langues: l'approche NooJ. Collection Sciences Cognitive et Management des Connaissances. Edition ISTE, London (2015)
7. Trouilleux, F.: A new French dictionary for NooJ: le DM. In: Automatic Processing of Various Levels of Linguistic Phenomena: Selected Papers from the NooJ 2011 International Conference, pp. 16–28. Cambridge Scholars Publishing (2012). 1-4438-3711-3 (2011).

Approach to the Automatic Treatment of Gerunds in Spanish and Quechua: A Pedagogical Application

Andrea Rodrigo[1]([✉]), Maximiliano Duran[2]([✉]),
and María Yanina Nalli[3]([✉])

[1] Facultad de Humanidades y Artes, Universidad Nacional de Rosario,
Rosario, Argentina
andreafrodrigo@yahoo.com.ar
[2] Université de Franche-Comté, Besançon, France
duran_maximiliano@yahoo.fr
[3] Facultad Regional Rosario, Universidad Tecnológica Nacional,
Rosario, Argentina
nalliyani@gmail.com

Abstract. This work aims to present an automatic processing of the Spanish and the Quechua gerunds to show the similarities and differences between an SVO and an SOV language [3] to teach Spanish as a foreign language for Quechua speakers, and Quechua as a foreign language to Spanish speakers. For this purpose, we use NooJ [7] to develop a preliminary formalization of the Spanish and the Quechua gerunds in order to examine their morphological features and their syntactic behavior according to their contexts of occurrence. The Spanish gerund uses the suffix *-ndo* after a thematic vowel which varies according to the verb conjugation: the vowel - *a*- belongs to the first conjugation, and the diphthong *-ie* (or its orthographic variant *-ye*) belongs to the second and third conjugations [5]. On the other hand, the Quechua gerund uses four suffixes: *-spa, -stin, -pti, -chka* and the reduplicated combination of the suffix *-n* in a verb stem, which is combined among them or with other verb suffixes to create different gerund forms, tenses, and aspects. In order to work with a standard use of Spanish, we used a corpus from a repository of the Ministry of Education of Argentina [10]. As the Spanish gerunds behave in different ways according to their context of occurrence, our research process includes NooJ grammars to analyze the Spanish gerund as part of a periphrasis or as a part of a subordinate clause with adjectival or adverbial value. Finally, we use NooJ to explore the syntactic and morphological richness of the Spanish and Quechua gerunds to show language learners the similarities and differences between them.

Keywords: Gerund · Spanish · Quechua · NooJ · Automatic processing

1 Introduction

Using NooJ as a working platform, the aim of the Argentina team (CETEHIPL, Centro de Estudios de Tecnología Educativa y Herramientas Informáticas de Procesamiento del Lenguaje, UNR, Argentina) is to examine and describe the Spanish and the

M. Bigey et al. (Eds.): NooJ 2021, CCIS 1520, pp. 135–146, 2021.
https://doi.org/10.1007/978-3-030-92861-2_12

Quechua gerunds for pedagogical purposes. Since these gerunds show different behaviors according to their contexts of occurrence, we find challenging intricacies in our search for the most appropriate formalization and classification, so this work is just a first approach to this issue.

1.1 Project Background

Since 2015, we have been working with the IES_UNR Argentina research team in the automatic processing of Spanish, and especially Rioplatense Spanish.[1] Our central hypothesis lies on the assumption that students using NooJ can play a researching role in creating their own dictionaries and grammars to develop the metalinguistic reflection. We strongly believe that metalinguistic reflection is a key step in the learning process of any language. This paper seeks to examine some key aspects of the Spanish and Quechua gerunds using NooJ for their automatic processing. Our intention is to provide a general and inspirational framework for teaching Quechua as a foreign language to learners whose mother tongue is Spanish (Quechua to Spanish relation) [8] and for teaching Spanish as a foreign language to learners whose mother tongue is Quechua (Spanish to Quechua relation) [9].[2]

1.2 Why Do We Use NooJ?

NooJ offers a computing environment that can be used with many different languages. Learners willing to learn Spanish or Quechua as a foreign language use common syntax from the modules developed for both languages. These modules are available in the NooJ platform as reference. Using NooJ, learners observe the data of their mother tongue and then they develop linguistic hypotheses to compare them with that data of the foreign language. Firstly, we present and examine some key aspects of the Quechua gerund to then present and examine some key aspects of the Spanish gerund, to finally bring them into comparison using NooJ as a common framework of analysis.

2 Considerations About the Quechua Gerunds

According to Greenberg's linguistic classification [3], Quechua[3] is a SVO language with binding features. As such, morphological information is a key aspect since syntactic information is also provided. The following section examines the morphology of the Quechua gerunds.

---

[1] Our book *Aprendo con NooJ* [1] summarizes this perspective of work.

[2] We have already presented some developments on this topic with [6] for Spanish learners with regard to other languages such as Italian and Portuguese.

[3] We take the Quechua spoken in Ayacucho (Peru) as our language of reference. Other dialect variants are also included.

2.1   Morphology of the Quechua Gerunds (QU)

The Quechua gerunds include the mark of person[4]: they provide grammatical information about the agent who performs the action described by the verb. Still, they do not include any information about the tense of the action from which it derives. At a syntactic level, the Quechua gerunds allow us to build subordinate clauses. The sentence below illustrates this point:

- *rima-spa-iki uya-ri-chi-ku-rja-nki* "hablando *tú/ vos*[5] te has hecho entender" "talking, you have made yourself understood"

Since gerunds are the adverbial form of the verb, they operate in the sentence as adverbs and they behave as adjuncts. In Quechua, the gerunds are formed by adding one of the four suffixes *-spa, -stin, -pti, -chka* and the reduplicated combination of the – *n* suffix[6] to a verb stem.

In the next sections, we will examine the suffixes *–spa, -stin y –pti*.[7] These suffixes are subordinating suffixes, i.e., they are used to build phrases containing two dependent clauses and create specific relationships between the subjects and the sequence of the actions described in the phrase. The tense of the subordinate clause depends on the tense of the main clause.[8]

Gerund with the Suffix *–spa*. The suffix *–spa* creates a gerund form that specifies that the action described in the subordinate clause takes place before the action described in the main clause. Table 1 shows the use of the suffix *–spa*.

Table 1. Some uses of the suffix *–spa*

Gerund		
SP (Spanish)	QU (Quechua) (static)	QU (Quechua) (dynamic)
hablar > hablando "talk > talking"	the *–spa* ending is used for all the grammatical persons *rimay > rimaspa*	Seven person TIM2[9] endings are used = (*i, iki, n, nchik, iku, ikichik, nku*) *rima-spa-i* "hablando (*yo*) + G + 1 + s" "(I) talking" *rima -spa-iki* "hablando (*tú/ vos*) + G + 2 + s" "(you) talking"

---

[4] Guardia Mayorga [4] considers the gerund as an impersonal form according to Spanish grammar.

[5] Both second person singular pronoun *tú* and *vos* Spanish forms are referred to since our language of reference is the Spanish spoken in the Río de la Plata, Argentina.

[6] For example, the verb to laugh "reír": a*si-n asi-n richkarqa* "iba riendo" "he went laughing" (verb in the present tense, third singular person, repeated).

[7] Due to space limitations, we will study the remaining suffixes in future works.

[8] This section does not examine the suffix *–chka* and the reduplicated combination of the suffix *–n*.

[9] The main endings of the verb conjugations are the indefinite time endings (TI) which make reference points for the present simple: TI = (*ni, nki, n, nchik, niku, nkichik, nku*), *miku-ni* "comí" "(I) ate", *miku-nki* "comiste" "(you) ate", *miku-n* "comió" "(he/she/it) ate", *miku-nchik* "comimos" "(we) ate"; (the T2 operator transforms the TI endings in the group of the TIM2 transformed endings = (*i, iki, n, nchik, iku, ikichik, nku*) which are used to conjugate verbs with the suffixes (*-pti, -spa,*).

The following example shows how a sentence is built using the gerund suffix *–spa*:

- *llamkaita tukuspa wasiikiman jamusaj* "*trabajando (después de trabajar) vendré a tu casa*" "working (meaning "after doing the job which somebody is paid for") I will come to your house."

To obtain the conjugated form of the gerund, the suffix *-spa* is placed between the verb stem and the TIM2 ending as shown below:

- (ñuqa) miku-spa-i ri-saq "comiendo (yo) iré" "eating (I) will go"

The suffix *-spa* can also be combined with other SIP[10] inter-positional and SPP[11] post-positional verb suffixes which generate all the other Quechua verb features (conjugations, moods, adjuncts, and aspects). All these combinations were obtained through the combinatorial matrices developed by [2]. Below we show one combination to illustrate this point:

- with one SIP: rqu-spa, ku-spa, ri-spa, ykacha-spa

In order to study all the possible automatic transformations of subordinate clauses containing these gerunds, we have constructed a NooJ grammar as shown in Fig. 2. If we take a phrase from the corpus[12] such as:

- yanapa-nku yacha-chi-spa-nku "(ellos) ayudan enseñando" "(they) help teaching"

we will get more than 3,700 transformed instances of the subordinate clause as seen in Fig. 1. At this stage of the study, the main clause will remain the same.

---

[10] SIP = (*chaku, chi, chka, ykacha, ykachi, ykamu, ykapu, ykari, yku, ysi, kacha, kamu, kapu, ku, lla, mpu, mu, na, naya, pa, paya, pti, pu, ra, raya, ri, rpari, rqa, rqu, ru, spa, sqa, stin, tamu, wa*).

[11] SPP = (*ch, chá, chik, chiki, chu, chusina, má, man, m, mi, ña, pas, puni, qa, raq, ri, si, s, taq, yá*) post-positional verb suffixes. Such suffixes are placed after the verb ending of the conjugation. See [2].

[12] The sample sentence has been taken from the corpus of work (repository of the Ministry of Education, Argentina) to develop this topic in the same way as that of the Quechua gerund [10].

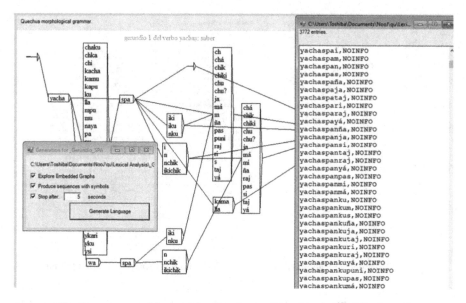

Fig. 1. -*spa* gerund form of the Quechua verb *yachay* *"saber"* "to know"

Gerund with the Suffix –*pti*. The inter-positional suffix –*pti*[13] creates a gerund form with two verbs. The suffix –*pti* specifies that the subject of the gerund is different from the subject of the main verb. The actions described by the verbs can occur simultaneously, but the action described by the gerund + -*pti* suffix usually occurs first or as a condition for the action specified by the main verb. The subordinate verb also includes a series of suffixes that specify its grammatical person, as shown by the TIM2 endings in Table 1. If the gerund includes one of the SPP modal suffixes (the assertive -*m*, -*mi*, the citative suffix -*s*, -*si*, or the conjecture suffix -*ch*, -*chá*), the suffix -*pti* usually expresses the cause of the action described by the main verb. Below we illustrate this point with an instance of the corpus:

- *rima-pti-i-mi puñu-ku-n "se durmió, cuando le estaba hablando"* "(he/she/it) fall asleep when (he/she/it) was talking to him"

In Fig. 2, we display the grammar which allows us to automatically generate all of the two suffix forms of the –*pti* gerund of the Quechua verb *rimay* "hablar" "to talk".

---

[13] -*pti* as a subordinating suffix indicates that the action described in the subordinate clause occurs before the action described in the main clause. In Spanish, this suffix means *cuándo* "when", *porque* "because", *debido a que* "due to", *"si"* "if". *jajchawaptinja manam takisajchu "Si me regaña, no voy a cantar".* "If he scolds me, I will not sing".

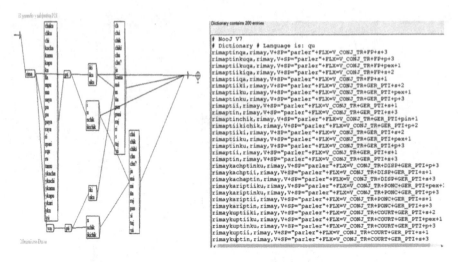

Fig. 2. Generated *-pti* gerunds forms of the Quechua verb *rimay "hablar"* "to talk"

Gerund with the Suffix *–stin.* The suffix *–stin* specifies that the action described by the subordinate verb and the action described by the main verb are simultaneous. The gerund + suffix *–stin* does not include any inflectional mark for the grammatical person. Still, there are two elements to be taken into consideration:

1. The subject can be the same for both verbs:

   - *Rosaja takistin yanukun "Rosa cocina cantando"*. "Rosa cooks while singing."

2. If the verbs have different subjects, the verb with the suffix *–stin* is followed by the verb *ka,* which is inflected by the combination *–chkapti,* i.e., *-chka + -pti*:

   - *rimanakustin kachkaptinku wawanja wichiikurja "el niño se cayó cuando ellos estaban conversando"*. "The boy fell when they were talking."

Figure 3 shows the finite transducer which generates the *–stin* gerund forms of the Quechua verb *rimay "hablar"* "to talk". The box on the right shows a sample list of the generated forms.

Due to space limitations, we will not examine the *–chka* gerund forms neither the V-n, V-n forms. In the following section, we present and examine some key aspects of the Spanish gerund.

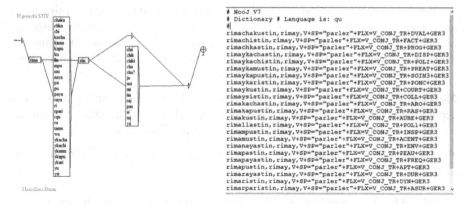

Fig. 3. The *-stin* gerund generator and the generated forms

3 Considerations About the Spanish Gerunds

Many works about the Spanish gerunds are largely focused on normative prescriptions to avoid using the gerund excessively. In contrast, our aim here is to identify and formalize the gerund according to its context of occurrence. To this effect, we will use an institutional repository[14] from the Ministry of Education of Argentina [10] as our corpus of work to define a standard use of Spanish.[15] By this way, we will focus on two central and well-differentiated aspects. First, we will discuss some key concepts about morphology and, second, we will examine the syntactic behavior of the Spanish gerunds. Unlike Quechua, the Spanish gerunds do not include any morphological information about tense or grammatical persons. Yet, the clauses containing gerunds can specify that the action described by the verb can occur before, simultaneously or after the action described by the verb in the main clause, but this is due to syntactic and semantic aspects and not morphological ones.

3.1 Morphology of the Spanish Gerund

Generally, the Spanish gerunds are formed by adding the suffix *-ndo* after a thematic vowel which varies according to the verb conjugation. Thus, the vowel *-a-* belongs to the first conjugation, and the diphthong *-ie-* or its orthographic variant *-ye-* belongs to the second and third conjugations.[16] See the examples below:

- *jugar - jugando "pukllay-pukllaspa"* "to play – playing"
- *volver - volviendo "jampuy- jampuspa"* "to return – returning"

---

[14] This corpus is a collection of regulations from several historical periods.

[15] We are referring to the Rioplatense Spanish variant, although some features are common to the Iberian Spanish.

[16] RAE [5], p. 2037.

This led us to the question of what kind of approach should we take in using NooJ to analyze the morphological information of the Spanish gerunds. On this basis, we have designed five files.*nof* models[17] which allow us to examine the Spanish gerunds in their basic forms.[18] In the following models, each phrase and clause have been translated into Quechua for comparative purposes.

Model ONE. This model includes the Spanish infinitive verbs ending in *–ar*. The gerund form is derived by keeping the thematic vowel *–a* plus the suffix *–ndo*. Below we show an instance taken from the corpus to illustrate this model:

- *enmarcando las estrategias "imay na_ruraikunata qinchaspa"*[19] "framing the strategies"

Model TWO. This model includes the Spanish infinitive verbs ending in *–er* or in *–ir*. The gerund is derived by adding the suffix *–iendo* to the verb stem. Below we show an instance taken from the corpus to illustrate this model:

- *siendo un objeto social "sasirayku-ima kaspa"*[20] "being a social object"

Model THREE. This model includes the Spanish infinitive verbs ending in *–er* or in *–ir*. This gerund form is a geographical variant of the Model TWO gerund, and it is derived by adding the suffix *–yendo* to the verb stem. Below we show an instance taken from the corpus to illustrate this point:

- *excluyendo del análisis a aquellos planes "chay rurana-qellqaikunata mana qawapayaspa"* "excluding from the analysis those plans"

Model FOUR. This model includes the Spanish infinitive verbs ending in *–er* or in *–ir*. The gerund is derived by adding the suffix *–iendo* plus a vowel change in the verb stem. Thus, the vowel /–e–/ is replaced by the vowel /–i–/, and the vowel /–o–/ is replaced by the vowel /–u–/. The vowel change is made automatically using NooJ's command <Y> for the .nof files. Below we show a series of instances taken from the corpus to illustrate this model:

- *siguiendo esta línea "kay imayna-ruraita qatispa"* "following this line"

Model FIVE. This model includes the Spanish infinitive verbs ending in *–er* or in *–ir*. The gerund is derived by adding the suffix *–endo*. In contrast to Model FOUR, there is

---

[17] ONE = <B2> ando/ger; TWO = <B2> iendo/ger; THREE = <B2> yendo/ger; FOUR = <B2> <Y> iendo/ger; FIVE = <Y> <B2> endo/ger.

[18] Due to space limitations, we will not study here the compound forms of the Spanish gerunds. Just as a mere reference, compound forms are made by the auxiliary verb *haber* "to have" in its gerund form plus a participle form standing as the main verb. Example: *habiendo pensado en eso* "having thought about that".

[19] Similarly, *qinchaspa* if the action occurs before the main event, *qinchastin* if the action occurs simultaneously.

[20] *kaspa* can be replaced by: *kachkaspa* "siendo" (meaning "being"); *kaptin* "siendo" (meaning "on the condition that").

no /-i-/ in the gerund ending yet the vowel /-e/ is replaced by the vowel /–i-/. The vowel change is made automatically using NooJ's command <Y> for the .nof files. This rule applies to such verbs as *ceñir "watapakuy"* "to fasten", *constreñir "qarkapakuy"* "to constrain". The verb list for this model is short and we do not have any specific example to take from the corpus to illustrate this point.

In the next section, we present some general syntactic considerations about the Spanish gerunds.

3.2   Syntax of the Spanish Gerunds

The Spanish gerunds can be part of a subordinate clause or can be part of a periphrastic form. The use of a preceding comma or coordinating conjunction before the gerund is a distinctive feature and determines the gerund's syntactic behavior. In the following sections, we will examine the different behavior of the Spanish gerunds.

Periphrastic Gerund. The gerund can occur as a periphrastic form. In this case, the gerund is part of a verb periphrasis and cannot be separated from the conjugated verb. The following example illustrates this point:

* *algunas provincias fueron incorporando la modalidad de adultos.* (periphrastic gerund) "wakin provinciakunaqa, yuyaq-runakunapa ruraininkuta yaykurichispa" "Some provinces were incorporating the modality for adults."

The key aspects which have to be highlighted here are: a) an auxiliary verb, which occurs as a conjugated form (*fueron "kanku"* "(they) were"); and b) a main verb which occurs in its gerund form (*incorporando "yaykuchispa"* "incorporating") and provides the semantic content. Figure 4 below shows the NooJ grammar for this sentence.

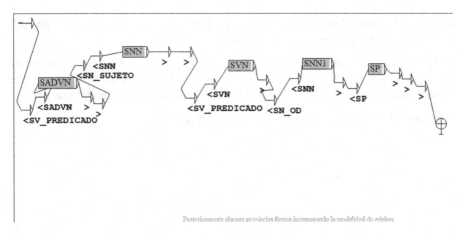

Posteriormente algunas provincias fueron incorporando la modalidad de adultos

Fig. 4. Sentence grammar of a periphrastic gerund

Predicative Gerund. The gerund has an adjectival value [+adjective] which modifies the noun head (*lengua* "language"). The following sentence is an example:

- *La lengua escrita, siendo un objeto social[21], no se distribuye equitativamente.* "qillqasqa simiqa, sasirayku-ima kaptin, manam chaykaqllaqa achurasqachu" "being a social object, written language is not distributed evenly."

Figure 5 below shows the NooJ grammar of this sentence.

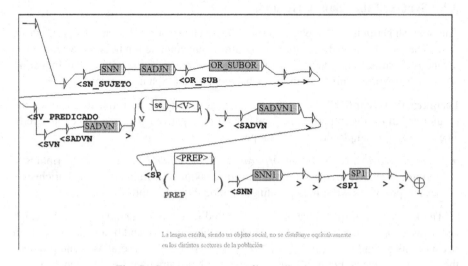

La lengua escrita, siendo un objeto social, no se distribuye equitativamente en los distintos sectores de la población

Fig. 5. Sentence grammar of a predicative gerund

Adverbial Gerund. The gerund is part of a subordinate clause that modifies the verb head. The following sentence is an example:

- *Los contenidos se abordan teniendo en cuenta la gran expectativa de las personas* "yachaikunataqa llamkarinchik runapa suyasqanta qawaspa" "Contents are addressed taking into account people's high expectations." (adverbial gerund)

Figure 6 below shows the NooJ grammar of this sentence.

---

[21] In this case, the gerund is part of a subordinate clause that modifies the noun head. Such occurrences are no longer allowed by the present-day Spanish grammar normative. In this context, this gerund can also be understood as an adverb of cause.

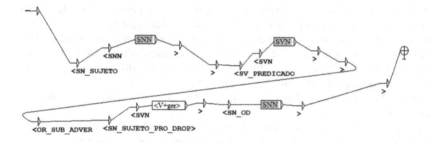

Los contenidos se abordan <teniendo en cuenta la gran expectativa y urgencia de las personas por aprender>.

Fig. 6. Sentence grammar of an adverbial gerund

4 Conclusion

From a linguistic point of view, we have seen that it is possible to formalize the generation of Quechua gerunds containing one of the suffixes -*spa, -pti, -stin*, or any other combination among them or other SIP or SPP verbal suffixes. As it has been shown, the paradigms which generate these gerunds can be rational expressions as well as graphic automata following NooJ's formalization patterns. We have shown that the gerunds in Quechua have a personal verb form and that they can be conjugated. Our approach to the Spanish gerunds, on the other hand, was initially made from a morphological point of view. In contrast to Quechua gerunds, Spanish gerunds cannot be conjugated and they do not have any personal verb form. We, then, made a syntactic approach to examine the contexts in which the Spanish gerunds can occur, that is, as part of a verb periphrasis, as an adjective with predicative value, or as part of a subordinate clause with an adverbial value. We schematically presented some specific aspects which must be taken into account for a Spanish speaker to learn the Quechua gerunds or for a Quechua speaker to learn the Spanish gerunds. This work is just a first approach to address this issue. We believe this is a fertile field of study and these studies can be a useful start for a joint work about Quechua and Spanish using NooJ as an integral platform for their automatic processing.

References

1. Bonino, R., Rodrigo, A.: Aprendo con NooJ: de la Lingüística Computacional a la Enseñanza de la lengua. Ed. Ciudad Gótica, Rosario, Argentina (2019)
2. Duran, M.: Dictionnaire électronique français-quechua des verbes pour le TAL. Thèse de doctorat, Université de Franche-Comté, Besançon (2017)
3. Greenberg, J.: Some universals or grammar with particular reference to the order of meaningful elements. In: Greenberg, J. (ed.) Universals of Language, 2nd edn, pp. 72–113. MIT Press, Cambridge (1966)
4. Guardia Mayorga, C.: Gramatica Kechwa. Ediciones Los Andes, Lima, Perú (1973)

5. Real Academia Española: Asociación de Academias de la Lengua Española: Nueva gramática de la lengua española. Espasa-Calpe, Madrid, España (2009)
6. Rodrigo, A., Reyes, S., Mota, C., Barreiro, A.: Causal discourse connectors in the teaching of Spanish as a foreign language (SLF) for Portuguese learners using NooJ. In: Fehri, H., Mesfar, S., Silberztein, M. (eds.) NooJ 2019. CCIS, vol. 1153, pp. 161–172. Springer, Cham (2020). https://doi.org/10.1007/978-3-030-38833-1_14
7. Silberztein, M.: Formalizing Natural Languages: The NooJ Approach. Iste Ediciones, London (2016)
8. Spanish Module: http://www.nooj-association.org/resources.html. Accessed 11 May 2021
9. Quechua Module: http://www.nooj-association.org/resources.html. Accessed 11 May 2021
10. Ministerio de Educación y Deportes, Presidencia de la Nación Argentina. Repositorio institucional: http://repositorio.educacion.gov.ar/dspace

Using NooJ to Formalize French Cooking Expressions

Tong Yang[✉]

North China Electric Power University, Beijing, China
tongyang@ncepu.edu.cn

Abstract. Our study fits the teaching method FOS [27] for Chinese cookers who come to work in French restaurants or who have chosen catering as a specialty. French gastronomy is internationally renowned, and the expressions of the cooking dishes often have informative and explanatory functions, and the large number of expressions of the cooking dishes that have the same structure (nominal group + à la/à l '/ au/aux + name) attract our attention. Before teaching these expressions to our learners, the extraction of these expressions constitutes the problem of our study. Indeed, the extraction of multiple words sequences is also a problem in NLP (automatic language processing). In order to choose an appropriate software for our study, in this article, we first modeled the lexical data of these expressions of dishes having the same structure (nominal group + à la/à l '/ au/aux + name) to choose NooJ as our appropriate software from among NLP extraction software. Then, we implemented the lexical data in NooJ by developing some grammars in the form of a transducer and will compile our data respecting the codes of the NooJ, in particular the operator + EXCLUDE (prefixed by the character "/") and the colored nodes (prefixed by the character ":"). Finally, the result of our extraction with NooJ was satisfactory for teaching.

Keywords: NooJ · Automatic extraction · Cuisitext · Routines · Modeling · Disambiguation · Expressions of cooking dishes

1 Introduction

Known throughout the world, French gastronomy attracts many foreign cooks each year who come to work in French restaurants or have chosen catering as a specialty. As Wilson states, France is reputed to be the land of gastronomy [38]. As Hervé Fleury, director of the Paul Bocuse Institute, in Écully (Rhône), testifies in a report (published on 04/02/2008): if there is a sector in which France has not lost its attractiveness is gastronomy. Applications from other countries to our establishment are even constantly increasing. In addition, Fleury adds that of the 330 students at the institute, half are foreigners of 37 different nationalities. These French-speaking cooks find themselves in a professional environment where - as in many professions - the language is important to master in order to do the job well: the learner must quickly understand the professional instructions and must be understood as briefly to his co-workers. As a result,

This article is supported by the Fundamental Research Funds for the Central Universities (JB2021059).

due to the expansion of professional and student mobility [5], French language training oriented towards the culinary field is increasingly in demand. But non-native cook-learners will find it difficult to acquire knowledge, not only because of the novelty of the French restaurant industry, but also because of their language level which is sometimes inadequate for the situation. These integration difficulties in French catering mainly concern allophone learners at level A2 of the CEFR (Common European Framework of Reference for Languages), because the latter is the minimum level for foreigners to obtain a visa to study in France.

2   Purpose of Our Study: Expressions of Cooking Dishes

Designed for any learner who needs to acquire the language used in the profession they practice, the FOS, a methodology derived from French as a Foreign Language, analyzes the language needs of learners and responds to them with a teaching methodology appropriate to the professional world. Regarding the needs of learners in FOS, the lexicon often holds a central place. As [6] puts it, the first skill among specialists is lexical. Binon and Verlinde also underline the importance of the lexicon in the FOS and say that the vocabulary plays a key role in the teaching/learning of French for specific purposes, no one will dispute that [3]. The meaning of a lexicon should be studied in its lexical contexts, such as [28] point out, lexical combinatorics determine the meaning of a word or a lexis. Linguistic concepts are invented and used to account for lexical combinatorics, and in the context of this article, we will compare some of them. The objective of this non-exhaustive comparison is to differentiate important linguistic concepts from lexical combinatorics and to circumvent the object of our study. The "patterns" are made up of syntactic or sequential molds with a more or less restricted lexical combinatorics. They can be of the order of the phrase or the proposition (syntactic pattern), or even have an inter-propositional span (sequential pattern) [29]. These syntactic/sequential molds can be the determinant/preposition lexical combinatorics (for example, à son, à la, de la) or noun/adjective (for example, round table, red car, open door). Indeed, the "patterns" are essentially formal. [30] join this formal notion with the concept of "motif émergent". The latter also takes into account syntactic/sequential molds and syntactic categories. But the concept "motif" is defined in the work on Latin texts by [24], as well as by [25] on the functional level: its function is to bring to the study of the internal structuring of texts and its characterization within a contrasting corpus of recurring expressions [24]. The concept of "motif" seeks, so to speak, to highlight textual specificities. The concept of "routine" is defined in the projects of the academic writings of [37] and of [36] on the formal and functional levels: on the formal level, these expressions constitute recurring statements, often built around a verb; nominal or adjectival expressions are in principle not routines, although expressions of this type can be integrated into routines;... with regard to the functions of these routines, we observe that they fulfill a specific discursive and/or rhetorical function. This description notes that routines must be built around a verb, and that they perform specific discursive and/or rhetorical functions. In the culinary field, what interests us the most is the lexico-syntactic pattern (syntactic mold): noun + adjective (for example, "steak haché", "fromage râpé") and the latter has been extracted and analyzed as part of our thesis [39]. Then what catches our attention is the pattern:

verb + noun (e.g., "préchauffer le four", "émietter le thon"), and we also studied it [40]. French cuisine is renowned and the expressions of the cooking dishes are interesting to study on the functional and formal levels: on the functional level, these expressions have the function of informing and explaining the ingredients (e.g. petits pois nouveaux à l'anglaise), the cooking methods (e.g. pommes de terre entières à la vapeur) or the cooking methods (e.g. salade au chou blanc) of the dishes; formally, these expressions have the same structures: nominal group + à la/à l '/ au/aux + noun (e.g. "filet de boeuf aux truffes", "moules au vin blanc", "quiche aux poireaux", "soupe aux 7 légumes", "salade au chou blanc") or nom + de + nom (e.g. "beignets de crevettes marinées", "tartare de thon rouge", "carpaccio de boeuf", "velouté de haricots verts"), etc. In this study, we will focus on extracting expressions from cooking dishes having the first structure: nominal group + à la/à l '/ au/aux + nom. Before starting the extraction, we present our corpus to you.

3 Corpus

Our corpus called Cuisitext contains the written and oral corpus. For the part of the written corpus, we recovered, by the software Gromoteur, thousands of French recipes from French culinary sites, such as Marmiton, 750 g, Cuisine AZ, etc. In the professional context of cooks, speeches are also frequently oral. Thus, our corpus has three types of oral corpus in video format (cf. Table 1).

Table 1. Three types of oral corpora in our study

Oral corpus	Number of video	Mins/video	Year	Source
Food videos on the internet	100	5	After 2010	TV channels
Filmings in a hotel school	20	3–5	2016	Mangiante J.M. (University of Artois)
Filmings in two kitchens	20	60	2015	Ourselves

The culinary video clips were selected on the Internet, based on the three types of French dishes (entrée, main course, dessert). These clips are edited by various websites and TV channels, like *750 g*, *Marmiton*, *Cuisine rapide*, etc. The second videos were filmed in a hotel school[1]. The videos taken in two kitchens were made by us at a rate of 20 h of recording corresponding to the time of service in two restaurants in Font Romeu at the end of December 2015. Recall that our corpus was built for the teaching/learning

---

[1] These twenty short films are made within the framework of partnership agreements with the Marguerite Yourcenar hotel school in Beuvry (The town of Beuvry is located in the Pas-de-Calais department in the Nord-Pas-de-Calais-Picardie region). These videos were donated by J-M. Mangiante.

of the culinary lexicon in FOS, the CLAN tool [26] was used to help us with spelling transcription and the latter allows lexical, syntactic or interactional study. Cuisitext is currently searchable online for free on the Lexicoscope[2] platform. In order to extract the expressions of the dishes having the structure (nominal group + à la/à l '/ au/aux + nom) from our corpus, modeling is often presented as an efficient method to easily access the text. In addition, the needs of modeling then impose the choice of an appropriate software [2].

4   Lexical Modeling of Data

In our study, the modeling objective is to perform the extraction exhaustively, and it is a mold with all semantic and syntactic properties. Inspired by [35], our modeling is constructed from observations made in Cuisitext and in the dictionary: Grand Dictionnaire de cuisine [12]. In this part, the grammar modeling requirements [nominal group + à la/à l '/ au/aux + noun] will be taken into account in choosing our appropriate software. In this grammar, a nominal group (GN) could be written in multiple ways. As proposed by linguists (among others, [11]), GN grammars can be written according to three assertions presented in Fig. 1 below.

Définition du GN
= Déterminant + Adjectif ou pas + Nom + Adjectif ou pas
= GN + à/de + Nom
= que + phrase

Fig. 1. GN grammars

The definition of GN becomes our first requirement for our modeling. GN grammars should be inserted into the main grammar [nominal group + à la/à l '/ au/aux + noun] as shown in Fig. 2.

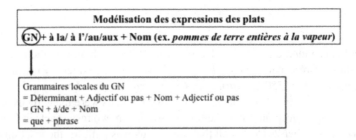

Fig. 2. Modeling of expressions of cooking dishes

---

[2] Lexicoscope, an online tool for studying combinatorial profiles and extracting lexico-syntactic constructs: http://phraseotext.univ-grenoble-alpes.fr/lexicoscope/ (accessed 08/10/2020).

In the GN grammars, we notice that there is another GN (circled in Fig. 2 above). If we try to define that GN circled in GN grammars, we will end up having a new GN. This procedure of defining GN never ends, as shown in Fig. 3, and it is therefore recursive.

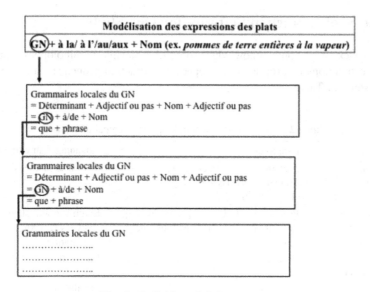

Fig. 3. Definition of GN grammars

Therefore, the GN grammars should refer to itself. In other words, the recursion of grammars is the second requirement of our modeling.

We realize that some unwanted expressions can be included in our modeling, for example, "la pâte à l'intérieur", "fumée à l'aide", "sandwich à la forme". In these examples, the words "intérieur", "aide", "forme" are neither the ingredients nor the cooking methods. In order to eliminate irrelevant expressions, we must therefore perform a lexical disambiguation, as shown in Fig. 4.

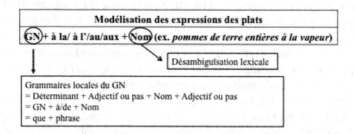

Fig. 4. Modeling and disambiguation of expressions of cooking dishes

Disambiguation is, therefore, the third requirement of our modeling. The three requirements of our lexical data modeling (definition of local grammar, grammar recursion and lexical disambiguation) will be taken into account in our choice of the appropriate extraction software.

5   Choice of Extraction Software for Our Study

Due to a lack of computer knowledge, some didacticians, terminologists, and translators use functions or programs developed for extracting sequences, and we briefly present some in Table 2.

Table 2. Programs developed for phraseological extraction

Type	Examples	Advantages in extraction
Textometry software	AntConc [1], Lexico 3 [20, 31], Trameur [14], Hyperbase [4], TXM [18], DtmVic [21]	Statistical analysis
Software dedicated to polylexical extraction	Programme de Lin [23], FipsCo [16], Programme de [17], Sketch engine [19]	Linguistic and statistical analyzes (Z-score, Mutual information)
Language formalization software	NooJ [32]	Linguistic and statistical analyzes Flexibility

In Table 2, the inventory of repeated segments of Lexico 3 or "n-gram" from Antconc makes it possible to identify the segments whose frequency is greater than or equal to 2 [31] and to constitute the starting point of interesting statistical experiments which go beyond traditional lexicometric descriptions because they take charge of the syntagmatic dimension [20]. This query could be used to locate more or less frozen sequences [13]. For example, [22] uses such a query to help learners acquire a repertoire of collocations. Some NLP specialists have realized the difficulty of phraseological extraction and devote their time to the development of software for the extraction of polylexical expressions [16, 19, 23, 34]. Note that only statistical analyzes (for example, Z-score, Mutual information) are integrated for this extraction [8–10]. It is true that this integration ensures the accuracy of the extraction result, but it still lacks linguistic analyzes, which every linguist is regularly confronted with. For example, we need morphosyntactic labeling for the extraction. Then, specialists associate linguistic processing with statistical analysis in programs developed as indicated in Table 2 above: program of Lin [23], FipsCo [16], and program of [17]. Lin's first program can analyze sentences with more than 25-word occurrences, and the second FipsCo can perform many grammatical transformations for direct subject processing, while Grefenstette and Teufel's last program can only perform some verb disambiguation. Compared to the developed programs, there is also a language formalization software that allows the extraction of the targeted expressions through the linguistic description of languages: NooJ [32]. In theory, NooJ is able to describe all languages exhaustively [33]. The Chomsky-Schützenberger hierarchy [7] is used to describe the four generative grammars: unrestricted grammar, contextual grammar, algebraic grammar, and rational grammar. At the algebraic grammar level, we can use a local grammar (colored node) to define the nominal group. In addition, the advantage of algebraic grammar enables the recursion of the grammar. Our first two requirements (definition of the local grammar and recursion of the grammar) can therefore find answers thanks to the algebraic grammar. Additionally, our third requirement (lexical disambiguation) can be satisfied using rational grammar, as shown in Fig. 5.

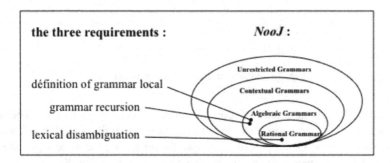

Fig. 5. The three requirements of our modeling and NooJ

Since NooJ can meet the three requirements of our lexical data modeling (local grammar definition, grammar recursion, and lexical disambiguation), we choose it as our appropriate extraction software and proceed to the next step: implementation of lexical data in NooJ.

6   Implementation of Lexical Data in NooJ

We implement the grammar [nominal group + à la/à l '/ au/aux + noun] in Fig. 6.

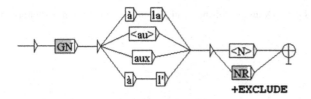

Fig. 6. Grammar implementation [nominal group + à la/à l '/ au/aux + noun]

In this automaton, names are already disambiguated using the + EXCLUDE operator. We write, under the NR tag (names rejected), names that have no direct relation to the ingredients or the cooking methods, for example, "intérieur", "extérieur", "aide", "forme", "aide". The imbricated graph of the grammar GN is shown in Fig. 7.

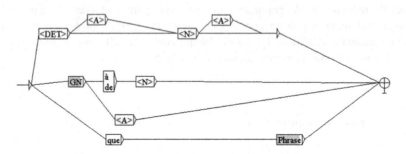

Fig. 7. Imbricated graph of the grammar GN

Recall that algebraic grammar allows a rule to be defined on its own. The imbricated graph of the grammar GN, therefore, refers to itself, and this reference is recursive because the GN is part of the graph. By respecting the same logic, the local grammar of the sentence ("Phrase") can also be defined as in Fig. 8.

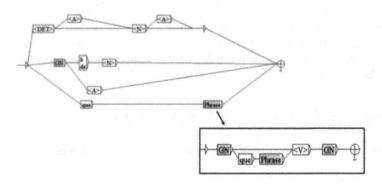

Fig. 8. Definition of the local grammar of the sentence ("Phrase")

Once we have completed the data implementation in NooJ, we can run our query, and the first result (846 sequences) we got is shown in Fig. 9.

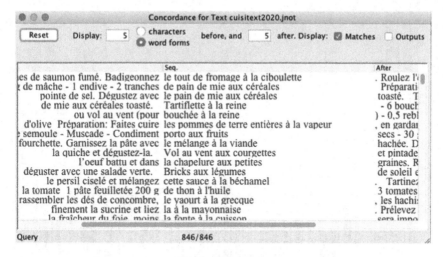

Fig. 9. First results

The identification and selection of expressions of types of [nominal group + à la/à l '/ au/aux + noun] have become our main task that follows.

7   Identification of Expressions [Nominal Group + à La/à l '/ Au/aux + nom]

High frequency is often taken into account in the selection of lexical combinations, as some researchers do [3, 10, 15]. Using NooJ, the extracted phrases can be sorted in descending order of word occurrences, as shown in Fig. 10.

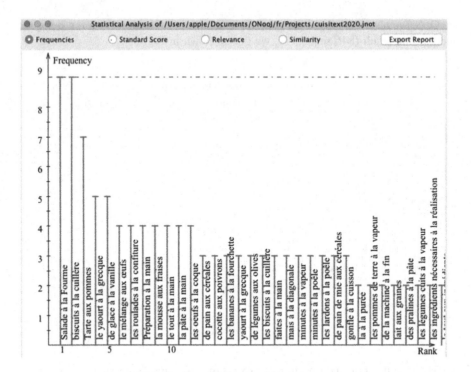

Fig. 10. Extract of extracted sequences.

As shown in Fig. 10, the most common expression in our survey is "salade à la fourme" (9 occurrences). Our selection of expressions for dishes of types of [nominal group + à la/à l '/ au/aux + nom] stops at the threshold of two occurrences, because expressions extracted at one occurrence contain irrelevant expressions, such as "du congélateur à l'instant", "quelques feuilles de laurier à la surface", "du bord opposé à la pointe", "le plat est fait à l'avance", etc. But we also check the expressions extracted from the threshold of an occurrence so as not to miss the relevant expressions, because a low frequency can hide a high relevance for the specialized domain (Binon & Verlinde, 2004), for example, in our extraction, the expressions "soupe de vermicelles au curry", "huitres gratinées au parmesan", "artichauts sauce crémeuse au citron" appears only once in our corpus, but it is part of the expressions for dishes of types of [nominal group + à la/à l '/ au/aux + nom]. Also, beware of false friends in our extraction, such as "biscuits à la cuillère" (9 occurrences), "mélange aux œufs" (4 occurrences), "préparation à la main" (4 occurrences).

8   Conclusion

By respecting the Chomsky-Schützenberger hierarchy, NooJ is able to describe all natural languages. Following with the three requirements of our lexical data modeling (definition of local grammar, grammar recursion, and lexical disambiguation), we have chosen NooJ as our extraction software, because NooJ can define local grammar using a colored node, do lexical disambiguation by applying the + EXCLUDE operator. In addition, the recursion of the grammar can be achieved with the algebraic grammar. By implementing a simple grammar, we extracted the expressions of the type dishes of [nominal group + à la/à 1 '/ au/aux + noun]. In our study, the selection of these expressions is mainly based on the frequency of extracted expressions. The expressions extracted above the threshold of two occurrences are retained, and we also check the expressions at one occurrence to not miss the relevant expressions. Finally, we managed to get 646 expressions out of a corpus of one million. Thanks to NooJ, we were able to extract some irregular expressions, such as "terrine aux courgettes et au basilic", "soupe au fenouil et à la courgette", "soupe aux carottes, topinambours et pommes de terre", "salade de champions crus à la crème", etc. After extracting these expressions from the type dishes of [nominal group + à la/à l '/ au/aux + noun], we will move on to the step of teaching/learning these extracted expressions.

References

1. Antony, L.: AntConc: design and development of a freeware corpus analysis toolkit for the technical writing classroom. In: Professional Communication Conference Proceedings, pp. 729–737 (2005)
2. Aussenac-Gilles, N., Condamines, A.: Entre textes et ontologies formelles: les Bases de Connaissances Terminologiques. In: Zacklad, M., Grundstein, M. (eds.) Ingénierie et capitalisation des connaissances, pp. 153–176. Hermès (2001)
3. Binon, J., Verlinde, S.: L'enseignement/apprentissage du vocabulaire et la lexicographie pédagogique du français sur objectifs spécifique (FOS): le domaine du français des affaires. Études de linguistique appliquée 3(135), 271–283 (2004)
4. Brunet, É.: Hyperbase, Logiciel documentaire et statistique pour la création et l'exploitation de bases hypertextuelles, Manuel de référence, Université de Nice (2006)
5. Carras, C., Tolas, J., Kohler, P., Sjilagyi, E.: Le français sur objectifs spécifiques et la classe de langue. CLE International (2007)
6. Challe, O.: Le français de spécialités. CLE International (2000)
7. Chomsky, N., Schützenberger, M.P.: The algebraic theory of context-free languages. In: Braffort, P., Hirschberg, D. (eds.) Computer Programming and Formal Systems, pp. 118–161. North-Holland, Amsterdam (1963)
8. Choueka, Y., Klein, S.T., Neuwitz, E.: Automatic retrieval of frequent idiomatic and collocational expressions in a large corpus. J. Assoc. Literary Linguist. Comput. 4, 34–38 (1983)
9. Church, K.W., Hanks, P., Hindle, D.: Using statistics in lexical analysis. In: Zernik, U. (ed.) Lexical Acquisition: Exploiting On-Line Resources to Build a Lexicon, pp. 115–164. Lawrence Erlbaum, Hillsdale (1991)
10. Curado, F.A.: Lexical behaviour in academic and technical corpora: implications for ESP development. Lang. Learn. Technol. 5(3), 106–129 (2001)
11. Dubois, J.: La nouvelle grammaire du français, Larousse (1973)
12. Dumas, A.: Le grand dictionnaire de Cuisine, Couverture reliée, Jaquette illustrée couleur, gravures et planches noir et blanc, préface: Daniel Zimmermann. Phébus (2000)
13. Fiala, P., Habert, B., Lafon, P., Pineira, C.: Des mots aux syntagmes, figements et variations dans la Résolution générale du congrès de la CGT de 1978. Mots 14, 45–87 (1987)

14. Fleury, S.: Le Métier Textométrique: Le Trameur, Manuel d'utilisation (2007). http://tal. univ-paris3.fr/trameur/
15. Gledhill, C.: Collocations in Science Writing. Gunter Narr Verlag, Tübingen (2000)
16. Goldman, J.P., Nerima, L., Wehrli, E.: Collocation extraction using a syntactic parser. In: Proceedings of the ACL 2001 Workshop on Collocation, pp. 61–66 (2001)
17. Grefenstette, G., Teufel, S.: Corpus-based method for automatic identification of support verbs for nominalizations. In: Proceedings of the Seventh Conference of the European Chapter of the Association for Computational Linguistics, pp. 98–103 (1995)
18. Heiden, S., Magué, J.P., Pincemin, B.: TXM: une plateforme logicielle open-source pour la textométrie – conception et développement. In: JADT 2010, vol. 2, pp. 1021–1032. Edizioni Universitarie di Lettere Economia, Roma (2010)
19. Kilgarriff, A., Tugwell, D.: WORD SKETCH: extraction, combination and display of significant collocations for lexicography. In: Proceedings of the Workshop on Collocations: Computational Extraction, Analysis and Exploitation, ACL-EACL 2001, pp. 32–38 (2001)
20. Lafon, P., Salem, A.: L'inventaire des segments répétés d'un texte. Mots **6**(1), 161–177 (1983). https://www.persee.fr/doc/mots_0243-6450_1983_num_6_1_1101
21. Lebart, L.: DtmVic: data and text mining - visualization, inference, classification. Exploratory statistical processing of complex data sets comprising both numerical and textual data (2015). http://www.dtmvic.com/
22. Lewis, M.: There is nothing as practical as a good theory. In: Lewis, M. (eds.) Teaching Collocation: Further Developments in the Lexical Approach, Language Teaching Publications, pp. 10–27 (2000)
23. Lin, D.: Extracting collocations from text corpora. In: First Workshop on Computational Terminology, Montréal, pp. 57–63 (1998)
24. Longrée, D., Luong, X., Mellet, S.: Les motifs: un outil pour la caractérisation topologique des textes. In: Heiden, S., Pincemin, B., Vosghanian, L., l'équipe Lexicometrica (eds.) Actes des 9ème Journées internationales d'analyse statistique des données textuelles – JADT 2008, pp. 733–744 (2008)
25. Longrée, D., Mellet, S.: Le motif: une unité phraséologique englobante? Étendre le champ de la phraséologie de la langue au discours. Langages **189**, 68–80 (2013)
26. Macwhinney, B.: The CHILDES Project: Tools for Analyzing Talk. Mahwah, Lawrence Erlbaum Associates, New Jersey (2000)
27. Mangiante, J.M., Parpette, C.: Le français sur objectif spécifique: de l'analyse de besoins à l'élaboration d'un cours. Hachette (2004)
28. Mel'čuk, I., Arbatchewsky-Jumarie, N., Iordanskaja, L., Mantha, S., Polguère, A.: Dictionnaire explicatif et combinatoire du français contemporain: recherches lexico-sémantiques IV. Les Presses de l'Université de Montréal (1999)
29. Née, É., Sitri, F., Veniard, M.: Les routines, une catégorie pour l'analyse de discours: le cas des rapports éducatifs. Lidil **53**, 71–93 (2016)
30. Quiniou, S., Cellier, P., Charnois, T., Legallois, D.: What about sequential data mining techniques to identify linguistic patterns for stylistics? In: Gelbukh, A. (ed.) CICLing 2012. LNCS, vol. 7181, pp. 166–177. Springer, Heidelberg (2012). https://doi.org/10.1007/978-3-642-28604-9_14
31. Salem, A.: Pratique des segments répétés: Essai de statistique textuelle. Klincksieck, Paris (1987)
32. Silberztein, M.: NooJ: an oriented object approach. In: Royauté, J., Silberztein, M. (eds.) INTEX pour la Linguistique et le Traitement Automatique des Langues. Presses universitaires de Franche-Comté, Besançon (2002)
33. Silberztein, M.: Formalizing Natural Languages: The NooJ Approach. Wiley (2016)

34. Smadja, F.: Retrieving collocations form text: Xtract. Comput. Linguist. **19**(1), 143–177 (1993)

35. Tutin, A.: Pour une modélisation dynamique des collocations dans les textes. In: Actes d'Euralex, Lorient, pp. 207–221 (2004)

36. Tutin, A., Kraif, O.: Routines sémantico-rhétoriques dans l'écrit scientifique de sciences humaines: l'apport des arbres lexico-syntaxiques récurrents. Lidil **53**, 119–141 (2016)

37. Tutin, A.: La phraséologie transdisciplinaire des écrits scientifiques: des collocations aux routines sémantico-rhétoriques. In: Tutin, A., Grossmann, F. (eds.) L'écrit scientifique: du lexique au discours. Autour de Scientext, pp. 27–44. Presses universitaires de Rennes (2013)

38. Wilson, A.: Les Tables du Monde: Recettes et Ingrédients de A à Z. Könemann, Cologne (1977)

39. Yang, T.: Constitution et exploitation d'une base de données pour l'enseignement/apprentissage des phrasèmes NAdj du domaine culinaire auprès d'apprenants non-natifs. Thèse de doctorat. Université Sorbonne Nouvelle – Paris 3 (2019)

40. Yang, T.: Automatic extraction of verbal phrasemes in the culinary field with NooJ. In: Mauro Mirto, I., Monteleone, M., Silberztein, M. (eds.) NooJ 2018. CCIS, vol. 987, pp. 83–94. Springer, Cham (2019). https://doi.org/10.1007/978-3-030-10868-7_8

Natural Language Processing Applications

Paraphrasing Tool Using the NooJ Platform

Amine Alassir[1]([📧]), Sondes Dardour[2], and Héla Fehri[2]

[1] University of Gabes, Gabes, Tunisia
[2] MIRACL Laboratory, University of Sfax, Sfax, Tunisia

Abstract. The dissemination of scientific research is gaining momentum and provides an opportunity for novice and established researchers to contribute to their field. Therefore, there is a particularly great and growing demand for paraphrasing tools, which can effectively and efficiently aid researchers in rewriting sentences to avoid plagiarism. Moreover, paraphrasing is useful in several NLP applications such as question-answering, summarization or machine translation. The aim of paraphrasing is to generate different expressions with the same meaning. Over the past decades, several paraphrase tools have appeared. Nevertheless, these tools give unsatisfied results. For example, the generated sentence maybe does not jibe well the specificities of the given language such as the sentence structure. Nowadays, this issue can be achieved with the advent of new NLP tools. The aim of this paper is to propose a method to paraphrase sentences in French. Our proposal is based on transducers and dictionaries. It consists in replacing some words of the sentence by synonyms or antonyms with negation, or in switching to the passive form. In addition, we have divided these words into two parts – one part related to words starting with a vowel and another part for words that do not start with a vowel – in order to eliminate the ambiguity of the apostrophe form case. The linguistic resources are implemented using the NooJ platform. Experimentations of our paraphrasing tool show interesting results.

Keywords: Paraphrasing · Natural Language Processing · NooJ

1 Introduction

The evolution of language gives rise to a wide range of linguistic phenomena and characteristics which have been the subject of a wide variety of studies. Among these characteristics, we cite the fact that the same idea can be expressed in several forms. The variety of forms of expression reflects the richness of the vocabulary of languages and defines a linguistic phenomenon considered to be a major challenge in the field of Natural Language Processing (NLP). Speakers of a language use paraphrases to express the same idea in different formulations using a few methods (e.g., synonymy, antonymity, repetition, and translation). Many students find it difficult to paraphrase either in changing structure and grammar or in changing a word.

In this article, we propose a method based on the analysis of data in French and going as far as reformulating these data by applying the chosen methods.

The remainder of this paper is organized as follows: we begin by giving a brief overview of the state of the art. After that, we describe the strategy used and the process

© Springer Nature Switzerland AG 2021
M. Bigey et al. (Eds.): NooJ 2021, CCIS 1520, pp. 163–173, 2021.
https://doi.org/10.1007/978-3-030-92861-2_14

followed to paraphrase French language text. Then, we present the experiment and the evaluation results obtained with a test corpus. Finally, we will conclude with some perspectives.

2 Related Works

According to our study, we can classify the existing work on three approaches: The first is the linguistic or rule-based approach is based on human vision, with the manual construction of analysis models, most often in the form of contextual rules. These rules take the form of extractions structures that allow you to describe the sequence of certain sentences. These structures generally use components of standard sentences in French (such as; Noun, Verb, Adjective…). These components exist in resources (lexicons or dictionaries). From the research on using this approach, we mention the work of (Milicevic 2007) who considers that modeling a speaker's paraphrastic capacity amounts to proposing linguistic rules that describe the paraphrastic links between expressions. Also, we can cite the work elaborated by (Barzilay 2003) who defined paraphrase according to two aspects: atomic paraphrase and composite paraphrase.

The second approach is the statistical or learning-based approach is the extraction of analysis rules from large volumes of data (or corpus). These can take different forms such as decision trees, sets of logical rules or even probabilistic models. From the research on using this approach, we mention the work of (Martin 1976) that highlighted the difficulties in formulating a definition of paraphrase and subsequently presented a definition of paraphrase as an equivalence relation. The notion of logical equivalence refers to three classic properties in mathematics: symmetry, transitivity and reflexivity. In this context, (Levrat 1995) confirmed the limitations of Martin's claim. Indeed, if symmetry is often admitted, it is not easy to consider the paraphrase as content of the initial sentence. In addition, the succession of paraphrases induces semantic deformations, which causes the transitivity of the sentences to be lost. Finally, a sentence is rarely considered to be a paraphrase of it (so no reflexivity).

The third approach is the hybrid approach that based on a rigorous linguistic study to find linguistic filters that allow a first collection of sensitive sequences. On these selected sequences, we apply various statistical models (depending on the data). From the research on using this approach, we mention the work of (Bhagat 2009) who asserts that while some paraphrases are not logically equivalent, they should be considered paraphrases or quasi-paraphrases.

3 Proposed Method

As shown in Fig. 1, the proposed method for paraphrasing is composed of four main steps: The segmentation based on the separator ".". The list of segmented sentences then allows us to extract the rules defining the different structures of the sentences to be paraphrased; which represents the second step. The third step is the resources identification that involves identifying the dictionaries and grammars needed for paraphrasing. The last step is based on applying the chosen methods on the segmented sentences to have new sentences well reformulated and coherent.

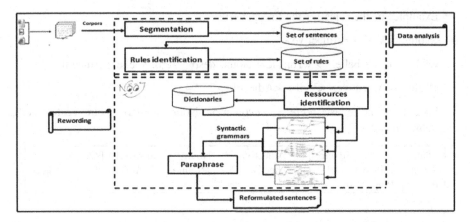

Fig. 1. The proposed method

3.1 The Segmentation

In our study, we built a study corpus containing easy texts in French available on the Internet to learn the French language and from the specialized site[1] to teach the French language to the student and enrich their knowledge. Thus, the study corpus contains 5 texts and 1200 words which cover 400 nouns, 330 adjectives and 300 verbs. The content of our corpus is segmented to obtain a list of simple sentences for paraphrasing. This segmentation is based on the separator "." The list of segmented sentences then allows us to extract the rules defining the different structures of the sentences to be paraphrased.

3.2 Rules Identification

A sentence is composed of a set of words placed in a logical order in order to have a meaning and to express an action or a state. Within a sentence, the coherent set of words that alone have meaning is called a clause. A sentence can therefore include one or more clauses. Each proposition is made up of several elements: a subject, a verb expressing an action or a state and a complement. The rules describe the sequence of the components of the sentences to be paraphrased. These components can be adjectives, nouns or verbs. In our work, we have identified a set of simple patterns. From each pattern, several rules can be derived. We can cite a few examples:

---

[1] www.dixmois.eklablog.com.

<Pattern 1> := [<Adverb>]* [<Adjective>]* <Noun> [<Adverb>]* <Verb> [<Adverb>]* [<Adjective>]*[<Preposition> <Noun>]*

Examples of the rules for the first pattern:

- <Noun> <Verb> <Adjective>

La Tunisie est belle. ⇒ «Tunisie»: Noun, «est»: Verb, «belle»: Adjectif

- <Noun> <Adjective> <Verb> <Adjective>

La couleur noire est morte. ⇒ «couleur»: Noun, «noire»: noire «est»: Verb, «morte»: Adjective

<Pattern 2>:= [<Adverb>]* [<Adjective>]* <Noun> [<Adverb>]* [<Adjective>]* <Verb> [<Adverb>]* [<Adjective>]* <Noun> [<Adverb>]* [<Adjective>]*[<Preposition> <Noun>]*

Examples of the rules for the second pattern:

- <Noun> <Verb> <Noun>

Les étrangers adorent la Tunisie.⇒ «étrangers»: Noun, «adorent»: Verb, «Tunisie»: Noun

- <Noun> <Verb> <Noun> <Adjective>

La Tunisie est une ville touristique.⇒ «Tunisie»: Noun, «est»: Verb, «ville»: Noun, «touristique»: Adjective.

3.3   Ressources Identification

Resource identification involves identifying the dictionaries and grammars needed for paraphrasing.

Identification of Dictionaries. As a dictionary, we used that of Jean Dubois and Françoise Dubois-Charlier "_dm". This is an open-source dictionary that contains all the entries we need. Each entry is described as follows: a lemma (considered as a basic form), a label (which will indicate the grammatical category to which it belongs), a possible list of alphanumeric codes (designating the inflectional and derivational models to be applied to it), and an optional list of syntactic-semantic information. To these entries we have added other information necessary for the application of the proposed methods for paraphrasing. This information is collected through a website specializing in the learning and understanding of the French language for basic education students[2]. Thus, each entry contains this additional information: A synonymy model given by the technical word "SYN" to represent all synonyms of the entry (ex., #abecquer, V+a+FLX=AIMER +vSYN=affriander+vSYN=embecquer+SYN=nourrir). An antonymy model given by

---

[2] http://dixmois.eklablog.com.

the technical word "ANT" to represent all the antonyms of the entry (ex., abêtir, V+a+FLX=FINIR+vSYN=abrutir+SYN=diminuer+vSYN=abasourdir+vANT=éveiller +ANT=dérouiller+ANT=réveiller). Note that we have tried to eliminate the ambiguity of attaching a negation to a verb by using the apostrophed negation (ex., Il ne aime pas jouer ⇒ il n'aime pas jouer).

Identification of Syntactic Grammars. The rules identified helped identify useful methods for paraphrasing sentences from our corpus. Indeed, the sentences will be reformulated in a different way and these using three methods. In what follows, we detail these methods with the grammars corresponding to each.

Method 1: Synonymy. The first method is to use synonymy to paraphrase a sentence. Synonymy is a semantic relation between words of the same language. The semantic similarity between these two words indicates significant equivalence. Terms related by synonymy are synonyms. These terms can be adjectives, nouns or verbs.

The Fig. 2 shows the different rules for paraphrasing sentences based on synonyms of an adjective.

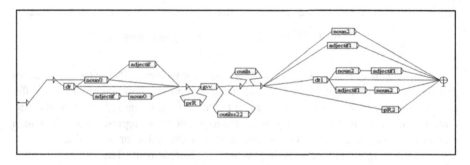

Fig. 2. Transducer of the synonymy of an adjective

The purpose of applying the transducer in Fig. 2 is to recognize the sentence given as input, then to modify the adjectives by their synonyms. The subgraphs "noun0" and "noun2" represent the nominal groups. The sub-graphs "gvv" subgraph represents a G. V. The subgraph "dt1" represents the set of determinants. The subgraph "adjectif1" contains at least one adjective and optional word such as adverbs and determinants… The subgraphs "outils", "outils22" define the use of conjunctions, prepositions, etc.

Figure 3 represents the transformation of an example sentence using the synonymy of adjectives.

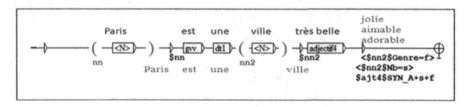

Fig. 3. A path of the transducer of the synonymy of adjectives

As shown in Fig. 3, the sentence (Paris est une ville très belle) follows the rule: Nom+verbe+nom+adverbe+adjectif. This rule is derived from <Pattern 2>.

The annotation/<$nn2$Genre=f><$nn2$Nb=s>$ajt4$SYN_A+s+f displays the synonyms ("jolie", "aimable" and "adorable") of the adjective "belle".

The Fig. 4 shows the different rules for paraphrasing sentences based on synonyms of a noun.

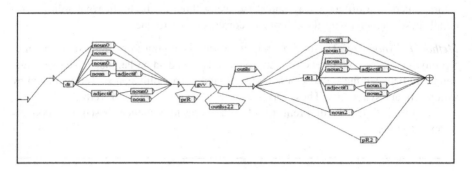

Fig. 4. Transducer of the synonymy of a noun

Each transducer path in Fig. 4 explains a rule for patterns <Patron1> and <Pattern 2>. The subgraphs "noun0", "noun1" and "noun2" represent nominal groups that differ from one example to another. The subgraphs "noun1" and "noun2" contain the permutation of names by their synonyms. The sub-graph "gvv" represents a G.V. which contains a word, or group of words, that indicates the action or state. The G.V. can consist of a single verb or a verb plus a verb complement. The sub-graph "dt1" represents the set of determinants. The sub-graph "adjectif1" contains at least one adjective and optional word such as adverbs and determinants... The sub-graphs "outils" and "outils22" define the use of conjunctions, prepositions, etc.

The Fig. 5 shows the different rules for paraphrasing sentences based on synonyms of verbs.

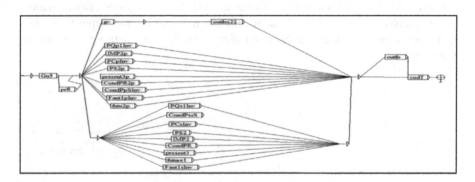

Fig. 5. Transducer of verb synonymy

The transducer depicted in Fig. 5 contains 24 sub-graphs. The "Gn5" sub-graph allows us to recognize some forms of nominal groups. "PrR" represents the relative pronouns which can follow the nominal group. Since our transducer aims to process the synonyms of the verb, these synonyms must respect the same tense of the verb given as input with or without the negation. For this, we have taken into account some tenses such as the present, the simple past, the compound past, the simple future, the future prior, the imperfect, the more than perfect, the present conditional and the past conditional. The two sub-graphs "gv" and "outils22" deal with verbal groups, that is, a verb followed by another verb in the infinitive. The "outils" sub-graph describes the tools for the connections between the G.V and the complement represented by the "codT" sub-graph which can be simple or compound. However the method of synonymy can meet the difficulty of a set of synonyms. This multitude can influence the meaning of the initial sentence. Since we don't deal with semantics in our work, we give the user the choice of the most appropriate synonym.

Method 2: Anonymy. The second method is to use antonymity to paraphrase a sentence. Two words are in an anonymous relationship if there is semantic symmetry between the two terms. Words in an anonymous relationship are called antonyms or opposites. These words can be adjectives or verbs in this part. In order to succeed with the antonymity method for paraphrasing, we have used negation to keep the meaning of the sentence the same. Note that there are rules to follow for negation. Among these rules, we cite the following:

- With a conjugated verb: in a single tense, the negation frames the verb (ex, Je ne crois pas qu'il va arriver). At a compound beat, the negation frames the auxiliary (ex: Je n'ai pas voulu en arriver là). Note that the negation always precedes the personal pronouns which are placed before the verb (ex: Je ne lui dis pas), in addition the two elements of negation are always separate (ex, Il m'a expliqué le cours pour que je ne m'échoue pas).
- With a verb in the infinitive: ne and not are glued and placed in front of the verb in the infinitive (Il a décidé de ne pas me donner la correction de l'exercice).
- The negation can be marked by various expressions (Ne…pas, ne…plus, ne… jamais, ne…rien, ne…guère, ne…ni…ni, etc.). I no longer watch advertisements ⇒ The transformation to the antonym requires the use of these phrases according to a semantic trait whose adverb must be transformed into its antonym (ex, Je regarde encore les publicités ⇒ Je ne regarde plus les publicités).

In the second method, we get a total of 2 graphs to paraphrase the sentences based on the use of antonyms (verbs and adjectives). Each graph deals with the "pattern 1" and "pattern 2" patterns. Note that we have not dealt with the antonyms of the nouns since the use of the latter will change the semantics of the sentence.

The Fig. 6 shows the different rules for paraphrasing sentences based on antonyms of adjectives.

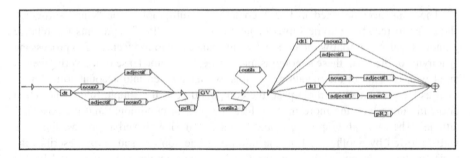

Fig. 6. Transducer of the antonym of an adjective

The transducer of the Fig. 6 is used to recognize the sentence given as input and to modify its adjectives by the appropriate antonyms. The sub-graphs of this transducer are the same sub-graph as the synonymy of adjectives transducer.

The Fig. 7 shows the different rules for paraphrasing sentences based on verb antonyms.

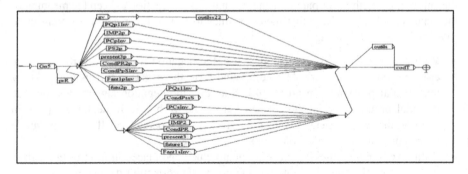

Fig. 7. Transducer of the antonym of a verb

The "Gn5" sub-graph allows us to recognize some forms of nominal groups. The sub-graph "prR" represents the relative pronouns which can follow the nominal group. Since our transducer aims to process the antonyms of the verb, these antonyms must respect the same tense of the verb given in input with or without the negation. For this, we took into account the same tenses cited at the level of verb synonymy. As we have already mentioned at the level of verb synonymy, the two sub-graphs "gv" and "outils22" deal with verbal groups, that is to say a verb followed by another verb in the infinitive. The "outils" sub-graph contains the tools of the links between the G.V and the complement described by the "codT" sub-graph which can be simple or composite.

The same remark of the synonymy method is presented in the antonymity; the context of the sentence is a constraint to choose the best antonym. We therefore give the choice to the user.

Method 3: The Change of Active/Passive Voice. This method consists in describing the passage from the active voice to the passive voice. It is enough just to substitute the subject by the complement and the complement by the subject if this is possible with the transformation of the verb. The active voice presents the subject as the agent of the action. By reversal, the passive voice presents the subject as an agent undergoing the action.

In addition, passive transformation is only possible with verbs which accept a direct object complement (transitive verbs). It cannot be used in the passive voice when: The verb of the sentence does not admit an object complement. It is an intransitive verb (tomber, courir, rire, nager…). Moreover, the verb of the sentence must be constructed with an indirect object complement (parler de, penser à, croire en…).

Besides, the passive transformation of a sentence that has a personal pronoun as the active subject does not provide a complement for the passive voice. Finally, the verb in the passive voice consists of two parts: The auxiliary being (which is conjugated according to the mode, the time, the person and the number) and the past participle of the verb, which indicates action.

The Fig. 8 shows the different rules for paraphrasing sentences based on the transformation from active voice to passive voice.

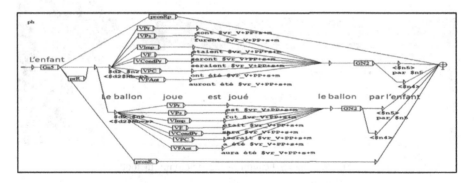

Fig. 8. The transformation to the passive voice

As shown in Fig. 8, the sentence (l'enfant joue le ballon) follows the rule: Nom +verbe+nom. On the one hand, the annotation/<$n5> par $n5 or/<$n4> will transform the subject into a complement. On the other hand, the annotation/d2 $n2 <$d2$Nb=s> will transform the complement into an active subject.

3.4   The Paraphrase Step

In this step, we have applied all the possible combinations between the methods used to have well reformulated and coherent sentences of which the worst case is to go through at least one method among those identified at the level of the syntactic grammars. The best case is to go through all the methods: synonymy, antonymy and passive trans-formation. So we have seven possible combinations; the first case is to apply only synonymy. The second case is to apply only the antonymity. The third case is to apply only the passive transformation. The fourth case is to apply the antonymity to the result of the synonymy (or vice versa). The fifth case is to apply the passive transformation on the result of the synonymy (or vice versa). The sixth case is to apply the passive transformation to the result of the antonymity (or vice versa). The 7th case is to apply the three reformulation methods at the same time.

4 Experimentation and Evaluation

The experimentation of the tool of the paraphrase is carried out in a Java application, using noojapply, syntactic grammars and specialized dictionary that has already been designed and edited with the NooJ platform (Silberztein 2018).

The Fig. 9 shows a view of our Java interface, the input of which is an extract of the text, the output represents a reformulation of the text given as input.

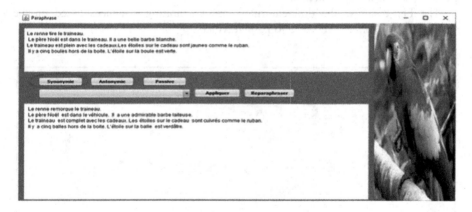

Fig. 9. The application of the synonymy method

As shown in the Fig. 9, paraphrase is done by importing or entering a sentence or a set of sentences. The test corpus contains 50 different rule phrases. In addition all the methods used can be combined to have coherent and well reformulated sentences.

The results of paraphrasing these sentences are interpreted by the following metric calculations: precision, recall, and F-measure. The following table illustrates the calculations of the metrics obtained (Table 1).

Table 1. Summarizing the measure values

	Results
Number of sentences	571
Precision	86%
Recall	65%
F-measure	74%

The values of the measures in the table above show the existence of some unresolved issues. Some are due to the absence of a few synonyms and a few antonyms in the built dictionaries. Others are related to the variety of sentence rules that can be found in the corpus. These rules are not taken into account in our syntactic grammars. So we sometimes have to add other paths and other subgraphs to the already constructed graphs. However, we are not led to rebuild all grammars from the start, this causes silence.

Note also that other problems are linked to the complexity of the French language. For example, we can find in a text a word which belongs to two different grammatical categories such as the word "small", which can be a noun or an adjective. It will then be described twice at the dictionary level with the synonyms and antonyms relating to each category. The surprisingly low percentage of recall is explained by the diversity of synonyms and antonyms.

5 Conclusion

We have developed a system for recognizing and paraphrasing sentences in French. This system is based on a set of rules extracted from a study carried out on the set of sentences in the corpus. This system is based on three methods of paraphrasing: synonymy, antonymity and the transformation from active voice to passive voice. Each method admits syntactic grammars necessary for the transformation phase.

References

Milicevic, J.: La Paraphrase. In Modélisation de la Paraphrase Langagière. Open J .Mod. Linguist. 4, (Cited pages 9, 15) (2007)

Barzilay, R.: Information Fusion for multidocument summarization: praphrasing and generation. Ph.D. thesis, Columbia University (2003)

Martin, R.: Inférence, antonymie et paraphrase : éléments pour une théorie sémantique. Inférence, antonymie et paraphrase, (Cited pages 9, 12, 14, 18, 21, 22, 23), (Klincksieck, Éd.) Paris (1976)

Levrat, B.: Paraphrase et reformulation: une présentation. In Rapport technique, Université Paris-Nord (1995)

Bhagat, R.: Learning paraphrases from text. University of Southern California. (Cited page 16) (2009)

Silberztein, M.: Using linguistic resources to evaluate the quality of annotated corpora. In: Proceedings of the First Workshop on Linguistic Resources for Natural Language Processing, pp. 2–11 (2018)

The Recognition and the Automatic Translation of Dative Verbs

Hajer Cheikhrouhou$^{(\boxtimes)}$

University of Sfax, LLTA, Sfax, Tunisia
hajer.cheihkrouhou@flshs.usf.tn

Abstract. This paper aims at studying French dative verbs extracted from Jean Dubois and Françoise Dubois Charlier's LVF dictionary. In this database, dative verbs are classified according to three semantic-syntactic categories (D1, D2, D3) and fifteen syntactic subcategories (D1a, D2b, D3a…). In this study, we seek an automatic recognition of dative verbs and also a French-Arabic automatic translation using the NooJ platform. The automatic recognition phase is problematic because the majority of dative verbs are used in different contexts and placed in different syntactic-semantic constructions.

Keywords: Dative verbs · LVF · Verbal polysemy · Automatic recognition and translation · NooJ

1 Introduction

Beth Levin defines the dative verbs as such: In some languages, including English, verbs such as give, send, and throw, which can be used to describe events of transfer, show two options for expressing their arguments, jointly referred to as the dative alternation, illustrated in (1)

(1) a. Terry gave Sam an apple.
b. Terry gave an apple to Sam.[1]

In this respect, this paper attempts to study French dative verbs extracted from Jean Dubois and Françoise Dubois Charlier's LVF dictionary [1].

In this database, dative verbs are classified according to three semantic-syntactic categories (D1, D2, D3) and fifteen syntactic subcategories (D1a, D2b, D3a…). This semantic-syntactic classification is put according to the oppositions "Animate/ Inanimate" and "Literal/Figurative", and also according to their syntactic and lexical paradigm. We have added another classification, based on their syntactic structures (T1100, N9a, T1308 P3000, P10a0…).

In this study of dative verbs, we sought an automatic recognition of verbs and also a French-Arabic automatic translation using the NooJ platform.

The automatic recognition phase is problematic because the majority of verbs are used in different contexts and placed in different syntactic-semantic constructions.

---

[1] Beth Levin, Dative verbs: Across linguistic perspective, in https://web.stanford.edu/ ~ bclevin/pal08. pdf.

© Springer Nature Switzerland AG 2021
M. Bigey et al. (Eds.): NooJ 2021, CCIS 1520, pp. 174–186, 2021.
https://doi.org/10.1007/978-3-030-92861-2_15

In our analysis of dative verbs, we found different polysemic predicates where one predicate can have two, four, five polysemic meanings. We encountered many problems in the recognition and automatic translation of these verbal entries. Examples include: donner (give: 16 uses); fournir (provide: 7 uses), livrer (deliver: 6 uses) ...

Our objective is related to the field of applied linguistics; we basically seek:

- The production of a system to recognize the syntactic patterns of dative verbs [2].
- Linguistic solutions for the disambiguation of verbal polysemy.
- An adequate and reliable French - Arabic automatic translation for dative verbs using the NooJ platform.

2   Creation of a Bilingual French-Arabic Dictionary

According to Dubois' verbs classification, the generic class of the dative verbs contains nine hundred fifty-three verbal entries which are divided into three semantic categories:

- D1: the semantic operator is: «Donner qn à qc/qn» (to give something to someone/to give someone to someone), «donner aide à qn» (to give help to someone).
- D2: the semantic operator is: «Donner qc à qn» (to give something to someone), «obtain something to someone/to something»
- D3: the semantic operator is: «Figurative of D2» (Table 1 and Figs. 1, 2).

Table 1. Generic Class D.

Generic Class D (953 entries)			
D1	«Donner qn à qc/qn» «donner aide à qn» (to give help to s.o)	4 subclasses (D1a → D1d)	Donner 01 (to give)
D2	«Donner qc à qn» (to give s.th to s.o) «obtenir qc de qn/qc» (obtain s.th from s.o)	5 subclasses(D2a → D2e)	Vendre 01 (to sell)
D3	«Figurative of D2»	6 subclasses(D3a → D3f)	Fournir 08 (to provide)

C1			fx	CLASSE						
A	B	C	D	E	F	G	H	I	J	K
M	DOM	CLASSE	OPER	SENS	PHRASE	C	CONST	DER	N	L
abandonner 0	DRO	D2a	dat qc A qn	laisser,léguer	On a~ses biens à ses enfants,à une fondation.	1aZ	T13a0	----D --RB--	3*	1
abandonner 0	MAR	D3a	dat mvt A qc	laisser aller	On a~sa barque à un fort courant.	1aZ	T13a8 P30a8	----D----	3*	5
abloquer 02	COMp	D2a	dat qc A qn ct arg	vendre(abloquir)	On a~à P une fringue défraîchie.	1aZ	T13a0	--- -- ----	.	6
abloquir	COMp	D2a	dat qc A qn ct arg	vendre(abloquer)	On a~à P une fringue défraîchie.	2aZ	T13a0	--- --RA--	.	6
abouler 01	MON	D2a	dat arg A qn	casquer,verser	On a~du fric à P.	1aZ	T13aq	-- -- ----	.	5
accenser 01	DRO	D2a	dat A qn c cens	louer	Le seigneur a~un domaine à un fermier.	1aZ	T13a6	----1------	-l	5
accepter 01	SOC	D2e	abda qc D p don	recevoir de	On a~un cadeau d'un ami.	1bZ	T13b0	2-1-- RBRA--	.	1
accepter 05	DRO	D3c	dat.val à loi	ratifier,approuver	On a~une loi.Ce projet ne peut s'a~dans cet état.	1bZ	T1300	2---- RB---	.	5
accolader 02	MIL	D1d	dat accolade à qn	donner l'accolade	Le ministre a~P lors de la remise de la décoration.	1aZ	T1100	--- -- ----	1*	5
accorder 03	DRO	D2a	dat qc A qn	octroyer	On a~un congé à P.On s'a~un jour de repos.Le congé est a~.	1aZ	T13a0 P30a0	21-- ------	2*	5
accorder 04	SOC	D3b	dat abs A qc	donner	On a~de l'importance à ce projet.	1aZ	T13a0	--- -- ----	.	5
accorder 07	PSY	D3b	dat abs A qn	prêter	On a~sa confiance,son attention à P,à ce qu'il dit.	1aZ	T13a0	--- -- ----	.	5
accoter 03	BAT	D2b	dat appui av accots	soutenir avec accot	Les ouvriers a~une façade avec des étais.	1aZ	T1308 P3008	----1-----	2*	5
acenser 01	DRO	D2a	dat A qn c cens	accenser	Le seigneur a~une terre à un fermier.	1aZ	T13a6	----1-----	-l	7
acenser 02	DRO	D2c	abda qc A qn loué	louer	Le fermier a~une terre au seigneur.Cette terre peut s'a~.	1aZ	T13a6 P3006	----1-----	.	5
acheter 01	COM	D2c	abda qc A qn pr soi	payer	On a~cher des fruits à un marchand.On s'a~une voiture.	1jZ	T13a6 P3006	2-- -D--RA--	4X	1
acheter 02	ECN	D2c	abda qc A qn cadeau	payer à	On a~un cadeau au bijoutier pour sa femme.	1jZ	T13a6 P3006	----D-----	4X	5
acheter 04	SOC	D3e	abda pr soi abs arg	payer	On a~cher sa liberté.Le bonheur s'a~à ce prix.	1jZ	T1308 P3000	----D-----	4X	5
acliquer (s)	SOCp	D1b	dat soi A qn	se maquer	La prostituée s'a~à un souteneur.	1aZ	P10a0	--- -- -----	.	6
acquérir 01	DRO	D2e	abda qc D p achat	acheter à	On a~cette maison d'un riche propriétaire.	3jZ	T13b0	---- 2NRA--	.	2
acquérir 02	ENS	D3e	abda pr soi abs arg	obtenir	On a~des connaissances par le travail.La souplesse s'a~.	3jZ	T1308 P3000	-1-- 2N---	.	5
acquérir 03	PSY	D3e	abda pr soi abs	réussir à obtenir	On a~la preuve de son innocence.Ce point est a~.	3jZ	T1308 P3000	-1-- ------	.	5

Fig. 1. Sample of dative verbs.

Fig. 2. The verbal entry "accorder04" (to accord).

For example, the verb accorder (04)/(to accord) belongs to the subclass D3b "Donner qc abstraite à qc" (give something or someone special attention) and it is classified in the syntactic structure T13a0, which means that the verb is transitive when the subject is human, its direct complement is an object, and its indirect complement is an object too.

In this step, we integrated the dative verbs in a bilingual French-Arabic dictionary. This dictionary contains 954 verbal entries (Fig. 3).

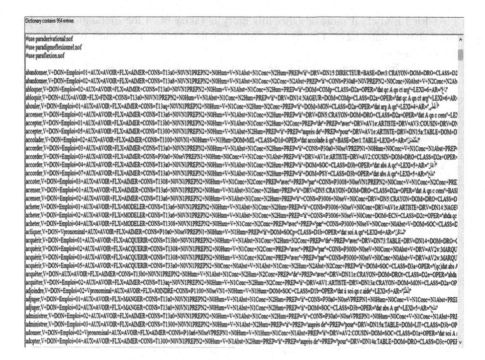

Fig. 3. Extract from the «verbes de don et de privation.dic» dictionary.

We have mentioned that we re-wrote verbal entries with the operators of NooJ. For example, the lexical entry "offrir 01" (to present) is described as follows:

offrir, V+DON+Emploi=01+AUX=AVOIR+FLX=COUVRIR+CONS= T13a0+ N0VN1PREPN2+N0Hum+V+N1Abst+N1Conc+N2Hum+PREP="à"+DRV= AV3: COUSIN+DOM=SOC+CLASS= D2a+OPER="datqcAqnecadeau"+BASE= Dev12: TABLE+LEXI=1+AR="أهْدَى" (to present).

For example, this entry describes the verb «*offrir*» (to offer) and denotes that the verb is a dative verb «V+DON» whose employment is 01. This verb is conjugated with the auxiliary «AVOIR» and follows the inflectional paradigm «COUVRIR». It has the syntactic construction [T13a0] which indicates that the verb is transitive, when the subject is human, its direct complement is an object, its indirect complement is a human and it is introduced by the preposition "à" (to).

Concerning the derivation, the verb "offrir" is associated with the derivational paradigm "AV3" to form the adjective «*offert*» inflected as the paradigm «COUSIN» [3]. This verb belongs to the domain SOC which means «*sociologie*». Offrir (01) belongs to the class D2, subclass D2a "Donner qc à qn ou à qc" [give something to someone or something]. The operator is «dat qc A qn e cadeau» that is to say give someone a gift. To obtain the derivative noun (déverbal), we use the derivational paradigm "Dev12" which will derive «*offre*», which inflects as the paradigm «TABLE» [4].

As for LEXI=1, it indicates that this entry is taken from the *dictionnaire fonda-mental* (basic dictionary). Finally, we indicated the Arabic translation of the word, which is «أَهْدَى».

e.g.: Il offre un diamant à sa femme. [He offers a diamond to his wife.]

By applying this dictionary on «Les liaisons dangereuses» de Laclos, we got these results (Fig. 4):

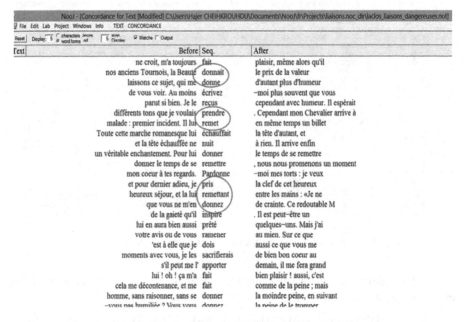

Fig. 4. Extraction of dative verbs.

After the first step in our investigative procedure of automatic translation, we proceed to the second step which consists in the automatic recognition of different syntactic and semantic schemas of dative verbs.

3 The Creation of Grammars for the Analysis and Recognition of Syntactic Patterns

In this phase, we attempted to create formal grammars to analyse the sentences. Accordingly, we sought to recognize the different arguments found in a text or corpus and to sort the suitable syntactic constructions without any ambiguity. The constructed grammars are called grammars of syntactic disambiguation [5] (Fig. 5).

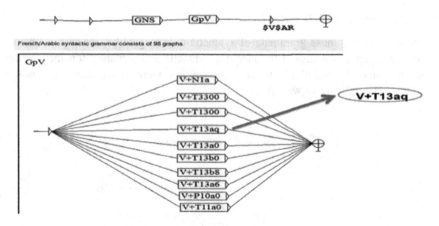

Fig. 5. The transduces of dative verbs.

Example: Il a payé les impôts au percepteur. (He paid the taxes to the collector.)

The predicate «**payer 01**» (to pay) is a dative verb that means "give money to someone"; the syntactic construction of this usage is [**T13aq**].This predicate is direct transitive when the semantic feature of the direct object N1 is [+ inanimate], and the semantic feature of the indirect object N2 is [+ human]; the latter is introduced by the proposition "à" (to). The translation of this verbal entry in Arabic is "دَفَعَ" (to pay) (Fig. 6).

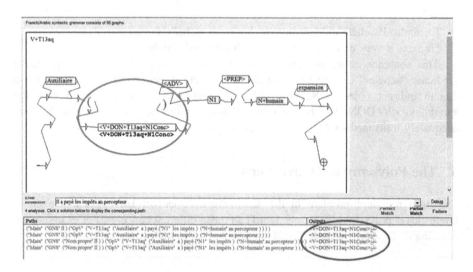

Fig. 6. The automatic recognition of the grammar of syntactic disambiguation

<V+DON+T13aq+N1Conc>.

When applying these grammars of syntactic disambiguation, we remark that sentences were properly analysed by adequate syntactic and semantic schemes. Furthermore, the analysis and the automatic recognition were exact, and the automatic translation was reliable as well (Fig. 7).

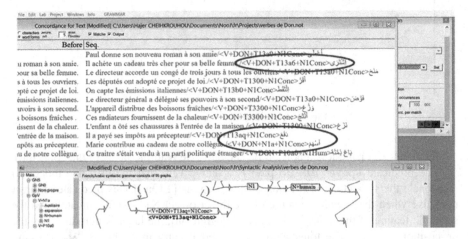

Fig. 7. The automatic recognition of different syntactic and semantic schemes of the dative verbs.

Example: Il achète un cadeau très cher pour sa belle femme.

He buys a very expensive present for his beautiful wife.

This sentence is recognized by the syntactic scheme T13a6 where the dative predicate "acheter" (to buy) necessitates a concrete direct object [+N1Conc] and a human indirect object [+N2Hum]. This sentence was properly marked with the annotation <V+DON+T13a6+N1Conc>. Consequently, the predicate "acheter" was adequately translated to Arabic into «اشْتَرَى».

4   The Polysemy of Dative Verbs

The most recurrent problem in the automatic treatment of languages and even in linguistics is polysemy, where one word can mean different concepts. For example, the meaning of the verb "remettre" can vary according to the context (Fig. 8):

748	remettre 12	OBJ	D2a	dat qc A qn	confier,donner	On r^les clefs au gardien.	5fZ	T13a0 P30a0 ---A----
749	remettre 13	DRO	D3b	dat abs A qn	dispenser de	On r^sa peine à P,sa dette à un débiteur.	5fZ	T13a0 P30a0 ---A 5D--
750	remettre 21	DRO	D1b	dat qn A autorité	livrer à	On r^P à la police.On se r^à la police.	5fZ	T11a0 P10a0 ---A----

Fig. 8. Polysemic verbal entry «remettre».

➤ **Remettre 12:** means "give somethings to someone". It can have the construction direct transitive [T13a0] with the indirect complement as human [+Hum] and the translation in Arabic is + AR="أَعْطَى".
Example: Il a remis les clefs au gardien.
     He gave the keys to the keeper.
→ [T13a0] + AR = "أَعْطَى " (to give).

➤ **Remettre 13:** means "give abstract to someone". It can have the construction direct transitive [T13a0] with the indirect complement [+Hum]and the translation in Arabic is + AR= " عَفَا "
Example: On a remis sa dette à un débiteur.
     We wrote off his debt.
→ [T13a0] + AR = "عَفَا "

➤ **Remettre 21:** means "give someone to an authority". It can have two constructions:
a/ Direct transitive [T11a0] with the direct complement [+Hum] + AR="سَلَّمَ"
Example: On a remis Paul à la police.
     We gave Paul up to the police.
→ [T11a0] + AR = "سَلَّمَ " (to give sb up to the police).

b/ The pronominal construction [P10a0] with the translation is "سَلَّمَ نَفْسَهُ"
Example: Le criminel s'est remis à la police.
     He gave himself up to the police.
→ [T11a0] + AR = "سَلَّمَ نَفْسَهُ"

We notice that the syntactic constructions of the verb «remettre» are very similar and the distinction between them is a little bit difficult, especially between direct transitive constructions.

While using the grammars of syntactic disambiguation, we notice that polysemic verbs were analysed by all verbal entries and consequently by all syntactic constructions, without taking into consideration the syntactic and semantic properties of each verbal use. This syntactic and semantic analysis involving all different polysemic verbal entries will systematically entail wrong and imprecise translations (Fig. 9).

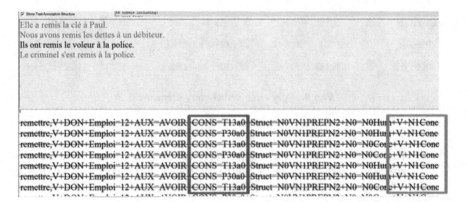

Fig. 9. The semantic-syntactic ambiguities of the polysemic uses of the predicate "remettre".

The predicate «remettre» used in the sentence "Ils ont remis le voleur à la police» (They gave the thief up to the police) was annotated with the syntactic-semantic construction [T13a0], where the direct object is concrete [+N1Conc]. This analysis is incorrect because the predicate in this sentence represents the use "remettre 21" where the direct object is human and the syntactic-semantic construction is [T11a0].

In this study, we not only sought to find an adequate syntactic-semantic analysis of dative predicates but also to provide essentially a reliable and precise automatic translation using the NooJ platform.

In fact, polysemy constitutes a big problem in the domain of automatic processing of natural languages. To resolve this linguistic ambiguity, Gaston Gross invented a theory of object classes which determines the semantic nature of arguments for each predicate [6].

In his article, the object classes, he presents the linguistic role of these classes:

> "These classes are a means to separate in a very precise manner the different uses of predicates, to construct synonyms and antonyms in context, and to automatically detect metaphors and metonyms. Object classes also yield a way to account for the behavior of predicative nouns and in particular for their conjugation. Their most general use is to be found in accounting for the different uses of predicates in terms of their argument schemas and in associating with these the set of all properties that characterize them."[2]

When adopting the theory of object classes in the process of automatic translation of the dative verbs, we have to apply the principles of this linguistic description on the different verbal entries of our dictionary to guarantee acceptable translations [7].

To achieve this end, we re-wrote the syntactic-semantic schemes of each verbal entry adding the semantic properties of each argument according to the context which determines the exact meaning of each predicate. In this respect, Gross maintains that «the notion of context, which is one of the most important concepts in linguistic

---

[2] Gaston Gross, Les classes d'objets, in https://excerpts.numilog.com/books/9782728804108.pdf.

analysis is in as much as all predicates are polysemous, which entails that only their distribution can determine the appropriate interpretation»[3].

- remettre+T13a0+N1Conc:Objet + AR = أَعْطَى (to give)
- remettre+T13a0+N1Conc:obligation + AR = عَفَا (to forgive)
- remettre+T11a0+N2Hum:Autorité + AR = سَلَّمَ (to give s.o up to the police)
- remettre+P10a0+N2Hum:Autorité + AR = سَلَّمَ نَفْسَهُ (to give oneself up)

e.g.:

remettre,V+DON+Emploi=21+AUX=AVOIR+FLX=METTRE+CONS=T11a0+N0VN1PREPN
2+N0Hum+V+N1Hum+N2Hum:Autorité+PREP="à"+DRV=DN11f:TABLE+DOM=DRO+CL
ASS=D1b+OPER="dat qn A autorité"+LEXI=3+AR="سَلَّمَ"

This step is conditioned by another one, that of defining the names by the appropriate semantic features; the names are registered in the "dm.dic" dictionary (Figs. 10, 11, 12 and 13).

e.g.: dette,N+Sem=**Conc:obligation**+FLX=F_S

clé,clef,N+Sem=**Conc:Objet**+FLX=F_S

police,N+Sem=**Hum:Autorité**+FLX=F_S

After the first step, we will move to the second one where we will change the filter of disambiguation of each syntactic-semantic scheme by specifying the semantic property of each argument:

- T13a0+N1Conc:obligation
- T13a0+N1Conc:objet
- T11a0+N2Hum:Autorité
- P10a0+N2Hum:Autorité

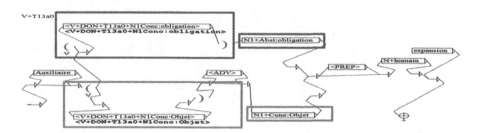

Fig. 10. The transducer of T13a0+N1Conc: Objet and N1Conc: obligation.

---

[3] Gaston Gross, Sur la notion de contexte, in https://www.erudit.org/en/journals/meta/1900-v1-n1-meta3696/039612ar.pdf.

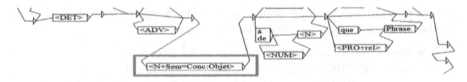

Fig. 11. The transducer of argument N+Sem=Conc: Objet.

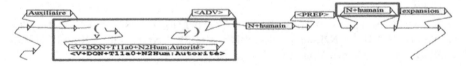

Fig. 12. The transducer of T11a0+N2Hum:Autorité.

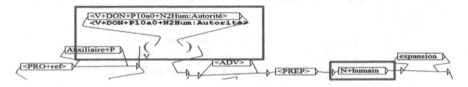

Fig. 13. The transducer of P10a0+N2Hum:Autorité.

After carrying out the necessary modifications, by adding the semantic properties of the arguments of each predicate in the dictionary and readjusting the filters of disambiguation of each syntactic-semantic scheme, we re-applied our process of automatic translation on the selected corpus; we obtained the following results (Fig. 14):

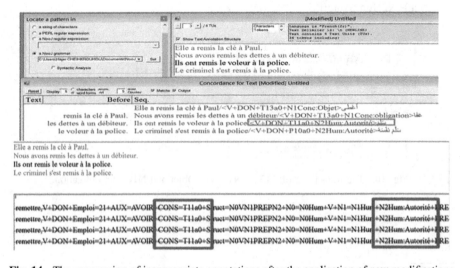

Fig. 14. The suppression of inappropriate annotations after the application of new modifications brought to the filters of disambiguation.

Indeed, the semantic details we added removed all ambiguities since the extra modifications had assigned to each sentence its adequate syntactic construction with the precise semantic property of each argument. We also noticed the suppression of annotations that are incompatible with the filters of disambiguation. This grammar, which is essentially based on the theory of object classes, resolved all ambiguities at the level of analysis and automatic recognition and at the level of automatic translation as well.

We deduced that this syntactic-semantic method of analysis and recognition guarantees the disambiguation of polysemous uses and also an adequate and reliable translation.

e.g.: Ils ont remis le voleur à la police.
They handed the thief over to the police.

This sentence was analysed by the suitable annotation <V+DON+T11a0+N2Hum: Autorité> and appropriately translated.

5   Conclusion

In this study, we presented all the necessary steps followed in applying the automatic translation of dative verbs using the NooJ platform. This process of French-Arabic automatic translation was based on two fundamental steps:

1) The creation of bilingual dictionaries of the dative verbs.
2) The construction of formal grammars to recognize syntactic schemes of the predicates of class (D) where we integrated the theory of Gaston Gross, the object classes, to resolve syntactic-semantic ambiguities especially for polysemic predicates.

This approach enables us to prove the feasibility of our system and the utility of local grammars in improving the recognition and extraction of syntactic schemes, and also in ameliorating the quality of proposed automatic translation.

References

1. Dubois, J., Dubois-Charlier, F.: Les verbes français. Larousse, Paris (1997)
2. Cheikhrouhou, H.: The automatic translation of French verbal tenses to arabic using the platform NooJ. In: Mbarki, S., Mourchid, M., Silberztein, M. (eds.) NooJ 2017. CCIS, vol. 811, pp. 156–167. Springer, Cham (2018). https://doi.org/10.1007/978-3-319-73420-0_13
3. Cheikhrouhou, H.: Recognition of communication verbs with NooJ platform. In: Formalising Natural Languages with NooJ 2013, pp. 155–169. Cambridge Scholars Publishing, British (2014)
4. Cheikhrouhou, H.: The formalisation of movement verbs for automatic translation using NooJ platform. In: Formalising Natural Languages NooJ 2014, pp. 14–21. Cambridge Scholars Publishing, British (2015)

5. Silberztein, M.: La formalisation des langues l'approche de NooJ. Collection Science Cognitive et Management Des Connaissances. ISTE Editions (2015)
6. Gross, G.: Les classes d'objets. Lalies, Presses de l'ENS, Editions rue d'Ulm, pp. 111–165 (2008). https://halshs.archives-ouvertes.fr/halshs-00410784
7. Cheikhrouhou, H.: Automatic recognition and translation of polysemous verbs using the platform NooJ. In: Fehri, H., Mesfar, S., Silberztein, M. (eds.) NooJ 2019. CCIS, vol. 1153, pp. 39–51. Springer, Cham (2020). https://doi.org/10.1007/978-3-030-38833-1_4

From Laws and Decrees to a Legal Dictionary

Ismahane Kourtin[1,2(✉)], Samir Mbarki[2], and Abdelaaziz Mouloudi[2]

[1] ELLIADD Laboratory, Bourgogne-Franche-Comté University,
Besançon, France
[2] MISC Laboratory, Faculty of Science, Ibn Tofail University, Kenitra, Morocco

Abstract. The mass of information in the legal field, which is constantly increasing, has generated a capital need to organize and structure the content of the available documents, and thus transform them into an intelligent guide, capable of providing complete and immediate answers to queries in natural language. Therefore, the Question Answering System (QAS), which is an application of the Automatic Language Processing domain (NLP), responds perfectly to this need by offering different mechanisms to provide adequate and precise answers to questions expressed in natural language. The general context of our work is the construction of an ontology-based legal question-answering system, allowing users to ask questions about desired information using natural language without having to browse through documents.

In this article, we will mainly focus on the construction of a legal dictionary from textual laws and decrees, for the natural language automatic processing platform NooJ. The legal dictionary that we propose to build from laws and decrees, will bring together the terminological material that will serve as a linguistic resource for the automatic processing of users' questions in natural language, and in particular during the information extraction step which is necessary for the formulation of SPARQL queries equivalent to users' questions.

Keywords: Legal field · Information retrieval · Automatic Language Processing (NLP) · NooJ · Legal dictionary

1 Introduction

Question-answering systems (QASs) offer different mechanisms to provide adequate and precise answers to questions expressed in natural language. Indeed, this type of system allows user to ask a question in natural language and receive a precise answer to his request instead of a set of documents deemed relevant, as in the case of search engines.

The first process in QASs is to extract the information from users' questions that are expressed in natural language. One of the crucial steps in the extracting information from texts is the recognition of named entities. The term named entity appeared during the MUC6 conference (Message Understanding Conference) [1]. These are the entities that have a determined designator (e.g. "EDF", "Jules Verne"). They include proper names or expressions such as the species names (e.g. "Bengal tiger"), diseases, or

M. Bigey et al. (Eds.): NooJ 2021, CCIS 1520, pp. 187–197, 2021.
https://doi.org/10.1007/978-3-030-92861-2_16

chemicals. This definition has also been extended to temporal expressions such as dates and times, or to numeric values (e.g. 2.3 g/l).

By legal entities, we mean named entities specific to the legal field such as acts and facts. Detecting such entities requires the availability of resources describing the domain vocabulary and / or training corpus allowing the learning of the common characteristics to these entities.

Our goal in this article is to build a legal dictionary that will be used for the automatic analysis of the users' questions expressed in natural language in order to extract the information that is needed to formulate SPARQL queries equivalent to users' questions.

The rest of this document is organized as follows: First, Sect. 2 presents related work on extracting terms from texts. Subsequently, Sect. 3 presents the legal field and its complexity. Then, Sect. 4 describes the methodology used for the construction of the legal dictionary. Finally, we end this article with the results of the experimentation of the legal entities recognition by applying our legal dictionary in Sect. 5, and conclude in Sect. 6.

2   Extracting Terms from Texts

A term is an expression with a unique meaning for a particular domain [2]. In the legal field, the words "tax service" become a term in relation to the field, it has a unique meaning in this field.

Term extraction consists of identifying potential terms in a specific text or a set of texts (corpus) as well as the relevant information related to the use of these terms or to the concepts to which they refer (definition, context, etc.).

Extracting terms is an important step in building a dictionary from a corpus. Terms are words or expressions having a precise meaning in a given context, and represent the linguistic supports of the concepts. The problem of building up resources is at the heart of terminological activity. If the notion of "term", which appeals to that of concept and is often based on a particular act of reference, does not seem to lend itself to computer processing, a certain number of tools aiming to extract the terms of a corpus have seen the day [3].

The definition of the term given above exerts strong constraints on the form and the functioning of the terminological units. These constraints constitute the operational principles of terminology extraction software that have been developed in recent years. The objective of these software is to automatically provide a more or less structured lexicon of the domain.

We can distinguish three types of approaches for the automatic term extraction: (i) linguistic approaches that use lists of named entities and manually written recognition patterns [4, 5], (ii) statistical approaches based on learning techniques from annotated texts [6, 7] and (iii) hybrid approaches which integrate the first two methods [8, 9]. Table 1 gives a brief description of each approach for the automatic term extraction.

Table 1. Approaches for the automatic term extraction

Approach	Description
Linguistic methods	These methods generally call upon linguistic knowledge which can be syntactic, lexical or morphological
	Linguistic methods consider that the construction of the terminological units obeys more or less stable syntax rules, they are mainly phrases formed of nouns and adjectives. Based on this knowledge, these systems perform the extraction of candidate terms using syntactic schemes [10]
	We can also use grammars and a lexicon acquired during analysis or through collaboration with specialists to generate all the potential terms of a domain [11]
	These tools therefore require a preprocessing of the corpus by a syntactic analyzer. The quality of the results depends closely on the quality of these analyzers. They have the disadvantage of depending directly on the language of the texts processed and require linguistic resources (dictionaries, stop-word list, etc.). In addition, they are only effective on small corpora
Statistical methods	The statistical approach offers undeniable advantages, since it makes it possible to tackle large data sets that it would be completely impossible to process manually [11]
	The first works in this field, using statistical data, date from the 80s, they were carried out by Ludovic Lebart and André Salem on the repeated segments [12]. These works exploit similarity measures
	There are several statistical methods applied to term extraction, most of which are based on mutual information or the Dice coefficient [13]. The principle is that the recurring association of two words cannot be due to chance. Therefore, it is necessarily significant [14]
Hybrid methods	Hybrid models, as their name suggests, are at the crossroads between linguistic and statistical approaches. The existing studies adopt a varying order of treatment. Indeed, some authors prefer to start processing corpora with linguistic analysis, and then filter the results using statistical techniques, while others do the opposite

3 The Legal Field

The legal field is a complex field by its terms which can be:

- Terms with only a legal meaning;
- Terms with at least one legal and non-legal meaning;
- Terms designated by their synonyms in different texts;
- Terms appearing in different morphological forms;
- Non-synonymous terms with the same legal meaning.

In addition, there are different lexical forms that legal terms can take. Table 2 gives some examples of legal terms with their lexical form.

Table 2. Examples of legal terms with their lexical form

Legal term	Lexical form
acquisition	Noun
action nominative	Noun Adjective
adressé par lettre recommandée avec accusé de réception	Verb Preposition Noun Adjective Preposition Noun Preposition Noun
disposition d'ordre législatif	Noun Preposition Noun Adjective
domicile fiscal	Noun Adjective
droit social	Noun Adjective
ensemble immobilier	Noun Adjective
établissement des sociétés non résidentes	Noun Preposition Determiner Noun Adverb Adjective
groupement d'intérêt économique	Noun Preposition Noun Adjective
impôt sur les sociétés	Noun Preposition Determiner Noun
libre disposition	Adjective Noun
membre de la société	Noun Preposition Determiner Noun
nommément désigné	Adverb Verb (PP)
occupé en majeure partie	Verb (PP) Preposition Adjective Noun
opération à caractère lucratif	Noun Preposition Noun Adjective
organisme légalement assimilé	Noun Adverb Adjective
remise contre récépissé	Noun Preposition Noun
service des impôts	Noun Preposition Determiner Noun
société à objet immobilier	Noun Preposition Noun Adjective
société de fait	Noun Preposition Noun
société en participation	Noun Preposition Noun
société immobilière transparente	Noun Adjective Adjective
société nouvellement créée	Noun Adverb Verb (PP)

These examples of legal terms show the diversity and the infinity of the lexical forms of the legal terms. We find terms in the form of "Noun", "Noun-Adjective", "Noun-Preposition-Noun", etc. This lexical diversity makes it impossible to automatically extract the legal terms based on lexical grammars.

No resource on the legal terms has been developed for the legal field. Therefore, we decided to build a NooJ legal dictionary describing the legal terms and their categorization, which will be used for the automatic analysis of the users' questions that are expressed in natural language, using the natural language automatic processing platform NooJ [15]. The latter makes it possible to build, test and manage formal descriptions in a wide coverage of natural languages, in the form of electronic dictionaries and grammars.

4 The Legal Dictionary

The description of natural languages is formalized in the form of electronic dictionaries and grammars represented by organized sets of graphs. NOOJ dictionaries are used to represent, describe and recognize simple and compound words. Dictionaries are.nod files compiled from editable.dic source files.

Our goal is to build an electronic dictionary of legal terms for NOOJ. A term can be simple if it contains one word, or compound if it contains more than one. A compound word is built from simple words. Silberztein M. [16] defines a compound noun as a consecutive sequence of at least two simple forms and blocks of separators. A simple form is a consecutive nonempty sequence of characters of the alphabet appearing between two separators. A single word is a simple form that constitutes a dictionary entry.

The legal dictionary that we propose to build from laws and decrees, will bring together the terminological material necessary for the automatic processing of legal texts, and in particular during the stage of transforming users' questions, in natural language, to SPARQL queries in our question-answering system. We have adopted a methodological framework in 6 steps for the construction of the legal dictionary (see Fig. 1).

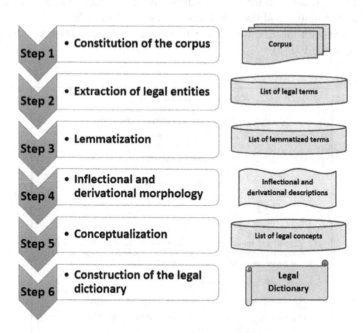

Fig. 1. Construction stages of the legal dictionary

4.1   The Constitution of the Legal Corpus

In this step we have built up a legal corpus from laws and decrees. We focused our study initially on the general tax code of Morocco. The general tax code has 3 books (see Fig. 2).

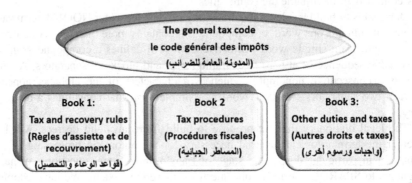

Fig. 2. The general tax code

The first book deals with the tax and recovery rules, and has 9 titles and 209 articles. Book 2 deals with the tax procedures and has 3 titles and 39 articles. Book 3 deals with other duties and taxes and has 5 titles and 40 articles.

We started with the first title of the first book of the general tax code, on "corporation tax" (see Fig. 3).

Fig. 3. The first title of the first book of the general tax code

4.2   Extracting the Legal Entities

In this step we have manually analyzed the corpus and extracted the legal entities. We identified 679 legal entities.

4.3   Lemmatization of Legal Entities

Then, we proceeded to the lemmatization of the extracted legal entities by passing words bearing inflection marks (plural, conjugated form of a verb…) to their reference forms (lemma or canonical form).

For example, the legal entity "Personnes imposables" (Taxable persons) becomes "Personne imposable" (Taxable person).

4.4   Inflectional and Derivational Morphology

In this step, we established the inflected and derived forms of the legal entities using NooJ grammars. An extract is given in Fig. 4.

```
# Language-Specific Commands:
# (None)
#
# Special Characters: '=' '<' '>' '\' '"' ':' '|' '+' '-' '/' '$' '_' ';' '#'
#

Genre = <E>/m | e/f;
Nombre = <E>/s | s/p;

ACHAT = <E>/m+s | <PW>s/m+p;
ACHAT_ADJ = <E>/m+s | <PW>s<N>s/m+p;
ACTION = <E>/f+s | <PW>s/f+p;
ACTION_ADJ = <E>/f+s | <PW>s<N>s/f+p;
ADRESSEE = <E>/m+s | e/f+s | s/m+p | es/f+p;
ANIMAL = <E>/m+s | <B>ux/m+p;
ANIMAL_ADJ = <E>/m+s | <PW><B>ux<N>s/m+p;
```

Fig. 4. An extract of the inflectional grammar

For example, the inflectional model "ACHAT" is defined by "ACHAT = <E>/m +s | <PW> s/m+p;" and means that the legal term that uses this inflectional model has two forms:

- The term as it is: masculine singular
- The term with an "s" at the end of the first word: masculine plural

4.5   Conceptualization

After having established the list of the legal entities, we proceeded to group these entities into semantic classes by establishing a list of concepts. We have established 42 concepts. Table 3 gives some examples of legal concepts with their description and some examples.

Table 3. Examples of legal concepts

Code	Meaning	Examples
ORGANIZATION	Organization	établissement d'animation touristique (tourist entertainment establishment)
COMPANY	Company	jeune entreprise innovante (young innovative company)
ADMINISTRATION	Administration	service des impôts (Tax service)
AGENCY	Agency	agence de développement social (social development agency)
ASSOCIATION	Association	association sportive (sports Association)
BANK	Bank	Banque Européenne d'Investissements (B.E.I.) (European Investment Bank)
PERSON	Person	adhérent, associé, bénéficiaire (member, partner, beneficiary)
VEHICLE	Vehicle	ambulance (ambulance)
ANIMAL	Animal	animal vivant (living animal)
STATE	State	capacité d'hébergement (accommodation capacity)
PURCHASE	Purchase	achat de marchandises revendus en l'état (purchase of goods resold as is)
ACQUISITION	Acquisition	acquisition de terrains (land acquisition)
ACTE	Act	autorisation, avance, agrément, exonération (authorization, advance, approval, exemption)
ACTIVITY	Activity	assistance technique (technical assistance)
HELP	Help	aide au logement (housing assistance)

4.6   The Construction of the Legal Dictionary

Finally, we proceeded to the structuring of the legal terms by building an electronic dictionary of legal terms. The electronic computer dictionary was developed with NooJ [17–19] and has 679 entries. An extract is given in Fig. 5.

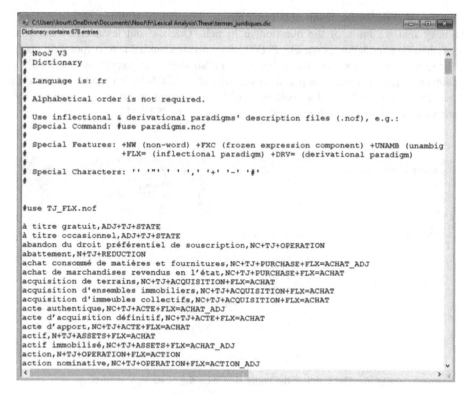

Fig. 5. An extract of the legal dictionary

For example, for the dictionary entry "acte d'acquisition définitif":
acte d'acquisition définitif, NC+TJ+ACTE+FLX = ACHAT.

- acte d'acquisition définitif: the legal entity
- +NC+TJ: the categories are compound noun and legal term
- +ACTE: the semantic class "ACTE"
- ACHAT: the inflectional model "ACHAT"

The inflectional model "ACHAT" is defined by "ACHAT = <E>/m+s | <PW>s/m +p;" which means that the legal term has two inflected forms:

- acte d'acquisition définitif: masculine singular
- actes d'acquisition définitif: masculine plural

5   Experimentation

The NooJ legal dictionary, which we have developed, is able to annotate and recognize legal entities in natural language text. However, with the legal dictionary one is able to automatically analyze and recognize legal terms in natural language questions, using the natural language automatic processing platform NooJ.

Figure 6 shows the result obtained from the annotation, with the NooJ legal dictionary that we built, of the question in French "Quelles sont les sociétés qui sont passibles de l'impôt sur les sociétés?" (Which companies are liable to corporation tax?). The result of the annotation shows that the term "société" (company) was identified by: noun and legal term masculin plural, of semantic class "COMPANY"; and that the term "passibles de l'impôt sur les sociétés" (liable to corporation tax) was identified by: noun and legal term masculin plural, of semantic class "STATE".

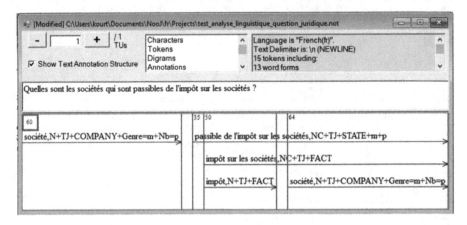

Fig. 6. The result of the annotation with the NooJ legal dictionary

6   Conclusion

In this work we have developed an electronic NooJ dictionary that allows annotating and recognizing legal terms in natural language texts. We have adopted a methodological framework in 6 steps for the construction of the legal dictionary: (1) we have constituted a legal corpus of laws and decrees focusing on the first title of the first book of the general tax code, on "corporation tax"; (2) we manually analyzed the corpus and extracted the legal entities by identifying 679 legal entities; (3) we lemmatized the extracted legal entities by passing words bearing inflection marks (plural, conjugated form of a verb...) to their reference forms; (4) we have built grammars describing the inflectional and derivational morphology of the legal entities; (5) we have grouped the legal entities into semantic classes by establishing 42 concepts; (6) we have structured legal entities by building a NooJ electronic legal dictionary capable of annotating and identifying legal terms in natural language texts.

As perspectives, we will integrate the legal dictionary into our question-answering system, by using it in the automatic processing of the users' questions in natural language, which the objective is to extract the information necessary for the formulation of SPARQL queries equivalent to users' questions.

References

1. Grishman, R., Sundheim, B.: Message understanding conference 6 - a brief history. In: Proceedings of COLING, Copenhagen, Denmark, (AUG 1996), pp. 466–471 (1996). (Cited pages 17 & 19)
2. Azé, J., Heitz, T.: Cours sur la Fouille de textes et Apprentissage (2004). http://www.lri.fr/ ~ aze/enseignements.php
3. Piwowarski, B.: Techniques d'apprentissage pour le traitement, d'informations structurées: Application à la recherche d'information, Doctoral thesis, University of Paris 6 (2003)
4. Poibeau, T.: Le repérage des entités nommées, un enjeu pour les systèmes de veille. In: Terminologies Nouvelles (actes du colloque Terminologie et Intelligence Artificielle, TIA'99, Nantes), no. 19, pp. 43–51 (1999). (Cited page 17)
5. Elkateb-Gara, F.: Extraction d'entités nommées pour la recherche d'informations précises. Dans 4e Congrès ISKO France, Grenoble (2003). (Cited page 17)
6. McCallum, A., Li, W.: Early results for named entity recognition with conditional random fields, features induction and web-enhanced lexicons. In: Proceedings of the Seventh Conference on Natural Language Learning at HLT-NAACL (2003). (Cited page 17)
7. Raymond, C., Wei, W.: Named entity recognition using hybrid machine learning approach. In: IEEE ICCI, pp. 578–583 (2006). (Cited page 17)
8. Kosseim, L., Poibeau, T.: Extraction de noms propres à partir de textes variés: problématique et enjeux. In: TALN 2001, pp. 365–371 (2001). (Cited page 1)
9. Fourour, N.: Nemesis: un système de reconnaissance incrémentielle des entités nommées pour le français. In: TALN 2002, pp. 255–264 (2002). (Cited page 17)
10. Malaisé, V.: Méthodologie linguistique et terminologique pour la structuration d'ontologies différentielles à partir de corpus textuels, Doctoral thesis, University of Paris 7 – Denis Diderot France (2005)
11. Drouin, P.: Acquisition automatique des termes: l'utilisation des pivots lexicaux spécialisés, Doctoral thesis, University of Montreal (2002)
12. Lebart, L., Salem, A.: Analyse statistique des données textuelles. Dunod, Bordas, Paris (1988)
13. Velardi, P., Missikof, M., Fabriani, P.: Using text processing techniques to automatically enrich a domain ontology. In: Proceeding of ACM-FOIS (2001)
14. L'Homme, M.-C.: Nouvelles technologies et recherche terminologique. Techniques d'extraction des données terminologiques et leur impact sur le travail du terminographe. In: L'impact des nouvelles technologies sur la gestion terminologique, Toronto (2001)
15. Silberztein, M.: NooJ manual (2006)
16. Silberztein, M.: Le dictionnaire électronique des mots composés. In: Langue Française, No. 87, septembre 1990
17. Aoughlis, F.: A computer science electronic dictionary for NOOJ. In: Kedad, Z., Lammari, N., Métais, E., Meziane, F., Rezgui, Y. (eds.) NLDB 2007. LNCS, vol. 4592, pp. 341–351. Springer, Heidelberg (2007). https://doi.org/10.1007/978-3-540-73351-5_30
18. Aoughlis, F.: Construction d'un dictionnaire électronique de terminologie informatique et analyse automatique de textes par grammaires locales. Thèse, Université Mouloud Mammeri, Tizi Ouzou (2010)
19. Hildebert, J.: Dictionnaire des technologies de l'informatique. vol. 2, Français/Anglais, La maison du dictionnaire (Paris), Hippocrene Books Inc., New York (1998)

Automatic Detection and Generation of Argument Structures Within the Medical Domain

Walter Koza[(⊠)] and Constanza Suy

Pontificia Universidad Católica de Valparaíso, Valparaíso, Chile
walter.koza@pucv.cl, constanza.suy.a@mail.pucv.cl

Abstract. Representing the predicate argument structure of the medical domain (ASMD) is important for automatic text analyses. This work aims to describe the ASMD through verbs and transformational possibilities. Computer resources were constructed from 100 selected biomedical verbs (corpus CCM2009). Firstly, these were analyzed to determine the quantity and type of arguments, and classified these arguments into object classes (OC). Secondly, we established possible transformations for each ASMD. With this information, we created computer models on NooJ for the detection and automatic creation of ASMD in a corpus. This work involved the elaboration of electronic dictionaries, syntactic recognition, and generative grammars. The detection was performed on a corpus of 188,000 words conformed by texts from the gynecology and obstetrics area, achieving the following results: 100% accuracy, 96.92% coverage, and 98% F-measure. NooJ grammars provided grammatical sentences of each ASMD involving different transformations admitted by each particular class.

Keywords: Predicate argument structure · Biomedical domain · Lexicon-grammar · NooJ

1 Introduction

Semantic analysis based on the treatment of argument structures (AS) is useful in the development of methodologies for the extraction and organization of information, automatic translation, and so on. This type of work tends to focus on specific domains, with more attention on medicine. However, a significant problem for automatic extraction tasks is the phenomenon of erroneous analyses due to polysemy, i.e., the multiple meanings projected by the same lexical unit [1]. For example, a verb such as 'encontrar' may have different meanings, and the possible AS may therefore contain different types of information (1).

(1)
a. El médico encontró el tumor. ('The doctor found the tumor')
b. El médico se encontró con el paciente. ('The doctor met with the patient')
c. El paciente se encuentra estable. ('The patient is stable')

As can be seen, in 1.a., the meaning is equivalent to 'to find'. In 1.b., on the other hand, it refers to the event of 'seeing another person'. Finally, in 1.c., *'encontrar'* takes on a semi-copulative value that supports the predicate *'estable'*.

© Springer Nature Switzerland AG 2021
M. Bigey et al. (Eds.): NooJ 2021, CCIS 1520, pp. 198–207, 2021.
https://doi.org/10.1007/978-3-030-92861-2_17

In the field of medicine, several studies have focused on automatic analysis of AS, either with machine learning or rule-based methodologies. However, these works tend to focus on specific aspects, such as the effects of drugs on patients [2] or concept identification [3], among others. In this regard, appealing to the morphosyntactic behavior of medical predicates and their arguments by means of a simple procedure, such as the one offered by Lexicon Grammar (LG) [4], can be an effective methodology that more broadly encapsulates different interests. This paper describes a method for the treatment of ASMD, in Spanish, based on the processing of lexical, morphological, and syntactic information within this theoretical framework.

The methodology followed three steps: (i) selection of one hundred medical verbal predicates from a corpus in the area of gynecology and obstetrics; (ii) following LG guidelines, descriptions of the predicates into object classes [5], i.e., nominal classes that give a predicate an equivalent meaning; and (iii) computational modeling for the automatic detection and generation of ASMDs. For the computational work, electronic dictionaries and computer grammars were built in NooJ [6]. The results obtained (100% accuracy, 96.92% coverage, and 98% F-measure) demonstrate the suitability of the proposed methodology for this type of task.

Below, we present the background in the area of automatic information extraction and the theoretical framework; the third section describes the methodological framework; the fourth section analyzes the results obtained; and finally, the fifth section presents the conclusions.

2   Background and Theoretical Framework

This section presents the state of the art in information extraction tasks, as well as general guidelines for the LG.

2.1   Automatic Data Extraction

Information extraction (IE) is the automatic identification and classification of user-specified instances, such as entities, relationships, terms, events, and so on [7]. According to Grishman [7], the output of this process is structured information, e.g., a database, which can be used for various purposes. For example, textual fragments of interest can be extracted and take structured forms.

In the field of medicine, both rule-based and machine learning-based information extraction studies can be found, such as drugs and their effects [2] or patient selection criteria [8], among others. Both rules-based and machine learning results are positive. However, the aforementioned works tend to focus on specific aspects of the domain, so further research may include methodologies for syntax knowledge.

2.2   Lexicon Grammar

Lexicon-Grammar (LG) is a descriptive model proposed by Gross [4]. This framework studies the set of formal rules of a language in relation to its lexical units, and in which analysis is performed on the basis of three conditions: (i) syntax is inseparable from the lexicon; (ii) the minimal unit is the simple sentence; and (iii) formalization is the result of a distributional and transformational analysis, which can be applied to any language [9].

First, the methodological steps in LG propose a distributional analysis to classify arguments according to the meaning they give to the predicate. Thus, for example, the case of 'eat' projects two classes of predicates with 4 types of nouns:

(2)
a. animate eat food ('The patient ate a sandwich').
b. rust eat metal ('The rust ate the metal').

Thus, whenever 'eat' is combined with an argument that is animate and an argument that corresponds to some food, it will have the meaning 'feed'. Conversely, when the combination of this verb is with 'rust' and metals, the meaning will be 'corrosion process'. Such groupings are called object classes and can be defined as semantic classes that give a predicate the same meaning [5].

Secondly, the LG framework seeks the specification of the transformations an AS can have. As an example, the verb 'eat' admits nominalization in one meaning ('feed'), but not in another ('corrode'):

(3)
a. O1: The patient ate an apple = O2: The patient's meal was an apple.
b. O1: The rust ate the metal = O2: The food of the rust was the metal.

The following section describes the implemented methodology.

3   Methodology

A total of 100 verbs were extracted from a corpus of all texts indexed under SciELO journals in the gynecology and obstetrics field from the first issue published until 2017. The corpus, which contains more than 6 million words, has been tagged with the resources developed in NooJ. The choice of lexical units followed the lexicographic and frequency criterion: the most frequent verbs found in the medical dictionary of the *Real Academia Nacional de Medicina* [10] were chosen. Using this procedure, we obtained the following list (Table 1):

Table 1. List of verbs studied

asegurar, avalar, ayudar, buscar, cambiar, carecer, causar, clasificar, coincidir, colocar, comentar, comparar, complicar, comprender, comprimir, comprometer, comunicar, condicionar, confirmar, conllevar, conocer, conservar, consistir, consultar, contener, contribuir, controlar, crecer, cumplir, cursar, decidir, depender, desarrollar, descartar, desconocer, describir, desear, desencadenar, detectar, detener, determinar, diagnosticar, dificultar, discutir, disminuir, disponer, durar, establecer, evaluar, evidenciar, evitar, evolucionar, experimentar, explicar, extraer, facilitar, fallecer, favorecer, fluctuar, generar, impedir, incluir, indicar, inducir, influir, informar, intentar, interrumpir, introducir, invadir, involucrar, manifestar, mantener, medir, mejorar, mostrar, observar, ocasionar, ofrecer, permanecer, persistir, pesar, plantear, producir, proponer, provocar, recibir, recuperar, reducir, registrar, reportar, representar, requerir, responder, sobrevivir, solicitar, sufrir, suspender, tomar, tratar

This group of verbs was analyzed following the LG parameters, as described in the following subsection.

3.1 Preparation of LG Tables for Medical Domain Predicates

For the construction of LG tables, we first identified the occurrences of each verb in the corpus and the arguments that appear in their contexts. As an example, Fig. 1 shows an excerpt for the occurrences of 'comunicar'.

Before	Seq.	After
arterial, y score de hirsutismo (Moncada). Se les solicitó que	comunicaran	espontáneamente cualquier efecto adverso a la droga, siendo cada paciente
Con respecto a los márgenes endocervical y exocervical se han	comunicado	tasas de persistencia de enfermedad que oscilan entre un 15-40%. Para
ncidencia con la literatura internacional y con experiencias más pequeñas	comunicadas	en nuestro medio. La utilización de el medio selectivo para
vida. El seguimiento de largo plazo de estos casos será	comunicado	posteriormente. Apoyados por la literatura creemos que para nuestro Servicio
y fetales variables según las distintas series. El presente reporte	comunica	una serie de seis casos manejados en nuestro servicio, respecto
ellas, se realizó histerectomía, lo cual es menor a lo	comunicado	Lo anterior, se explica, probablemente, por la baja paridad promedio
GTG, que dio como resultado 47, XY, +9. Ante lo cual se	comunica	a los padres el pronostico de esta patología, y decidimos
las 20 semanas. Por lo que podemos decir que probablemente hemos	comunicado	el caso de diagnóstico más precoz de esta enfermedad con
diámetro no suele ser superior a 3-5 cm, aunque se han	comunicado	quistes funcionales de hasta 11 cm de diámetro, aunque son raros
DISCUSIÓN Los resultados de este estudio son similares a los	comunicados	en la literatura extranjera y que señalan un aumento en
complicaciones y mantener una adecuada tasa de parto vaginal se	comunican	diversos métodos de inducción del parto y profilaxis antibiótica. Este
inducciones sin alterar la tasa de infecciones. El presente trabajo	comunica	la experiencia de un servicio de obstetricia nacional en el

Fig. 1. Excerpt of the search for verb contexts with 'comunicar'

This search allows for the identification of object classes and possible meanings of the predicate. In Fig. 1, we can see, as of argument 0 (A0), SNs of the type: 'the present work', 'the present report', etc., which give 'communicate' the meaning of 'exchange information' to be included in the object class 'Studies'.

Subsequently, the information obtained in the previous step was placed into LG tables. This allowed for distributional and transformational analysis for each verb, yielding predicative patterns in medicine (ASMD). Table 2 shows the case of '*comunicar*' with the meaning of 'information exchange':

Table 2. Example of the distributional analysis of 'comunicar'

A0		Lemma	A1		Prep. Asoc	A2	Example
Human	Study		Message		'a'	Human	
			SN	Completion			
+	−	*Comunicar*	+	−	+	+	*El médico (le) comunica la situación al paciente* *The physician communicates the situation to the patient*
+	−	*Comunicar*	−	+	+	+	*El médico le comunica que se debe operar al paciente* *The physician (le) communicates that the patient should be operated on*
−	+	*Comunicar*	+	-	−	−	*El reporte comunica la situación sanitaria* *The report communicates the sanitary situation*
−	+	*Comunicar*	−	+	−	−	*El reporte comunica que se deben mejorar las condiciones sanitarias de la region* *The report communicates that the sanitary conditions of the region should be improved*

Table 2 indicates that: (i) argument 0 can belong to the object classes of 'medicine professional'; (ii) the lemma mentions the corresponding verb; (iii) argument 1 belongs to the object class of 'finding'; (iv) argument 2 is part of the object class of 'patient'; and (iv) finally, accounts for the corresponding ASMD.

The transformational analysis took place for simple sentences of the obtained ASMD, considering seven possible transformations: negation; reflexive passive; periphrastic passive; nominalization; and construction with relative subordination for A0, A1, and A2. See the following example for the simple sentence 'The doctor told the patient the news':

(4)

a. [Neg] El médico comunicó la noticia al paciente = El médico no comunicó la noticia al paciente. (The physician communicated the news to the patient = Physician did not communicate the non-news to the patient).

b. [PasivRef] El médico comunicó la noticia al paciente = Se comunicó la noticia al paciente. (The physician communicated the news to the patient = The news was communicated to the patient).

c. [PasivPerif] El médico comunicó la noticia al paciente = La noticia fue comunicada al paciente por el médico. (The physician communicated the news to the patient = The news was communicated to the patient by the physician).

d. [Nom] El médico comunicó la noticia al paciente = El médico dio el comunicado de la noticia al paciente. (The physician communicated the news to the patient = The news was communicated to the patient by the physician).

e. [A0Rel] El médico comunicó la noticia al paciente = Fue el médico el que comunicó la noticia al paciente. (The physician communicated the news to the patient = It was the physician who communicated the news to the patient).

f. [A1Rel] El médico comunicó la noticia al paciente = Fue la noticia lo que comunicó el médico al paciente. (The physician communicated the news to the patient = It was the news that was communicated by the physician to the patient).

g. [A2Rel] El médico comunicó la noticia al paciente = Fue al paciente a quien se le comunicó la noticia. (The physician communicated the news to the patient = It was the patient to whom the news was communicated).

We used the information collected at this stage for the NooJ computational work, described below.

3.2   Construction of Electronic Dictionaries

An electronic dictionary was compiled from lemmas within a general language dictionary [11], a medical dictionary [10], and, partially, from the Snomed CT ontologies [12]. Each entry has a corresponding inflectional model and linguistic information from the distributional and transformational analyses specified in the LG tables. The entries that make up the lexicon are declared as shown in Fig. 2, which gives an example of class IV (communication predicates), Subclass 3 (response predicates):

Entry	S-Lemma	Category	clase	DRV	FLX	subclase
confirmar	confirmar	V	4	CION:ILUSIÓN	AMAR	iii
explicar	explicar	V	4	CION:ILUSIÓN	TRAZAR	iii
responder	responder	V	4	RESPUESTA:CASA	TEMER	iii

Fig. 2. Extract for verb contexts with '*comunicar*'

Nouns contain information regarding the different object classes to which they belong. Thus, for example, in the case of '*explain*', one of the argument structures it may project includes:

(5) +Human Explain +Event to +Human.

An example adapted from the corpus is 'the practitioner explained the clinical case to the medical board', and in order to parse this sentence the nouns must be stated as shown in Fig. 3:

Entry	S-Lemma	Category	DRV	FLX	subtipo	tipo	SynSem
caso	caso	N		COYOTE	est	-	
junta médica	junta médica	N		CASA<P>CASA	hum+pm	anim	UNAMB
practicar	practicar	V	NTE:ESTUDIANTE+PRACTICA:CASA	TRAZAR	-		

Fig. 3. Declaration of nouns

The electronic dictionary may be used to construct grammars for the recognition and generation of the argument structures of medical predicates. The following section describes the development of grammar models.

3.3 Construction of Grammars

The grammars developed in NooJ consider the different ways in which ASs may be projected, starting from the Subject-Verb-Internal Arguments structure and, from there, any transformations. Thus, the example presented above starts out as shown in Fig. 4.

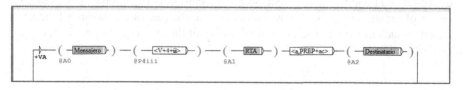

Fig. 4. Excerpt of generated grammar for the analysis of communication predicates

The sentence starts with an initial state, containing the first argument, followed by the predicate and the two internal arguments. The parentheses indicate the variables that make up the AS, i.e., argument 0 ('@A0'), the predicate ('@P4iii'), argument 1 ('@A1'), and argument 2 ('@A2'). The arguments, in turn, contain an embedded grammar indicated in yellow. An embedded grammar is an internal grammar where the structure of the arguments is declared. Figure 5 shows this using *Mensajero*:

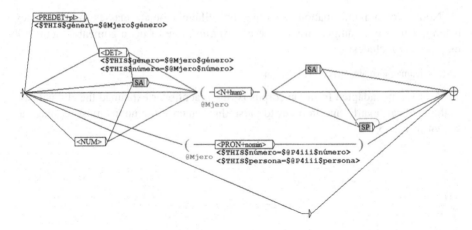

Fig. 5. Example of embedded grammar

Here, the head is a noun with the human trait ('+hum') and which carries on its left a determiner (<DET>) and an adjectival phrase (AP). The determiner agrees in gender and number (indicated by the command '$THIS') and, in turn, may also carry a predeterminer ('todos', 'todas'), which will also agree with DET. It is also possible for @Mjero to be determined by a number ('two doctors', 'three doctors', etc.). The SA, on the other hand, is made up of an adjective or verb in participle, which will agree in gender and number with @Mjero, and may be accompanied by an adverb ('*atento médico*', '*muy atento médico*'). On the right, @Mjero can also have a SA or a prepositional phrase (PP).

The sample structure in Fig. 4 enables transformations for example by adding the dative pronoun and the adverb 'not' yields the clitization of A2 and its negation. For others of greater complexity, possible positional changes of the arguments must be included, such as the modifications of categories of the predicate. Figure 6 shows such nominalization.

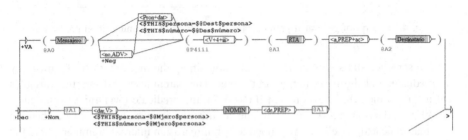

Fig. 6. Transformative grammar for obtaining AS with nominalization

Thus, the grammar containing all the combinatorial possibilities has the structure shown in Fig. 7:

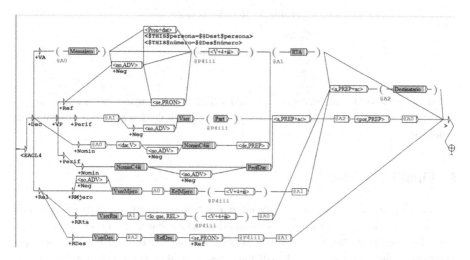

Fig. 7. Computed model for predicate grammar of "comunicar"

This grammar provides information on and generates 178 different sentences. Figure 8 shows an excerpt.

```
# Dictionary generated automatically
#
fue a la junta médica la que se le explicó eso,EACL4#+Dec#+Rel#+RDes+REF+Dat
fue a la junta médica la que se le explicó el caso clínico,EACL4#+Dec#+Rel#+RDes+REF+Dat
fue a la junta médica la que se explicó eso,EACL4#+Dec#+Rel#+RDes+REF
fue a la junta médica la que se explicó el caso clinico,EACL4#+Dec#+Rel#+RDes+REF
fue el caso clínico lo que explicó él a ella,EACL4#+Dec#+Rel#+RRta
fue el caso clínico lo que explicó él a la junta médica,EACL4#+Dec#+Rel#+RRta
fue el caso clínico lo que explicó el practicante a ella,EACL4#+Dec#+Rel#+RRta
fue el caso clínico lo que explicó el practicante a la junta médica,EACL4#+Dec#+Rel#+RRta
fue el practicante quien explicó eso a ella,EACL4#+Dec#+Rel#+RMjero
fue el practicante quien explicó eso a la junta médica,EACL4#+Dec#+Rel#+RMjero
fue el practicante quien explicó el caso clínico a ella,EACL4#+Dec#+Rel#+RMjero
fue el practicante quien explicó el caso clínico a la junta médica,EACL4#+Dec#+Rel#+RMjero
```

Fig. 8. Excerpt of automatically generated sentences

The following section presents the results obtained.

4   Results

From the distributional analysis of 100 medical verbs, 41 object classes were established. More description under LG tables determined the existence of 604 predicative patterns in medicine (ASMD) within the corpus of gynecology and obstetrics. Resources were tested on an annotated corpus (188,397 words) of clinical cases in the area of gynecology and obstetrics indexed in the SciELO platform [13]. The overall results obtained are presented in Table 3.

Table 3. Results obtained

Coverage	Accuracy	F-measure
96.2%	100%	98%

In sum, the study successfully validated ASMDs as proposed in the automatically generated LG tables. All the sentences generated complied with the grammaticality conditions.

5 Final Discussion

This paper presents a methodology for the computational treatment of medical domain ASs. For this purpose, we showed a formal description based on the LG proposal [9] and subsequently performed a computational implementation using the NooJ tool [6]. The methodology was shown to be adequate insofar as it presents adequate percentages of accuracy and coverage. Moreover, one of the most remarkable factors of this proposal is its ability to resolve ambiguities in polysemous lexical units. Briefly, by classifying nouns into object classes, grammars with high restrictive power are developed.

This paper thus contributes to information extraction tasks and greater validation of the LG theoretical proposal. It also furthers the potential of formal methods in simplifying the construction of resources through concatenation. As a result, we demonstrate the possibility of constructing context-dependent grammars overcoming the limitations of resources elaborated on the basis of finite states.

References

1. Pustejovsky, J.: The Generative Lexicon, 1st edn. MIT Press, Cambridge (1996)
2. Kim, Y., Meystre, S.: Ensemble method-based extraction of medication and related information from clinical texts. J. Am. Med. Inform. Assoc. **27**(1), 31–38 (2020)
3. Yehia, E., Boshnak, H., AbdelGaber, S., Abdo, A., Elzanfaly, D.: Ontology-based clinical information extraction from physician's free-text. J. Biomed. Inform. **98**, 1–7 (2019)
4. Gross, M.: Méthodes en syntaxe. Hermann, Paris (1996)
5. Gross, G.: Manual de análisis lingüístico. Aproximación sintáctico-semántica al léxico. Editorial UOC, Barcelona (2014)
6. Silberztein, M.: Formalizing natural languages. The NooJ approach. ISTE, London (2016)
7. Grishman, R.: Twenty-five years of information extraction. Nat. Lang. Eng. **6**, 677–692 (2019)
8. Chen, L., et al.: Clinical trial cohort selection based on multi-level rule-based natural language processing system. J. Am. Inf. Assoc. **26**(11), 1218–1226 (2019)

9. Messina, S., Langella, A.: Paraphrases V<-> in one class of psychological predicates. In: Monti, J., Monteleone, M., di Buono, M. (eds.) Formalizing Natural Languages with NooJ 2014, pp. 140–149. Newcastle, Cambridge (2015)

10. Real Academia Nacional de Medicina: Diccionario de Términos Médico. Editorial Panamericana, Buenos Aires (2012)

11. Real Academia Española: Diccionario esencial de la lengua española. Espasa Calpe, Madrid

12. Snomed CT: Guía de introducción a Snomed CT. https://confluence.ihtsdotools.org/display/DOCSTARTES. Accessed 24 Sept 2021

13. Burdiles, G.: Descripción de la organización del género Caso Clínico de la medicina a partir del corpus CCM-2009. Ph. D. thesis. Pontificia Universidad Católica de Valparaíso, Valparaíso (2012)

Meaning Extraction from *Strappare* Causatives in Italian

Ignazio Mauro Mirto[1] and Mario Monteleone[2(✉)]

[1] Dipartimento Culture e Società, Università di Palermo, Palermo, Italy
ignaziomauro.mirto@unipa.it
[2] Dipartimento di Scienze Politiche e della Comunicazione,
Università di Salerno, Fisciano, Italy
mmonteleone@unisa.it

Abstract. The work targets a little-known causative construction of Italian whose causative verb is *strappare* 'tear/extort/snatch' (e.g. *Ada strappò la confessione a Piero* 'Ada made Piero confess against his will'). In the active voice of this clause type, the subject, licensed by *strappare*, is invariably associated with the semantic role 'Causer' (as *fare* does in *fare* causatives, see [1]), whilst the post-verbal NP (e.g. *confessione* 'confession') is best analyzed as the predicate licensing the remaining syntactic function/s and the related semantic role/s. The NooJ grammar which the authors propose automatically extracts the meaning of *strappare* causatives by means of a novel type of semantic role. The latter is labeled as *Cognate Semantic Role* because its wording requires a verb whose content morpheme is the same as that of the predicate licensing arguments (e.g. *confessare* 'to confess'). The indirect object licensed by the predicate noun is typically associated with a semantic role expressing an Agent. However, a few predicate nouns, e.g. *vittoria* 'victory', determine an unusual pairing between syntactic functions and semantic roles. Importantly, a distinction must be made between cognate semantic roles which are guaranteed by entailments and others which hold true on pragmatic grounds.

Keywords: Causative constructions · Predicate nouns · Semantic role labeling · NooJ · NooJ local grammars

1 Introduction

This paper focuses on the automatic extraction of meaning from causative constructions in Italian, e.g. that occurring with the verb *fare* 'make/have' (or *lasciare* 'let'), exemplified in (1):

(1)   La polizia fece confessare l'uomo
       'The police made the man confess'

Italian also features a little-known causative clause type with *strappare* (detailed in [2]), a verb which more frequently occurs in non-causative, transitive uses, e.g. *Ada strappò la camicia a Piero* 'Ada tore Piero's shirt' and *Ada strappò la penna a Piero*

© Springer Nature Switzerland AG 2021
M. Bigey et al. (Eds.): NooJ 2021, CCIS 1520, pp. 208–218, 2021.
https://doi.org/10.1007/978-3-030-92861-2_18

'Ada snatched the pen from Piero'. The following example permits a comparison between the preceding non-causative types and the *strappare* causative illustrated in (2), whose surface structure is provided in (3):

(2)   La polizia strappò una confessione all'uomo
       'The police made the man confess'

(3) N_0 *strappare* N_1 a N_2

Our main interest lies in the clause type illustrated in (2), whose post-verbal noun, i.e. N_1, functions predicatively ([2]: 340–342), akin to the predication pattern of support verb constructions such as *Piero fece una confessione* 'Piero confessed' ([3]). That which catches the eye in the translation of (2) is that the sentence has the potential for being regarded as a paraphrase of (1) (albeit conditioned, see below), in so far as (1) and (2) share the semantic roles itemized in (4) below (these roles are introduced informally in [4], described in detail in [5–7], and compared to Case Grammar roles in [8]):

(4) **Semantic roles in sentence (2)**

a) >the one who confesses< (to be linked to the indirect object *the man*)

b) >those who bring about the confession< (to be linked to the subject *the police*)

Of importance, (1) and (2) do *not* convey the same meaning. A key difference relates to the man's stiff resistance to the confession. In this regard, (1) is neutral, whilst (2) expresses the man's unwillingness, which amounts to saying that the police somehow extorted his confession. The semantic role of the subject is thus comparable, although not identical, to that described by Maurice Gross ([3]: 24) with regard to the subject of *mettre* 'put' in French as a *Vsup causative* (e.g. *Max met en rage Luc* 'Max enrages Luc'). Despite this difference between (1) and (2), however, the meaning expressed in (4a) and (4b) remains constant in both sentences. Thus the truth of (2) guarantees the truth of (1), and therefore (2) entails (1).

This work is organized as follows: Sect. 2 will be devoted to the semantic-syntactic interface and to how machine-readable meaning is obtained by means of a novel type of semantic roles, labeled as 'cognate semantic roles'[1]; Sects. 3, 4, and 5 will illustrate differences in the representation of meaning which depend on N_1, i.e. the predicate noun combining with causative *strappare*. Finally, Sect. 6 will draw some conclusions.

2   Participants and Cognate Semantic Roles

A *strappare* causative always gives rise to two participants (beings or things), regardless of whether these are overt, as in (2) (whose participants are *la polizia* and *l'uomo*), or covert, as e.g. in *Strappò una confessione* 'Someone or something wrung a confession (from someone)'. In the model of meaning extraction proposed here, the

---

[1] The word *cognate* is used as researchers do either in diachronic linguistics (e.g. Latin MŪSCA 'fly' and Italian *mosca* are etymologically related, and therefore are cognate words) or with the so-called 'cognate objects' (*figura etymologica*).

number of semantic roles depends on the number of predicate-argument relations which the sentence expresses. Worthy of note is the fact that the direct object of (2), that is N$_1$, is not assigned a semantic role (henceforth, SR), but rather assigns semantic roles. Again, this is in line with the syntax and semantics of support verb constructions, since in (2) *una confessione* 'a confession' is predicative (see [2]).

Given the syntax-semantics interface outlined above, in (2) each of the participants is assigned a semantic role. Below, semantic roles are formulated by employing the verb cognate to the predicate noun (thus from *applauso* 'applause' the cognate verb *applaudire* 'to applaud' is obtained). As (4) illustrates, when the diathesis is active the SR assigned to the subject expresses the Cause of the event, whilst the SR originating from the indirect object expresses an Agent. However, whilst labels such as Agent, Patient, or Experiencer belong to the so-called Case Grammar roles ([9]), those in (5a) and (5b) below express meaning by means of cognate semantic roles (henceforth, CSR):

(5)   L'artista strappò un applauso ai ragazzi del pubblico
       'The artist managed to get a round of applause from the boys in the audience'
(5a)   CSR_Cause: >qualcuno determina l'applaudire<
       CSR_Cause: >someone brings about the applauding<
(5b)   CSR_Agent: >qualcuno applaude<
       CSR_Agent: >someone applauds<

By combining participants and cognate semantic roles, the matches shown in Table 1 obtain:

Table 1. Alignment between participants and CSRs in (5).

Participant		Cognate semantic role
The artist	>	He who brings about the applauding
The boys	>	Those who applaud

Each row in Table 1 can be considered as an equivalence, which in turn can be expressed with a statement (this approach is Harrisian, see below), more precisely, as an equative sentence (see [6, 8, 10]: 40), as Table 2 illustrates:

Table 2. Participants and CSRs combined into statements.

Participant		Cognate semantic role
The artist	is	he who brings about the applauding
The boys	are	those who applaud

The semantic core of sentence (5)—its propositional content (see [11]: 213)—is thus decomposed into two statements, each corresponding to a predicate-argument relation[2]. This approach is in line with the view taken by Z. S. Harris in relation to metalanguage and morphemic invariance (i.e. invariance of *signifié* and *signifiant*): "[T]he metalinguistic statements are themselves sentences of natural language" ([12]: 274). In a paper published posthumously ([13], see also [14]: 293–351, 377–391), Harris outlined the steps which led to "the recognition of the metalanguage as being part [a sublanguage] of natural language" ([13]: 1).

The NooJ graph below shows how the above statements are extracted automatically, thus providing a semantic representation of (5):

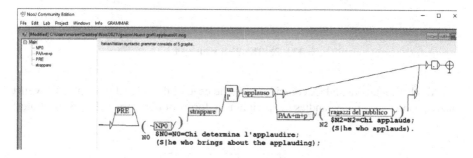

Fig. 1. NooJ graph for sentence (5).

The graph above contains four metanodes. As shown in Fig. 2, the metanode indicated by the acronym PRE relates to determiners and adjectives (if any) preceding the noun phrase fulfilling the subject function (i.e. *l'artista* 'the artist'):

---

[2] In *strappare* causatives such as (5), the verb cognate to the predicative N_1 is transitive. As a transitive predicate, *applaudire* (as well as the cognate *applauso*) can therefore assign two semantic roles: (i) >chi applaude< 's|he who applauds' and (ii) >chi è applaudito< 's|he who is applauded' (notice that for the wording of such roles the active voice is employed for the former role, whilst the latter requires the passive voice). In (5), the semantic role (i) is predictably present, unlike the other, which is not included. In the most common interpretation of (5), the semantic role (ii) does apply to N_0, the subject, and therefore *l'artista* 'the artist' is not only >s|he who brings about the applauding<, but also > s|he who is applauded<. The reason motivating the absence in (5) of the role in (ii) above is the following: whilst the semantic role paired to the indirect object is logically entailed (thus, if (5) is true, the sentence *The boys are those who applaud* must also be true), the role in (ii) is not, although this unit of meaning is normally assigned on pragmatic grounds (see e.g. Fig. 5). Indeed, the following variant of (5) is unlikely but possible: *L'artista strappò un applauso per il proprio collega* 'The artist managed to get a round of applause for his own colleague'. This point will be addressed again in Sect. 5.

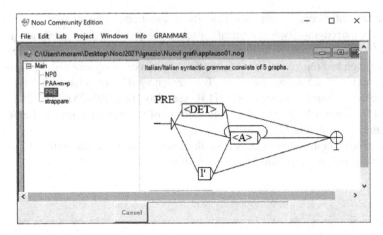

Fig. 2. The PRE metanode.

Another metanode, NPØ, coincides with the head of the subject noun phrase, whilst the metanode *strappare* handles the periphrastic forms of the verb, as Fig. 3 illustrates:

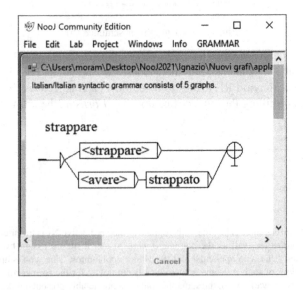

Fig. 3. The *strappare* metanode.

Finally, a metanode PPA regards the preposition *a* 'to', which in Italian introduces the participant fulfilling the indirect object function (when the preposition combines with a definite article, the two coalesce, e.g. *a+lo* 'the' → *allo*).

Figure 1 also shows the two CSRs which the sentence gives rise to: N_0 (i.e. the subject) is matched with the semantic role >chi determina l'applaudire< 'she/he who brings about the applauding' (in order to express causation, the verb *determinare* 'cause/bring about' is employed), whilst N_2 (i.e. the indirect object) is matched with the semantic role >chi applaude< ('she or he who applauds', see fn. 2). As these semantic roles illustrate, the content morpheme of the word functioning as a predicate (e.g. *confess-* in (2) and *applau(d/s)-*[3] in (5)) is employed, which is the reason why the label *Cognate semantic role* was chosen.

Approximately 80 nouns[4], capable of replacing *applauso* 'applause' in the *strappare* causative, were collated for this study. The automatic extraction of semantic roles such as those in (5a) and (5b) requires: (i) an inflected dictionary associating each of such nouns to the verb which shares the noun's root, e.g. *confessione* 'confession' / *confessare* 'to confess'; and (ii) the construction of a NooJ local grammar which employs variables (see [15]: 188–191, [16–18]). The latter will permit the automatic returning of units of meaning such as (4a) and (4b). Thus, unstructured texts containing instances of the *strappare* causative can be automatically annotated with semantic roles which clarify '*who-does-what-to-whom*' ([8, 19]: 1).

3 Suppletion: N_1 Has no Verbal Counterpart

In parallel with the predicate nouns of the support verb construction, some of the nouns entering the clause type with causative *strappare* do not have a verbal counterpart. When this happens, suppletion is required for the formation of CSRs. One such case is that of the noun *ovazione* 'ovation'. This case is close to (5) because *ovation* is a hyponym of *applause*. Since no verbal counterpart of *ovazione* exists, a semantically contiguous verb must be selected. Given the hyponym-hypernym relationship mentioned above, the cognate verb to be paired with *ovazione* obviously is *applaudire* 'to clap/applaud'. As pointed out above, this piece of information must be included in the dictionary. In this case, the NooJ graph for *L'artista strappò un'ovazione ai ragazzi pubblico* 'The artist managed to get an ovation from the public' will be the same as that shown in Sect. 2 above[5].

An additional case of suppletion is shown below:

(6)   L'artista strappò delle lacrime al pubblico
       'The artist made the audience shade tears'

This time, the predicate noun combining with *strappare* is *lacrime* 'tears'. The noun *lacrima* does have a verbal counterpart with the same root, i.e. *lacrimare*. However, the meaning of this verb does not normally relate to emotions, as e.g. in *Il*

---

[3] The noun *applauso* and the cognate verb *applaudire* illustrate a frequent case of allomorphy in Italian.

[4] Most of these nouns come from a research conducted on the Itwac corpus of SketchEngine (see [2]).

[5] This semantic representation does not capture the difference in meaning between the sentence with *applauso* and that with *ovazione*.

fumo mi fa lacrimare gli occhi 'Smoke makes my eyes water'. It follows that, again, a non-cognate verb must be used, i.e. *piangere* 'cry' and the cognate semantic roles will be as follows:

(6a)   CSR_Cause: > someone brings about the crying <

(6b)   CSR_Agent: > someone cries <

The graph below for sentence (6) has the same characteristics and the same metanodes as the one for sentence (5):

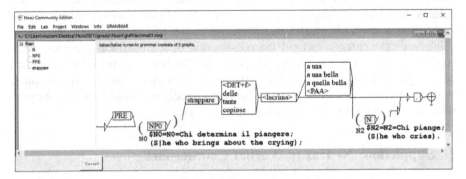

Fig. 4. NooJ graph for sentence (6).

4   N₁ is a Number

In another case, the noun combining with *strappare* is apparently a number (e.g. *sette*/ 7 = seven). This number (written either as a numeral or with letters) actually is the grade (score, mark) rating a student's work. In Italian the hypernym is *voto*[6] and in Italy we find grades either from 18 to 30 (at the university) or from 1 to 10 (at school). The latter case is exemplified in sentence (7):

(7)   L'alunno strappò un sette al professore

       'The pupil managed to get a seven from the teacher'

In sentence (7), *sette* 'seven' turns out to be a hyponym of *voto* 'grade', a noun that has no cognate verb (a verb *votare* does exist, but it is not related to 'giving grades'). Thus, once again, suppletion becomes necessary. In Italian (English translations are also provided below), the two cognate semantic roles might be expressed as follows:

(7a)   CSR_Cause: >chi determina il voto<

        CSR_Cause: >s|he who brings about the rating/grade<

(7b)   CSR_Agent: >chi attribuisce un voto<

        CSR_Agent: >s|he who gives a grade<

---

[6] Not to be confused with the homonyms meaning 'vow' and 'ballot'.

Pragmatically, however, the subject noun phrase, i.e. N_0, to which the SR_Cause is assigned, is simultaneously understood as she or he who receives the grade (see fn. 2). This is the reason why in the associated graph the CSR for N_0 is also rendered as >chi riceve il voto< 's|he who receives the grade':

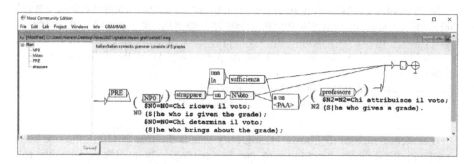

Fig. 5. NooJ graph for sentence (7).

If compared to the graphs above, Fig. 5 differs in at least three ways: the first, difference concerns the metanode N_Voto, which is split into two distinct lists. This is because the metanode must distinguish between grades at the university and grades at school. The second difference regards the inclusion of grades expressed with letters rather than numerals, for example *sufficienza* 'pass' (still a hyponym of *voto*), as e.g. in *Ha avuto una sufficienza in latino* 'He managed to scrape a pass in Latin'. Finally, the third difference regards N_0, the subject, which is assigned two cognate semantic roles instead of one. The reasons motivating this double assignment of cognate semantic roles will be provided in the next Section.

5   Inversion

A small number of N_1s give rise to partially distinct graphs because their occurrence produces an inversion of semantic roles, e.g. with (8):

(8)   Gli Ungheresi strapparono una sorprendente vittoria agli Italiani
       'The Hungarians pulled off a surprise victory over the Italians'

The subject still expresses the Cause of the event, thus >chi determina il vincere< 's|he who brings about the winning' (as pointed out above, this syntactic-semantic relationship is a regular feature of the causative construction). However, sentence (8) differs from the *strappare* causatives discussed so far for at least two reasons. Let us first consider the verb etymologically related to the N_1 *vittoria* 'victory', i.e. *vincere* 'to win'. Being transitive, this verb may give rise to two cognate semantic roles, one expressed in the active voice, as in (9a), the other expressed with the passive voice, as in (9b) (see fn. 2):

(9)   a. >chi vince< 's|he who defeats'
       b. >chi è vinto< 's|he who is defeated'

In most cases, for example in (4) and (5) above, causative *strappare* does not call into cause the cognate semantic role rendered by means of the passive voice, as seen in Figs. 1 and 4. In (5), for example, the verb *applaudire* 'to applaud/clap', cognate to the N_1 *applauso*, is also transitive, and might potentially yield the following cognate semantic roles:

(10)   a. >chi applaude< 's|he who applauds'
       b. >chi è applaudito< 's|he who is applauded'

A sentence such as (5), however, logically entails the role in (10a), the one associated with the indirect object function, but does not logically involve the semantic role in (10b) (the reasons are provided in fn. 2).

What distinguishes the *strappare* causative in (8) is the following: first, the cognate semantic role to be paired with the indirect object (i.e. N_2) is that in the passive voice, that is (9b)[7]; second, the cognate semantic role in the active voice, i.e. (9a), is to be associated to the subject function, that is N_0. Therefore, the sentence involves both the semantic roles in (9). (11) and (12) provide the core meaning of (8), rendered by means of cognate semantic roles:

(11)   Cognate semantic roles to be associated to the subject of (8)
       a. >chi determina il vincere< 'S|he who brings about the winning'
       b. >chi vince< 's|he who defeats'
(12)   Cognate semantic role to be associated to the indirect object of (8)
       c. >chi è vinto< 's|he who is defeated'

Therefore, the NooJ graph of sentences such as (8) differs from those shown in the Figs. 1 and 4 because they contain an additional semantic role as well as an inversion of semantic roles, as Fig. 6 illustrates:

---

[7] The same type of inversion takes place in the so-called *constructions converses* ([20]), for example in *John rilasciò un'intervista al giornalista* 'John gave an interview to the reporter'. For our purposes, the following difference is noteworthy: in *John fece un'intervista al giornalista* 'John interviewed the reporter', a support verb construction, the indirect object is to be associated with the cognate semantic role >he who is interviewed< (in the passive voice), whilst in *John rilasciò un'intervista al giornalista* the indirect object is associated with the semantic role >he who interviews< (in the active voice).

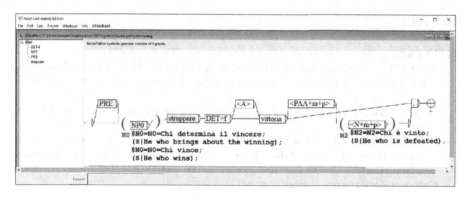

Fig. 6. NooJ graph for sentence (8).

6 Conclusion

Two causative clause types of Italian were presented in the Introduction, one with the verb *fare*, the other with *strappare*. In both, the causative verb licenses the subject and therefore a number of differences between the two types originate from the other licenser: whilst *fare* combines with a verbal predicate, *strappare* combines with a noun predicate. As suggested above, the two clause types are strictly interlinked also from a semantic point of view, given that they invariably establish an entailment relation. For example, the truth of sentence (2) guarantees the truth of sentence (1) (the opposite is not true, due to the semantic nuance which *strappare* introduces as a causative verb). This truth relation regularly holds true: each sentence built with the *strappare* causative entails the corresponding sentence built with the *fare* causative. For example, if (5) is true, the sentence *L'artista fece applaudire i ragazzi del pubblico* 'The artist made the boys in the audience applaud' is also true, just as the truth of (6) guarantees the truth of *L'artista fece piangere il pubblico* 'The artist made the audience cry'.

When meaning is represented by means of cognate semantic roles, the entailment relationship can be straightforwardly captured and easily become machine-readable. This means that, once a dictionary and a NooJ grammar become available also for the *fare* causative exemplified in (1), NooJ will permit the tracking or generation of entailment relations between *any* causative sentences such as the ones analyzed above. Other entailments will also become possible with ordinary verb sentences (e.g. *L'uomo confessò* 'The man confessed'), clefts (e.g. *Fu l'uomo a confessare* 'It was the man who confessed'), pseudoclefts (e.g. *Colui che confessò fu l'uomo* 'He who confessed was the man'), support verb sentences (e.g. *L'uomo fece una confessione* 'The man made a confession', *L'uomo rese una piena e dettagliata confessione al pm* 'The man gave a full, detailed confession to the Prosecutor'), as well as sentences such as *La polizia fece sì che l'uomo confessasse* 'The police made the man confess'.

References

1. La Fauci, N., Mirto, I.M.: *Fare*. Elementi di sintassi. ETS, Pisa (2003)
2. Mirto, I.M.: Italian *strappare*: unwilling vs. struggling agents. In: Kakoyianni-Doa F. (ed.) Penser le Lexique-Grammaire. Perspectives actuelles, Honoré Champion, Paris, pp. 335–348 (2014)
3. Gross, M.: Les bases empiriques de la notion de prédicat sémantique. Langages **63**, 7–52 (1981)
4. Mirto, I.M.: Dream a little dream of me. Cognate predicates in English. In: Camugli C., M. Constant, Dister, A. (eds.) Actes du 26ᵉ Colloque International Lexique-Grammaire, Bonifacio, Corse, 2–6 October 2007, pp. 121–128 (2007). http://infolingu.univ-mlv.fr/Colloques/Bonifacio/proceedings/mirto.pdf
5. Mirto, I.M.: L'estrazione automatica dei ruoli semantici corradicali: The importance of being cognate, online: https://www.academia.edu/39796685/Lestrazione_automatica_dei_ruoli_semantici_corradicali_The_importance_of_being_Cognate
6. Mirto, I.M.: The role of cognate semantic roles: machine translation support for support verb constructions. Paper presented at NooJ 2019, 7–9 July, Hammamet, Tunisia (2019)
7. Mirto, I.M.: Automatic extraction of semantic roles in support verb constructions. Int. J. Natural Lang. Comput. **10**(3), 1–10 (2021)
8. Mirto, I.: Measuring meaning. In: Arai, K. (ed.) Intelligent Computing. LNNS, vol. 283, pp. 1054–1067. Springer, Cham (2022). https://doi.org/10.1007/978-3-030-80119-9_70
9. Fillmore, C.J.: The case for case. In: Bach, E.W., Harms, R.T. (eds.) Universals in Linguistic Theory, Holt, Rinehart & Winston, New York, pp. 1–88 (1968)
10. Heasley, B., Hurford, J., Smith, M.B.: Semantics A coursebook. Cambridge University Press, Cambridge (1983)
11. Lyons, J.: Linguistic Semantics. An introduction. Cambridge University Press, Cambridge (1995)
12. Harris, Z.S.: A Theory of Language and Information. Clarendon Press, Oxford (1991)
13. Harris, Z.S.: The background of transformational and metalanguage analysis. https://zelligharris.org/HAR.pdf. Accessed 21 Nov 2020. Also published in: The Legacy of Zellig Harris: Language and information into the 21ˢᵗ Century, Vol. 1: Philosophy of science, syntax and semantics, B. Nevin (ed.), John Benjamins, Amsterdam/Philadelphia, pp. 1–15 (2002)
14. Harris, Z.S.: Papers on syntax. In: Hiz, H. (ed.) D. Reidel Publishing Company, Dordrecht (1981)
15. Silberztein, M.: Formalizing Natural Languages The NooJ Approach. Wiley, London (2016)
16. Monteleone, M.: Automatic text generation: how to write the plot of a novel with NooJ. In: Fehri, Héla., Mesfar, Slim, Silberztein, Max (eds.) NooJ 2019. CCIS, vol. 1153, pp. 135–146. Springer, Cham (2020). https://doi.org/10.1007/978-3-030-38833-1_12
17. Monteleone, M.: NooJ local grammars for endophora resolution. In: Barone, L., Monteleone, M., Silberztein, M. (eds.) NooJ 2016. CCIS, vol. 667, pp. 182–195. Springer, Cham (2016). https://doi.org/10.1007/978-3-319-55002-2_16
18. Monteleone, M.: NooJ local grammars and formal semantics: past participles vs. Adjectives in Italian. In: Okrut, Tatsiana, Hetsevich, Yuras, Silberztein, Max, Stanislavenka, Hanna (eds.) NooJ 2015. CCIS, vol. 607, pp. 83–95. Springer, Cham (2016). https://doi.org/10.1007/978-3-319-42471-2_8
19. Palmer, M., Gildea, D., Xue, N.: Semantic Role Labeling. Morgan & Claypool (2009). www.morganclaypool.com
20. Gross, G.: Les constructions converses. Droz, Genève (1989)

Terms and Appositions: What Unstructured Texts Tell Us

Giulia Speranza$^{(\boxtimes)}$, Maria Pia di Buono, and Johanna Monti

UniOr NLP Research Group, University of Naples "L'Orientale",
80121 Naples, Italy
{gsperanza, mpdibuono, jmonti}@unior.it

Abstract. Terminological resources, invaluable tools for language experts, translators, learners, among others, are widely employed in many applicative scenarios from Machine Translation (MT) to Natural Language Processing (NLP). Automatic terminology extraction from unstructured texts represents a useful, yet non-trivial task, in order to create terminological resources. In this study, we propose a methodology to extract domain terminology from unstructured texts, based on the recognition of appositive structures, as they may mark the presence of terms. Our hypothesis is that, due to their semi-fixed, easily recognizable structure and the semantic richness they convey, appositions are suitable linguistic constructions that can be exploited as markers within texts in order to identify terminology and from which to derive additional and valuable information about terms. Once several syntactic patterns identifying different types of appositional structures have been defined, we aim at automatically extracting them from a collection of unstructured texts in Italian, i.e., a domain corpus, by means of NooJ syntactic Grammars.

Keywords: NooJ · Terminology · Appositions · Domain Corpus · Specialized texts

1 Introduction

Terms, intended as simple and complex lexical units conveying special meanings in particular contexts [1], are highly used in specialized texts. That is due to the fact that terms represent denominations of items of knowledge [2], namely concepts, in the specific domain they belong to.

The entire set of terms suitable for representing domain concepts constitute a specialized vocabulary of knowledge for that domain, namely a terminology [3].

Terminologies, the core of every Language for Special Purposes (LSP), convey the most informative and salient information of specialized texts [4].

Thus, terminological resources, invaluable tools for language experts, translators, and learners, among others, are widely employed in many applicative scenarios from Machine Translation (MT) to Natural Language Processing (NLP).

Nevertheless, the development of such resources can often be demanding and time-consuming, especially when carried out manually.

For this reason, automatic terminology extraction from unstructured texts represents a useful, yet non-trivial task, in order to create terminological resources.

© Springer Nature Switzerland AG 2021
M. Bigey et al. (Eds.): NooJ 2021, CCIS 1520, pp. 219–230, 2021.
https://doi.org/10.1007/978-3-030-92861-2_19

In this study, we propose a methodology to extract domain terminology from unstructured texts, based on the recognition of appositive structures, as they may mark the presence of terms.

Our hypothesis is that, due to their semi-fixed, easily recognizable structure and the semantic richness they convey, appositions are suitable linguistic constructions that can be exploited as markers within texts in order to identify terminology and from which to derive additional and valuable information about terms.

The use of appositions within specialized texts is mainly related to a communication process between experts and non-experts, which requires text insertions to clarify and simplify terms, such as appositions, lowering the degree of technicism in specialized discourses.

Indeed, the communication of domain knowledge calls for different levels of specialism in the language used according to the actors involved in the communication process [5].

As remarked by [6–8], the communication can usually take place between:

- experts in the field (high degree of technicism)
- experts and semi-experts (medium degree of technicism)
- experts and non-experts (low degree of technicism).

The reason for lowering the degree of technicism when dealing with non-experts relies on the fact that terms result to be obscure to lay-people, sometimes making text comprehension very difficult. Indeed, the final users may often lack the domain knowledge to interpret and correctly understand technical concepts.

Therefore, we assume that appositions signal the presence of a technical concept - expressed by a term- which is further simplified in order to meet the intended audience's needs, receiving this kind of specialized texts.

To test whether the presence of appositive structures can be exploited in order to retrieve and extract terminology within texts, we focus on the Cultural Heritage (CH) domain. We compile a corpus of Italian texts in the specialized domain of archaeology, a sub-field of CH, and set up different NooJ syntactic Grammars [9] hinging on the syntactic nature of appositions to extract new terminology.

The remainder of this paper is structured as follows: Sect. 2 discusses the related works in the field of terminology extraction and appositional constructions investigation. Section 3 exposes our methodology, while Sect. 4 describes the experimental part, the NooJ syntactic Grammars, and the resources used in order to identify appositions in our domain corpus. In Sect. 5 we discuss and evaluate the results. Section 6 is dedicated to the conclusive remarks and future works.

2   Related Work

Automatic Terminology Extraction (ATE) tasks generally aim at extracting from specialized texts a list of candidate terms, i.e., hypothetical terms which are likely to be actual terms, which should be manually checked by experts.

As reported in [10, 11] computational terminologists, to perform ATE, traditionally employ (i) linguistic approaches in order to identify specific syntactic term patterns and linguistic features or (ii) statistical approaches to rank candidate terms according to a definition of termhood and unithood or (iii) a hybrid approach combining linguistic and statistical features. Recently, other approaches mainly based on machine learning techniques are also being applied to ATE [12].

Nowadays, there are many terminology extraction tools with graphical user interfaces, supporting several text formats, freely available on the web, or proprietary, for the extraction of monolingual and/or bilingual terms. A comparison among some of the most popular ATE tools is presented in [13, 14]. Nonetheless, some tools still present inaccuracies, being often unable to really discriminate among actual terms.

To the best of our knowledge, no previous experiments have tried to employ the syntactic features of appositive constructions in relation to terminology. Indeed, appositive constructions have usually been semantically and syntactically studied by linguistics scholars and grammarians for the sake of describing their usage, purpose, behavior, features, and history.

The main studies conducted on the English general language explored the nature of close appositions [15, 16], namely appositions where no punctuation separates the apposed substantives, or they focused on the definition of loose appositions [17], namely appositions which show a loose relation to their reference. In [18] an argument on the metalanguage to be used in relation to appositions is made. Whereas some studies focused on a specific type of appositional constructions such as those composed of nouns, as in [19].

Attestations about appositions and terminology mainly seem to pertain to text simplification tasks, as in [20], where the insertion of specialized terms between brackets and the explanatory simplification within the main sentence was found to decrease the level of difficulty in English technical medical texts. Furthermore, in [21] also for text simplification purposes, an apposition detector and classifier are developed for the Basque language.

3   Methodology

Our methodology is deeply linked to the syntactic nature and the characteristics of the appositive structures, from a purely linguistic point of view.

Appositive structures, appositional constructions, or, simply, appositions have been studied and defined in several ways according to different research perspectives. Most scholars agree on identifying appositions as constructions showing the juxtaposition of two or more noun phrases (NPs), though appositional constructions may also involve other types of syntactic classes.

Among the several meta-linguistic labels proposed within grammar books and linguistics manuals, in order to indicate the two elements composing the appositional construction, we choose to follow the one proposed by Huddelston and Pullum [22], who designates the first element of the appositive structure as *anchor*, and the second one as *supplement* (see Fig. 1), since that designation best avoids terminological confusion, allowing for two separate references for each of the elements composing the appositive structure.

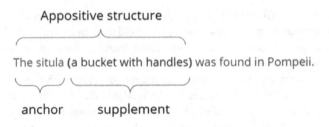

Fig. 1. Example of the two elements of an apposition

On a syntactical and graphical level, supplements can also be flagged with punctuation marks that enclose them, separating them from the main sentence [23]. Usually, supplements are placed between commas, but it is not rare to find them between brackets or dashes, which may contain even a single word. Among the punctuation marks, brackets seem to have a stronger separation effect, with the consequence of giving less attention to its content, hence considered as accessory and secondary, or alternatively, giving more prominence to it, as a key element in the understanding process.

On a pragmatical and semantic level, supplements are used with an explicative function in mind, aimed at providing additional information about the anchor they are referring to or reformulating previous concepts, by means of relations of synonymy, hyponymy, etc. [24].

A dichotomous classification of apposition is reported in [25], according to which appositions can be full or partial, strict or weak, and restrictive or non-restrictive. On a semantic level, they can be classified on a scale ranging from equivalence to inclusion.

In this study, we focus on the syntactic nature of appositive structures as markers of terminology within specialized texts intended for a non-expert audience. The syntactic feature we mainly focus our attention on is the presence of punctuation marks such as brackets, in order to retrieve appositional constructions in texts. The reason for selecting the brackets is that side experiments with other punctuation marks, such as dashes and commas, do not prove to be as effective in our corpus.

Our methodology is composed of two complementary steps (see Fig. 2): the *Supplement Identification Phase* and the *Terminology Discovery Phase*.

The former consists of a NooJ syntactic Grammar which uses as anchors a list of terms from the domain of archaeology, and recognizes any following word form between brackets, as we choose to start from the second element of the appositive construction, the so-called supplement, in order to understand and analyze the structure of appositions. This simple grammar applied to our domain corpus allows us to identify several examples of supplement structures, which are necessary for the second part of the experiment.

The latter takes as input the syntactic pattern of supplement structures previously recognized and the syntactic pattern of the domain terminology, formalized into a second NooJ syntactic Grammar to be applied to the same corpus in order to retrieve extra terms.

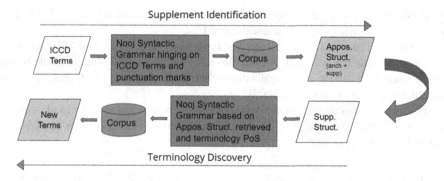

Fig. 2. Workflow of the applied methodology for the experiment

4   Experiment

In order to investigate appositive structures, we compile a domain corpus of 60 archaeological texts composed of museums and archaeological sites brochures, leaflets, and guides in Italian. To have a general overview of the linguistic data of the corpus, we calculate the total number of tokens, the number of types, the type/token ratio (TTR), and the average number of words per sentence (see Table 1).

These texts are informative and didactic by nature since the intended receivers are museum visitors with a diversified background and a general, non-specialist knowledge of the domain.

This type of texts can easily be framed within the communication between experts and non-experts. Therefore, it is possible to find interesting linguistic structures aiming at reformulating or simplifying technical specialism.

As a pre-processing step, the corpus has been cleaned from noise represented by para-textual elements as well as images.

Table 1. Statistics about our domain corpus of archaeological texts

Total number of texts	60
Total number of tokens	230,047
Total number of types	22,660
TTR	9,85%
Tokens Average	30,1 tokens/sentence

Based of the methodology we implemented, we process the corpus within the NooJ environment, by setting up different Grammars for the two phases of the experiment.

Supplement Identification Phase. For retrieving the supplements in our domain corpus, we set up a NooJ syntactic Grammar which takes as input a list of terms in the domain of archaeology. This list of terms is taken from the Thesaurus of Archaeological

Finds of the Italian Central Institute for Cataloguing and Documentation (ICCD - Istituto Centrale per il Catalogo e la Documentazione).[1]

The ICCD Thesaurus of Archaeological Finds consists of more than 4.000 terms, of which we include not only lemmas, but also other forms, such as plural and alternative forms since these are the actual realization of terms within texts, which present a great terminological variation (see Table 2).

This external resource is mainly employed in our experiment in order to identify the anchors, i.e., the first element of the appositive structure, which is further described or defined by the supplements.

Table 2. Examples of singular, plural, and alternative terms in Italian used as anchors

Singular term	Plural term	Alternative term
Cratere (krater)	*Crateri* (kraters)	
Antefissa (antefix)	*Antefisse* (antefixes)	
Fibula (fibula)	*Fibule* (fibulae)	*Fibulae* (fibulas)
Dinos (dinos)	*Dinoi* (dinoi)	*Dynos, deinos*
Dolio (dolium)	*Dolia* (doliums)	*Doglio, dogli, dolium, dolii*

In this phase, by setting the anchors, we aim at identifying supplements, hinging on the punctuation marks enclosing them, mainly brackets, as illustrated in the NooJ Grammar (see Fig. 3). Furthermore, intending to keep the Grammar clean and less noisy, we store the list of archaeological terms from the ICCD Thesaurus in a sub-graph (anchor). The sub-graph is followed by an opening bracket, followed by an unspecified number of repeated word forms (WF), followed by a closing bracket. Side experiments with other types of punctuation marks such as commas and dashes do not provide meaningful results within our corpus. Furthermore, the loop on WF lets us identify supplements without defining their syntactic structure a priori, which is exactly what we intend to retrieve and examine.

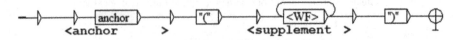

Fig. 3. NooJ grammar for the supplement identification phase

The output obtained with the Grammar of the first step constitutes the input for the second step of the experimental setup.

Terminology Discovery Phase. In the *Terminology Discovery Phase*, which constitutes the second step of the workflow, we conduct an analysis of the syntactic structures of the supplements retrieved in the previous step, by means of a Part of Speech (PoS) tagging. Furthermore, we also perform a PoS analysis on the anchors, to obtain an overall understanding of the syntactic structure of the terminology of archaeology. The PoS

[1] http://www.iccd.beniculturali.it.

tagging of the two elements composing the appositive construction allows us to generalize and abstract the investigation, by identifying the most frequent and productive syntactic patterns in Italian related to terms and supplements in the domain of archaeology, as far as our domain reference corpus is concerned. The PoS tagging is performed automatically, by means of the Python package Spacy. Nonetheless, a manual validation and correction of erroneous tags are also performed. Finally, since the PoS tags employed by Spacy are different from those used in NooJ, we choose to manually map Spacy's PoS schema onto the NooJ's PoS schema in order to ease the creation of the paths within the NooJ environment. PoS patterns of the terms are characterized by simple structures that may include adjectives and prepositions (see Table 3).

Table 3. Examples of part of speech patterns related to terms.

PoS pattern	Term
N	*Anfora* (amphor)
N–N	*Disco-corazza* (disc cuirass)
N + A	*Coppa biansata* (double-handed cup)
N + A + PREP + N	*Piede destro di statua* (right foot of statue)
N + PREP + N	*Cratere a campana* (bell krater)
N + PREP + N + A	*Fibula ad arco ingrossato* (enlarged bow fibula)

On the other hand, the supplements' syntactic patterns are more diversified and may vary from complete sentences to even a single word (see Table 4).

Table 4. Examples of part of speech patterns related to appositions.

PoS pattern	Apposition
A + N + PREP + N + PREP + V + CONJC + V + N + A	*Grandi contenitori in terracotta per contenere e conservare derrate alimentari* (large earthenware containers for holding and conserving food products)
N + PREP + N + A + PREP + N + CONJC + N	*Ossicini degli arti inferiori di capre e montoni* (small bones from the lower limbs of goats and rams)
DET + N + PREP + V + DET + N	*Le brocche per versare il vino* (the jugs for pouring wine)
N + PREP + N + PREP + N	*Coppa a forma di corno* (horn-shaped cup)
N + PREP + N + A	*Vasi per olii profumati* (vases for perfumed oils)
N + PREP + N	*Contenitori di unguenti* (ointments containers)
N	*Corridoi* (corridors)

We then formalize the several PoS patterns so far identified into a NooJ syntactic Grammar (see Fig. 4), which is composed of two sub-graphs: the first one containing the syntactic structures of the ICCD terms (anchors) (see Fig. 5), and the second one, enclosed between brackets, containing the syntactic structures of the supplements (see Fig. 6).

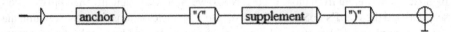

Fig. 4. NooJ syntactic grammar for the terminology discovery phase.

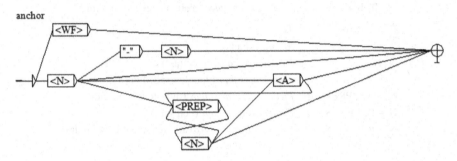

Fig. 5. Sub-graph containing the anchors' PoS patterns.

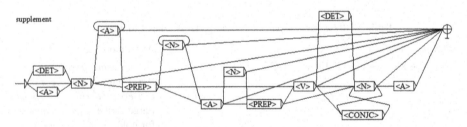

Fig. 6. Sub-graph containing the supplements' PoS patterns.

Finally, we also set another NooJ syntactic Grammar capable of identifying appositive constructions showing the reversed order (see Fig. 7), i.e., with the technical term (anchor) between brackets as the second element, and the supplement exemplification as the first element within the body of the sentence, as in the case of *testa in marmo (acrolito)* (marble head (acrolith)).

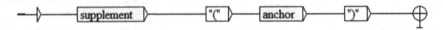

Fig. 7. NooJ syntactic Grammar for retrieving reversed order appositive structures.

5   Results and Evaluation

Results of our experiment (see Table 5) show that using a list of terms as anchors proves useful in order to make the output less noisy, even though this approach is limited to the external resource used. The main issue concerns the presence of terms in the resource, therefore, if a term is not in the list, it is not likely to be retrieved within the corpus even if there are occurrences. Furthermore, resource pre-processing is needed, and especially useful is the inclusion of plural and alternative forms of the terms, which in many cases constitute the actual realization of lemmas in the texts.

More specifically, making use of the NooJ syntactic Grammar for the *Supplement Identification Phase,* we are able to retrieve 57 appositive structures presenting the term between brackets, and 25 appositive structures when the term is outside brackets (reversed order).

Finally, following the approach we propose in the *Terminology Discovery Phase,* namely setting a NooJ syntactic Grammar based on the PoS patterns of terms and supplements, allows us to overcome the issue related to the a priori setting of terms. Indeed, this latter Grammar allows us to retrieve 30 more new terms, previously not identified.

Table 5. Summary of the results retrieved.

Type of grammar	Results
Supplement identification phase	57
Supplement identification phase (reversed order)	25
Terminology discovery phase	30
Total	112

Furthermore, from the analysis of the appositive structures retrieved from our domain corpus, we observed two main scenarios, reflecting two different aims:

- The technical term (anchor) is followed by a supplement between brackets to exemplify the meaning of the anchor it refers to, i.e., *kantharos (alto calice a due manici per bere il vino)* - kantharos (high goblet with two handles for drinking wine). This structure reflects the divulgative nature of this kind of specialized texts, whose aim is to convey concepts intelligibly.
- The technical term is between brackets with the aim of further specifying concepts, i.e., *spogliatoio (apodyterium)* - changing room (apodyterium). This structure reflects the informative nature of this kind of specialized texts, which aims at expanding the readers' knowledge by keeping, at the same time, specialistic rigor.

In addition, the nature of appositions related to archaeological terms, i.e., the semantic relation between the anchor and the supplement, can be very diverse.

Generally speaking, in our domain corpus, the appositive constructions are mainly composed of:

- Common noun used as synonym or quasi-synonym for the term
  i.e., *bracciali (armille)* - bracelets (armillas);
- Synonym/hypernym + function of the object
  i.e., *frigidarium (sala per il bagno freddo)* - frigidarium (cold bathing room);
- Synonym/hypernym + shape of the object
  i.e., *rhyton (coppa a forma di corno)* - rhyton (a horn-shaped cup);
- Synonym/hypernym + shape + function of the object
  i.e., arcosolio (una nicchia a forma di arco usata come sepolcro) - arcosolium (an arched niche used as a tomb).

6   Conclusions and Future Work

In this study, we focused on the syntactic features of appositive constructions within specific types of texts, i.e., specialized domain texts intended for a general, non-specialist audience, to identify and extract the surrounding technical terminology.

As a first step, we described the workflow for the experiment, consisting of using an external resource in the form of a list of terms in the domain of archaeology, to be employed as anchors. Secondly, in order to retrieve supplements, we hung on the punctuation marks, such as brackets, signaling the presence of appositive constructions.

The syntactic patterns identified for both the anchors and the supplements were useful to limit the foreseen noise and keep the output clean, while using punctuation marks was effective in the identification step, allowing the discovery of new terminology.

Finally, considering that different LSPs share many linguistic and textual features, we believe in the replicability of this methodology also in other domains of knowledge, provided that the corpus of texts shows the characteristics of the communication towards the general public.

In conclusion, we observed that the NooJ environment, especially the syntactic Grammars, has proved an indispensable and useful tool to conduct experiments based on specific linguistic features.

As future work, since the results obtained are also dependent on the corpus composition, we envision expanding the corpus size in order to retrieve more appositive structures. Furthermore, we also plan to replicate the same methodology on a parallel corpus, adapting the NooJ Grammars to the PoS patterns of the second language, ot create a bilingual glossary.

Acknowledgments. This research has been partially supported by the Programma Operativo Nazionale Ricerca e Innovazione 2014–2020 - Fondo Sociale Europeo, Azione I.2 "Attrazione e Mobilità Internazionale dei Ricercatori", Avviso D.D. n 407 del 27/02/2018 and the POR Campania FSE 2014/2020 funds. Authorship attribution is as follows: Giulia Speranza is author of Sect. 3, 4 and 5; Johanna Monti is author of Sect. 2, and Maria Pia di Buono is author of Sect. 1 and 6.

References

1. Gambier, Y., Van Doorslaer, L. (eds.): Handbook of Translation Studies, vol. 1. John Benjamins Publishing, Amsterdam (2010)
2. L'Homme, M.-C.: Terminologies and Taxonomies. The Oxford Handbook of the Word. Oxford University Press, Oxford (2014)
3. Zadeh, B.Q., Handschuh, S.: The ACL RD-TEC: a dataset for benchmarking terminology extraction and classification in computational linguistics. In: Proceedings of the 4th International Workshop on Computational Terminology (Computerm), pp. 52–63. Association for Computational Linguistics and Dublin City University, Dublin (2014). https://doi.org/10.3115/v1/W14-4807
4. Cabré, M.T.: Terminology: Theory, Methods, and Applications, vol. 1. John Benjamins Publishing, Amsterdam (1999)
5. Sobrero, A.A.: Lingue Speciali. Introduzione all'italiano Contemporaneo. La Variazione e gli Usi, pp. 237–77. Laterza, Roma (1993)
6. Dardano, M.: I linguaggi scientifici. Storia della lingua Italiana, vol. 2, pp. 497–551. Einaudi, Torino (1994)
7. Gotti, M.: Specialized Discourse: Linguistic Features and Changing Conventions. Peter Lang, Bern (2003)
8. Cortelazzo, M.: Lingue Speciali: la Dimensione Verticale. Unipress, Padova (1990)
9. Silberztein, M.: La Formalisation des Langues: L'approche de NooJ. ISTE Group, London (2015)
10. Pazienza, M.T., Pennacchiotti, M., Zanzotto, F.M.: Terminology extraction: an analysis of linguistic and statistical approaches. In: Sirmakessis S. (eds) Knowledge Mining. Studies in Fuzziness and Soft Computing, vol. 185, pp. 255–279. Springer, Berlin, Heidelberg (2005). https://doi.org/10.1007/3-540-32394-5_20
11. Castellví, M.T.C., Bagot, R.E., Palatresi, J.V.: Automatic term detection. In: Bourigault, D., Jacquemin, C., L'Homme, M.: Recent Advances in Computational Terminology. John Benjamins, Amsterdam (2001)
12. Rigouts-Terryn, A., Drouin, P., Hoste, V., Lefever, E.: Termeval 2020: shared task on automatic term extraction using the annotated corpora for term extraction research (ACTER) dataset. In: Proceedings of Computerm, pp. 85–94. European Language Resources Association (ELRA) (2020)
13. Chatterjee, N., Kaushik, N.: Automatic Extraction of Agriculture Terms from Domain Text: A Survey of Tools and Techniques. arXiv (2020)
14. Costa, H., Zaretskaya, A., Pastor, G.C., Seghiri, M.: Nine terminology extraction tools: are they useful for translators? Multilingual 27(3), 14–20 (2016). https://multilingual.com/product-reviews/?artid=2327. ISSN:1523–0309
15. Lee, D.W.: Close apposition: an unresolved pattern. Am. Speech 27(4), 268–275 (1952). https://doi.org/10.2307/453542
16. Haugen, E.: On resolving the close apposition. Am. Speech 28(3), 165–170 (1953). https://doi.org/10.2307/454129
17. Norwood, J.E.: The loose appositive in Present-Day English. Am. Speech 29(4), 267–271 (1954). https://doi.org/10.2307/454300
18. Hockett, C.F.: Attribution and apposition. Am. Speech 30(2), 99–102 (1955). https://doi.org/10.2307/454269
19. Burton-Roberts, N.: Nominal apposition. Found. Lang. 13(3), 391–419 (1975)

20. Gu, Y., Leroy, G., Kauchak, D.: When synonyms are not enough: optimal parenthetical insertion for text simplification. In: AMIA Annual Symposium Proceedings, vol. 2017, p. 810. American Medical Informatics Association (2017)
21. Gonzalez-Dios, I., Aranzabe, M.J., Díaz de Ilarraza, A., Soraluze, A.: Detecting apposition for text simplification in Basque. In: Gelbukh, A. (ed.) CICLing 2013. LNCS, vol. 7817, pp. 513–524. Springer, Heidelberg (2013). https://doi.org/10.1007/978-3-642-37256-8_42
22. Huddelston, R., Pullum, G.K.: The Cambridge Grammar of the English Language. Cambridge University Press, Cambridge (2002)
23. Burton-Roberts, N.: Parentheticals. In: Brown, K. (coord.), Encyclopaedia of Language and Linguistics, 2a ed., 9, pp. 179–182. Elsevier, Amsterdam (2006)
24. Meyer, C.F.: Apposition in contemporary English. Cambridge University Press, Cambridge (1992)
25. Quirk, R., Greenbaum, S., Leech, G., Svartvik, J.: A Comprehensive Grammar of the English Language. Longman, New York (1985)

Automatic Generation of Intonation Marks and Prosodic Segmentation for Belarusian NooJ Module

Yauheniya Zianouka$^{(\boxtimes)}$, Yuras Hetsevich, David Latyshevich, and Zmicier Dzenisiuk

United Institute of Informatics Problems of the National Academy of Sciences of Belarus, Minsk, Belarus

Abstract. The article depicts the problem of automated text segmentation into syntagmas at the punctuational and the semantic levels of Belarusian. It is aimed at generating prosodic transcription and delimiting long sentences. Its implementation is essential for improving the synthetic speech generated by Belarusian text-to-speech systems using prepared syntactic grammars in NooJ.

Keywords: Syntactic grammar · Intonation · Syntagma · Prosodic delimitation · Segmentation · Extraction · Text-to-speech systems

1 Introduction

The problem of localizing automatic intonation boundaries in a text is one of the main tasks of a prosodic processor, which is a mandatory unit in any speech and recognition system. The syntagmatic articulation of the speech flow allocates minimal semantic units and reflects the structural and semantic components of utterances [1]. The automatic selection of syntagmas is complicated by the lack of deep parsing, leading to the search for new approaches to the development of machine algorithms, methods and techniques by defining sequences of linguistic elements associated with certain semantic relationships.

To date, there are no general rules or mechanisms for an unambiguous definition of syntagmas in a written text or speech flow. The study of the prosodic speech organization is conducted on the basis of auditory and experimental analyses, with the help of which the parameters of super-segmental means are distinguished [2]. They are the limits of the speech flow segmentation, types of intonation constructions (IC), tonal, dynamic and quantitative signals of the IC center, changes in the speed and intensity of sound.

This work is a continuation of previous research where analyzed sentence parts were separated by punctuation [3, 4]. Most punctuation marks for sentences have been developed (up to 5 words) but the most frequent being three-word. Now the authors have expanded the study. The keystone is the number of syntagmas in a sentence that can significantly exceed the number of punctuation marks in the text. We applied a

M. Bigey et al. (Eds.): NooJ 2021, CCIS 1520, pp. 231–242, 2021.
https://doi.org/10.1007/978-3-030-92861-2_20

technique for automated phrase segmentation not only at the punctuational level but also at the semantic. It is also a system of marking intonation patterns in electronic Belarusian texts using NooJ [5, 6]. It widens the prosodic performance of the Belarusian text-to-speech system and may also serve to improve the Belarusian NooJ module with so-called prosodic transcription at different levels.

2   Types of Syntagmas in the Belarusian Language

Intonation components are primarily related to syntax that represents a set of rules, theoretical systems and language processes. The delimitation of syntagmas is connected with the sentence structure, word order, the presence of homogeneous members, the nature of word combinations and other linguistic parameters. All the mentioned components should be taken into account and noted in separate syntagmas while developing new syntactic and morphological NooJ grammars [7].

The problematic field of our research involves next points:

- Each language has specific rules for syntactic relations and their application. It should be noted that not all the results obtained for one language are suitable for developing similar mechanisms in other languages. It is necessary to specify prosodic rules of Belarusian speech organization.
- Most of the sentences can be read purely syntactically based on the surface syntactic structure, which in the Belarusian written text is quite fully displayed by punctuation marks. Based on the knowledge of the rules operating in the language, the most and least probable boundaries are predicted both when encoding speech by the speaker and when decoding it by the listener. But sometimes the syntactic information is not enough for the correct delimitation especially for the ambiguity of the context.
- Not all the context can be rendered by syntax with the help of punctuation. First of all, this is due to the stylistic and genre diversity. For example, if a literary text is focused on evoking an emotional response, influencing the psycho-emotional sphere of the reader/listener, it is characterized by the use of visual and expressive means and various syntactic structures, separated by punctuation marks. On the contrary, medical texts are characterized by a strict, almost expressionless nature of scientific and journalistic content using special vocabulary, terminology, abbreviations and less punctuation. Also, analytical languages convey grammatical relations through individual parts of speech (prepositions, modal verbs, etc.), fixed word order, where context and/or intonation variations. It also can be reproduced by a various system of inflection using dependent morphemes (endings, suffixes, prefixes, etc.) but less by punctuation.

Therefore, within the framework of this study, three groups of syntagmas are defined: **punctuation, grammatical and lexical.**

A punctuation syntagma (PS) refers to a sentence or part of a sentence that is limited to punctuation marks. Belarusian punctuation includes next marks: ".", ",", ";", ":", "-", "...", "!", "?", "?!", "!!!", "???".

Examples: *Karboksihiemahlabin, (PS) jaki utvarajecca pry hetym, (PS) nie zdolny pieranosic kislarod (PS).*

Skoda, (PS) vyklikanaja nikacinam, (PS) zakranaje nie tolki samich kurcoŭ (PS).

Grammatical Syntagma (GS) marks stable word combinations (phraseological units and collocations).

Lexical Syntagma (LS) is a short sentence of 2–3 words or a part of a sentence that is not limited to punctuation marks and is expressed according to personal lexical signs (through certain words or phrases) or rules.

Examples: *Na zaniatkach školy prafsajuznaha aktyvu (LS) abmiarkoŭvalisia pytanni (LS) ab matyvacyi prafsajuznaha člienstva (LS).*

Uračy pastajanna viaduc baracbu z kurenniem (GS) siarod moladzi (LS) i daroslaha nasielnictva (PS).

As the problem of extracting punctuation syntagmas is resolved in the previous works, the main and most difficult task of current research is to distinguish lexical syntagmas in a Belarusian written text.

3   An Algorithm for Dividing Texts into Syntagmas

Unfortunately, there are no general rules for the syntagma extraction of Belarusian speech. But the results of the statistical analysis of the experimental data fulfilled by the authors give grounds for developing a general algorithm for its delimitation. The system that is planned to be created to find the intonation boundaries of syntagmas is based on a superficial syntactic analysis with an emphasis on grammatical characteristics of speech parts. In programming, the syntax is determined by a set of rules applied in mathematical systems. Simplified versions of the original mathematical model of syntax and the method of its modeling on a computer are suitable for writing, on the basis of which these models are developed. The main task of this work is to develop rules and an algorithm of formal syntactic grammars that will divide a sentence into syntagmas. Types of syntagmas described above allow concluding that in order to develop an algorithm, it is necessary to take into account all punctuation marks, phraseological units and directly a list of formal rules dividing a sentence into lexical syntagmas.

An algorithm for determining syntagmas and intonation boundaries in sentences contains the next steps (see Fig. 1):

1. Dividing a text into sentences, according to punctuation marks emphasizing the end of the sentence. They are a period, a question mark, an exclamation mark, a question mark with an exclamation mark, three exclamation marks.
2. Delimiting a sentence into syntagmas:
   2.1 Searching punctuation marks in a sentence that mark syntactic relations within a sentence: comma, semicolon, dash, colon, brackets, quotation marks. Arranging syntagma boundary and inserting a marker instead of a punctuation mark in combinatorial variants of intonation types.
   2.2 Searching numbers, abbreviations, abbreviations and proper names. Splitting them off into a separate syntagma.

2.3 Searching phraseological units. Allocating them into a separate syntagma, arranging a syntagma boundary and inserting a marker according to the phraseological units.

2.4 Searching for conjunctions. Placing the marker of the syntagma boundary before conjunction according to their category by functional meaning: connective (combinative, enumerative-distributive, comparative, gradational) and subordinate (explanatory, temporary, conditional, causal, target, introductory, final, comparative, of place, mode of action, measures, of degrees).

2.5 Compiling a list of formal rules for dividing a text into semantic syntagmas.

3. The output of all sentences delimited by intonation boundaries with their formal markers.

   Steps 1–2.1 of the algorithm described above can be fulfilled on the basis of the syntactic grammar developed in the previous research (see Fig. 2). It consists of 10 graphs depicting punctuation syntagmas of the Belarusian language. The authors applied a technique for automated phrase segmentation at the punctuational level and a system of marking types of phrase intonation in electronic Belarusian texts using NooJ.

   Grammatical syntagmas can be searched for using formal markers with the help of the dictionary of phraseological units of I. Y. Lepeshev. For other steps, it is necessary to develop additional resources including a list of formal rules for delimiting grammatical and lexical syntagmas.

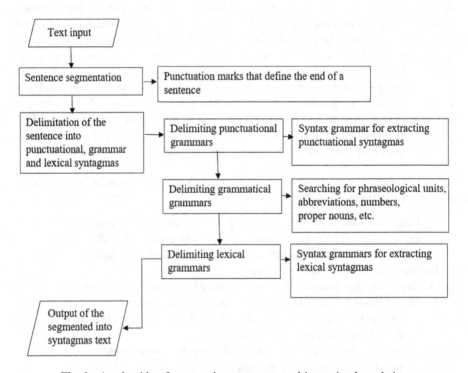

Fig. 1. An algorithm for extracting syntagmas and intonation boundaries.

A more difficult problem is separating lexical syntagmas, which are interconnected at the semantic and syntactic levels. This group of lexemes can be determined on the basis of creating general syntactic grammars for a computer expert system, which will search for similar syntactic constructions in a database or a corpus. Each grammar must be presented with a personal syntactic rule to isolate their intonation boundaries in a specific sentence.

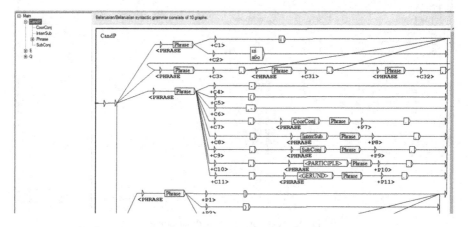

Fig. 2. Syntactic grammar for determining punctuational grammars.

4   Formal Rules for Extracting Semantic Grammars

Within previous research, the staff of speech synthesis and recognition laboratory created a text corpus of a medical domain (see Fig. 3). It was compiled on the basis of medical news published in next medical Internet portals:

- *Health Committee of Minsk City Executive Committee,*
- *Minsk City Gynecological Hospital,*
- *1st Central Regional Clinical Polyclinic of the Central district of Minsk,*
- *4th City Clinical Hospital named after M.J. Saŭčanka.*

Our laboratory works on Russian-Belarusian-English translations of these sites. On the rights of authors of bilingual translations, we took the news and formed the corpus. At the current stage of development, the authors have added new medical texts and supplement them. Now, created corpus of medical domain consists of:

- 627 texts;
- 23623 text units;
- 24212 digits;
- 63017 other delimiters;
- 336146 tokens;
- 248917 wordforms;
- 55208 different annotations.

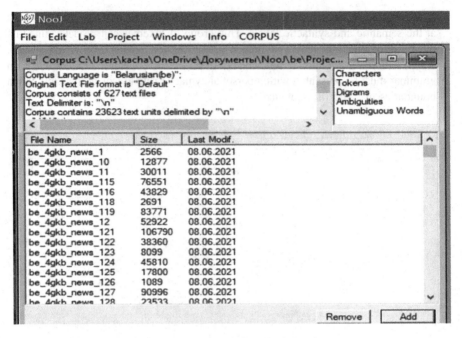

Fig. 3. Text corpus of medical domain.

The purpose of the corpus extension is to search and define syntactic constructions in the Belausian literary language, not separated by punctuation marks and a system of conjunctions. Their detailed analysis (mostly manual processing of each individual sentence) provides the basis for compiling a list of formal syntactic rules that will later be used by the expert system as a means of searching for identical structures in the input text and determining intonation boundaries within each sentence (Fig. 4).

Fig. 4. Applying syntactic grammar for extracting punctuational syntagmas.

In the research following syntactic rules were used for the arrangement of syntagmas boundaries. They are based on the semantic and formal union of two (or more) full-meaning words connected by subordinate relations of the Belarusian literary language. According to the number of principal parts of speech that can serve as the main component, there are 6 types of phrases: nominative, adjective, verbal, adverbial, prepositionaland conjunction groups. They are extracted according to the main word/component and some subordinate members of the sentence.

1. The boundary is drawn between a nominative group that includes a noun and several codependent or sub-dependent components: a noun and a group of words that convey the same related concepts; a noun and a complex name; a noun and a syntactically indivisible phrase. In these coordinated combinations of words, the main component is the noun.
2. The boundary is placed between the verbal group, where the verb is the grammatical and semantic core of the sentence and enters into subordinate relations with a large number of subordinate members of the sentence.
3. The boundary is drawn between phrases with an adjective as the main component, which include an adjective and a noun in different cases. They can be an adjective, a preposition and a noun in different cases; an adjective in the forms of degrees of comparison with adverbs and particles; an adjective with an infinitive; an adjective with pronouns; word combinations of adjectives; an adjective and several codependent or sub-dependent components; an adjective and a group of words that convey the same related concepts; an adjective and a complex name; an adjective and syntactically indivisible phrase; an adjective with a noun in different cases and determinators; an adjective, a preposition with a noun in different cases and a determinator.
4. The boundary is placed between the adverbial group, where the adverb acts as the main component in the following combinations: adverb and qualitative/quantitative/ qualitative-circumstantial adverb; qualitative/quantitative/qualitative-circumstantial adverb with a preposition and a noun in different cases; adverb and pronouns.
5. The boundary is placed between the prepositional group that separates long combinations of adjectives with nouns or the verbal group.
6. The boundary is placed before all types of conjunctions. With three or more homogeneous members, it combines the last two.

Using theoretical knowledge in the delimitation of Belarusian texts the authors have developed a list of formal rules for determining lexical syntagmas based on the medical text corpus (see Fig. 5). Each line describes a combination of speech parts that are included in one syntactic rule. The computer system must consistently analyze each rule until it finds the item that matches the combinations of certain words in the sentence and automatically sets the boundaries of syntagmas. The main principle is to take into account the right and the left context that separates syntagmas. Uppercase of Latin letters marks a part of speech and its case, the " +" signs a combination, the right arrow " →" indicates the parts of speech that separates previous and subsequent syntagmas (starts a new syntagma), forward slash "/" suggests possible variants of those parts of speech that begin the next syntagma. The"/PUNKT/" symbol describes any of the punctuation marks that possibly separates punctuational syntagmas. It is important to note that syntactic grammars are designed for the computer processing of syntactic-accent units at the machine level. For the moment, the list consists of 250 formal rules. However, their number may increase during the analysis of a larger volume of material and testing the system for defining new types of syntagmas.

104. P+N+R→C//PUNCT//V

105. P+I+P→V/C//PUNKT/

106. P+R+P→P+J+N+V

107. P+J+N+V→PUNKT//C

108. P+V+P+N→C//PUNKT/

109. D+J+J+N→I/C/V//PUNKT/L/PART2

110. J+J+J+N→I/C/V//PUNKT/L/PART2

111. R+N+N+J+N→I/C/V//PUNKT/L/PART2

112. R+IPL+N→I/C/V//PUNKT/L/PART2

113. R+I+J+J+N→I/C/V//PUNKT/L/PART2

114. R+P+INF→I/C/V//PUNKT/L/PART2

115. R+P+ЁСЦЬ→C//PUNKT//

116. R+I+N→I+N

117. R+MV+INF→N+I+N+N

118. R+V+I+N+N+N→I/C/V//PUNKT/

119. R+V+I+N+N→P

Fig. 5. The fragment of a list of formal rules for determining lexical syntagmas.

5 Application of Formal Grammars in NooJ

Based on the segmentation techniques proposed above, the authors have developed a NooJ syntactical grammar (see Fig. 6) representing the initial stage of prosodic processing for text-to-speech systems. It consists of 7 graphs: syntagmas which start a sentence, verbal, adverbialial, noun, pronoun, prepositional, conjunction groups. In their turn, some of them are also divided into subgraphs.

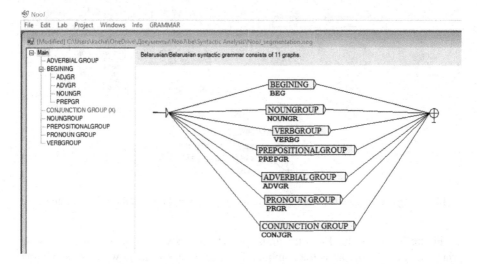

Fig. 6. Syntactic grammar for extracting lexical syntagmas in NooJ.

Firstly, the system automatically defines syntagmas that start the sentence. For this, it specifies punctuation marks that finish the previous sentence and uses a"Beginning" graph that is the combination of different speech parts (see Fig. 7, 8). It also subdivided into four subgraphs according to the main component of accentual unit. After finding the correct subgraph that corresponds to a certain rule from the list, the system analyzes the right context: formal markers that indicate the boundary between syntagmas (main/auxiliary parts of speech or punctuation). This marker is an indicator of a new syntagma. Thus, a boundary is drawn between the word combination of one subgraph and defined markers that begin a new syntagma. According to this principle, the syntactic grammar should work.

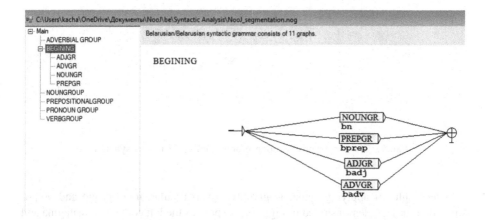

Fig. 7. A "Beginning" graph of the syntactic grammar for extracting lexical syntagmas in NooJ.

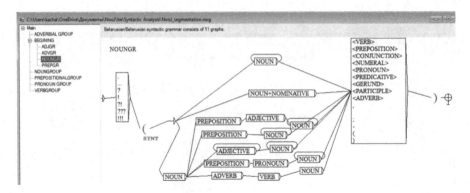

Fig. 8. Syntactic grammar for extracting noun groups at the beginning of the sentence.

Figure 9 shows the Pronoun graph which consists of 6 subgraphs. The main principle of this grammar is the combination of pronouns as main words of syntagmas and their subordinate components. It's very important to consider the right and the left context (words/expressions) which surround this syntagma for delimiting its boundaries. For greater clarity let's consider the first subgraph. The left context can be a conjunction, a numeral adverb, or some punctuation marks represented in this figure. The syntagma is a combination of a pronoun, an adjective and a noun or some nouns that close it in case if the next sign is a verb, a preposition, a conjunction, a numeral, an adjective, a pronoun, a predicative, a gerund, a particle, an adverb, or any punctuation mark. The other 6 graphs have the same structure and principle of working out.

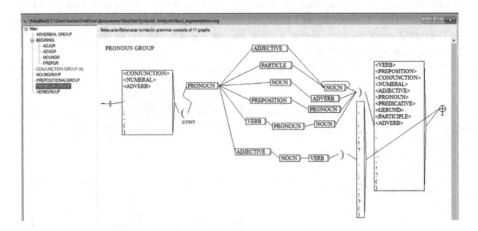

Fig. 9. The graph for extracting pronoun group of lexical syntagmas.

The results of applying syntactic grammar (in particular, noun group and prepositional group) are demonstrated in Fig. 10. It separates the left context, a syntagma and the right context. The grammar has some flaws and demands follow-up revision. The main hypothesis of the grammar is sequential processing of each subgraph from the most complex to the simplest. The same is necessary for graphs. Except this, there is a problem with homonyms, numbers and abbreviations which are not taken into account in the grammar. The next step of the research is detailed grammar testing on the whole corpus on a medical domain for searching new word combinations into syntagmas, their adding into graphsand correcting mistakes and bugs (Fig. 11).

Reset | Display | 50 ⊙ characters before, and | 50 after. Display: ☑ Matches ☑ Outputs / ○ word forms

Before	Seq.	After
грышыню прычыняецца да цыгарэты, ён не задумваецца	аб тых цяжкіх наступствах./PREPGR	да якіх можа прывесці курэнне. Л
утнясць кантактаў з курцамі дапамогуць пазбавіцца	ад тытуню і/PREPGR	пагрозы захворвання на рак, на хр
ачаць мер прафілактыкі захворванняў, не адмовіцца	ад шкодных прывычак./PREPGR	Дым цыгарэт павольна падточвае
бівающца не адразу, а праз шэраг гадоў і залежаць	ад яго інтэнсіўнасці./PREPGR	колькасці цыгарэт, якія скурваюц
овай дзейнасці, курэц затым няўхільна адчувае яго	адваротны ход./NOUNGRадваротны ход	Але кавярства нікаціну не толькі ў
рванне адной цыгарэты эквівалентна знаходжанню на	ажыўленай аўтамагістралі на/NOUNGRажыўленай аў...	працягу 36 гадзін. Цыгарэта змян
Абдамінапластыка Абдамінапластыка – аб'ёмнае	аперацыйнае ўмяшанне./NOUNGRаперацыйнае ўмяш...	якое ажыццяўляецца з мэтай адна
й. і наадварот. Курцы бышцам бы імкнуцца насыціць	арганізм пэўнай дозай нікаціну./NOUNGRарганізм пэ...	Якой менавіта? Ды той, пры якой
не сказаць пра тое, што чалавечы арганізм валодае	вялікім запасам трываласці дзякуючы/NOUNGRвялік...	наяўнасці ў ім ахоўных механізм
цікава: калі нікаціну ў цыгарэце мала, частата і	глыбіня залягае аказваецца большай/NOUNGRглыбі...	. і наадварот. Курцы бышцам бы іл
есці непатрэбную шкоду здароўю. Калі ж далучаюцца	да курэння?/PREPGR	У асноўным у школьным узросце
удах, страўнікава-кішачным тракце, што прыводзіць	да развіцця цяжкіх хвароб і/PREPGR	ўкарочвае жыццё. На даных дакл
я, працу, якая развівала б творчыя задаткі і вяла	да рэалізацыі здольнасцей./PREPGR	І тым самым супрацьстаяць прыв
якіх можа прывесці курэнне. Легкадумна ставячыся	да свайго здароўя./PREPGR	курэц лічыць сябе непаражальным
орванні – гэта доля іншых, больш слабых, схільных	да хвароб людзей./PREPGR	Але, на жаль, такі аптымізм нельг
Шкода курэння Калі чалавек уперашыню прычыняецца	да цыгарэты,/PREPGR	ён не задумваецца аб тых цяжкіх н
да. Бо мозгу патрэбны адпачынак. Зрушваючы звыклы	да сябе мантнік разумовай/PREPGR	дзейнасці, курэц затым няўхільна
йна мяркуюць, што ім зауседы будзе спадарожнічаць	добрае самаадчуванне./NOUNGRдобрае самаадчуван...	а Усякія захворанні – гэта доля ін
ці позна ў курсоў узнікаюць паталагічныя змены ў	дыхальных шляхах./NOUNGRдыхальных шляхах	сэрцы, сасудах, страўнікава-кішач
арганізма. Як правіла, большая частка пацыентаў –	жанчыны пасля родаў./NOUNGRжанчыны пасля род...	УПЛЫЎ НІКАЦІНУ НА ЗДАРОЎ
лёгкіх, хваробы сэрца і эмфіэма. Курэнне – адна	з асноўных прычын узнікнення ракавых/PREPGR	захворвання ў ЗША. Тут у сярэд

Fig. 10. Applying lexical grammars of noun and prepositional groups in the corpus of a medical domain.

```
Corpus contains 627 texts.

Corpus contains 1970166 characters.

Rank    Term    Frequency
1       юрыдычная дапамога;/NOUNGRюрыдычная дапамога      2
2       сацыяльнае суправаджэнне;/NOUNGRсацыяльнае суправаджэнне       2
3       эмацыянальная падтрымка;/NOUNGRэмацыянальная падтрымка  2
4       для асоб,/PREPGR      1
5       за дапамогай у/PREPGR      1
6       тэрытарыяльных цэнтраў сацыяльнага/NOUNGRтэрытарыяльных цэнтраў  1
7       сацыяльнага абслугоўвання насельніцтва вы/NOUNGRсацыяльнага абслугоўвання насельніцтва  1
8       часовы прытулак./NOUNGRчасовы прытулак       1
9       за дапамогай у рэлігійныя арганізацыі,/PREPGR      1
10      правядзення першнай кансультацыі і/NOUNGRправядзення першнай кансультацыі  1
11      тэлефона для асоб,/NOUNGRтэлефона для асоб       1
12      цэнтраў сацыяльнага абслугоўвання насельніцтва вы/NOUNGRцэнтраў сацыяльнага абслугоўвання насельніцтва  1
13      тлушчавых адкладаў,/NOUNGRтлушчавых адкладаў       1
14      грамадскіх арганізацый,/NOUNGRграмадскіх арганізацый      1
15      са стацыянарнага тэлефона /PREPGR      1
16      у рэлігійныя арганізацыі,/PREPGR      1
17      пакарання ў выглядзе штрафу альбо/NOUNGRпакарання ў выглядзе штрафу       1
18      Грамадскія арганізацыі./NOUNGRграмадскія арганізацыі      1
19      па сацыяльнай рабоце для правядзення першнай/PREPGR      1
20      стацыянарнага тэлефона /NOUNGRстацыянарнага тэлефона       1
21      арганізавана работа крызісных/NOUNGRарганізавана работа  1
22      па сацыяльнай рабоце./PREPGR      1
```

Fig. 11. Statistical analysis of applying lexical grammars in the corpus of a medical domain.

It is also planned to develop a syntactic grammar for extracting collocations and combine three types of grammars (punctuation, grammatical and lexical).

6 Conclusion

This paper represents an algorithm for extracting grammars and the grammar for automatic highlighting the intonation boundaries between syntagmas at the syntax level. The main core is the morphological and syntactic principle. The approach is confined in the ability of a particular speech part to match with words of other lexical and grammatical classes and occupy certain syntactic position. The concept is grounded in a superficial syntactic analysis of a text with the emphasis on grammatical characteristics of speech parts that combine accentual units. The results can be used for further research in phrase delimitation of Belarusian. Identified prosodic rules for dividing speech flow not only at punctuation level estimate value of intonation peculiarities of a certain language. This grammar is also wholesome to create an algorithm for segmenting textual information in the Belarusian speech synthesis systems.

References

1. Lobanov, B., Levkovskaya, T.: Multi-stream word recognition based on a large set of decision rules and acoustic features. In: Proceedings of the 5nd International Title Suppressed Due to Excessive Length 9 Workshop Speech and Computer SPECOM 2000. Revised Selected Papers, pp. 75–78. St.-Petersburg (2000)
2. Lobanov, B., Tsirulnik, L., Zhadinets D., Karnevskaya, E.: Language- and speakerspecific implementation of intonation contours in multilingual TtS synthesis. In: Speech Prosody: proceedings of the 3-rd International conference, Dresden, Germany, 2–5 May, V. 2. Revised Selected Papers, pp. 553–556. Dresden (2006)
3. Okrut, T., Hetsevich, Y., Lobanov, B., Yakubovich, Y.: Resources for Identification of cues with author's text insertions in Belarusian and Russian electronic texts. In: Monti, J., Silberztein, M., Monteleone, M., di Buono, M.P. (eds.) Formalising Natural Languages with NooJ 2014. Revised Selected Papers, pp. 129–139. Cambridge Scholars Publishing, Newcastle (2015)
4. Hetsevich, Y., Okrut, T., Lobanov, B.: Grammars for sentence into phrase segmentation: punctuation level. In: Okrut, T., Hetsevich, Y., Silberztein, M., Stanislavenka, H. (eds.) NooJ 2015. CCIS, vol. 607, pp. 74–82. Springer, Cham (2016). https://doi.org/10.1007/978-3-319-42471-2_7
5. NooJ: A Linguistic Development Environment. http://www.nooj-association.org. Accessed 18 Feb 2021
6. Silberztein, M.: Formalizing Natural Languages: the NooJ Approach. Wiley, Hoboken (2016)
7. Silberztein, M.: NooJ Manual (2003). http://www.nooj4nlp.org

Author Index

Printed in the United States
by Baker & Taylor Publisher Services